Walking A TIGHTROPE BACKWARD in HIGH HEELS

Walking A TIGHTROPE BACKWARD in HIGH HEELS

A MEMOIR

BLONDELL REYNOLDS-BROWN

A work of Nonfiction
Walking a Tightrope Backward in High Heels

All rights are reserved. No part of this book may be used or reproduced in any manner without the copyright owner's written permission except for quotations in book reviews.

Copyright @ 2025 Blondell Reynolds-Brown

ISBN: 978-1-959811-83-1 (Hardcover)
ISBN: 978-1-959811-67-1 (eBook)

Library of Congress Control Number: 2024919549

Book Cover Design: Okamoto
Interior Design: Amit Dey
Editor: A.E. Williams
Author Photo Credit: Whitney Thomas

2nd Edition

Website: www.wordeee.com
Twitter.com/wordeeeupdates
Facebook: facebook.com/Wordeee/
e-mail: contact@wordeee.com
Published by Wordeee in the United States, New York, New York 2024

Printed in the USA

DEDICATED TO...

My daughter, Brielle Autumn Brown, Esq. Be you. Be unique. Resist being a copy, only an originaloriginal . . . YOU. Be inspired by the fact that there are things only you can do. Be authentic, even when it is uncomfortable and especially when it's inconvenient. Dream big, and when that doesn't work, Dream bigger! Go for the gold charm even when the odds are not in your favor. Understand that no one gets a pass with challenges. You will grow and learn because of, and despite the hurdles and disappointments that are sure to come. With effort, you will know that adversity will be one of your greatest teachers. So always with a smile, *carpe diem*. Seize the day and pursue your dreams with excellence, enthusiasm, integrity, grace, and a mustard seed of faith. To Sadie Toney Reynolds, the kindest woman and role model life ever gave me. And to Debbie Johnson Lankford, my dear friend, now an angel, was my forever comrade and confidant in the talking walls of city hall.

Together we *"stood in the storm and when the wind did not blow our way, we adjusted the sail."* —Elizabeth Edwards.

ADVANCE PRAISE

"Blondell, a mother in the unforgiving world of the electoral process, looked in the mirror and after twenty years, dared to stretch herself beyond the walls of the Philadelphia City Council. She succeeded in this heartfelt memoir sharing stories and anecdotes of both the joy, the dreadful, the ugly, and the blessings and, most importantly, the lessons learned. Her season of weariness was matched and smothered by the generosity of spirit manifested by the selfless angels. In the end, Blondell's reelection in 2015 symbolized stick-to-itiveness, persistence, and strength. You will find her unvarnished story inspirational. You will be enlightened by Blondell's transparency of her personal failure and career stumble that left her stronger and clear-eyed because of her faith. "Everyone has a copyright on their own life," including Blondell."

—Sheryl Lee Ralph Hughes, Actress, Singer,
Author, Soror & State Senator Vincent Hughes,
Seventh Senatorial District, Philadelphia, PA

"My forever Councilwoman Blondell reveals the good, the bad, and everything in between of electoral politics in Philadelphia. I had the awesome opportunity to have a front-row seat during her journey. Through this deeply personal memoir, she shows if something as frail as a butterfly can emerge from the darkness victorious, so can you."

—Honorable Katherine Gilmore Richardson,
City Councilwoman at-large, Philadelphia, PA

"*Walking a Tightrope Backward in High Heels* is a must-read guide for every woman who is considering a career in politics. Ms. Reynolds-Brown's story gives it to you straight—no chaser. From the smoke-filled back rooms packed with male party bosses dictating who gets to sit at the decision-making table; Reynolds-Brown broke down barriers by not only demanding a seat at the table but bringing other women along with her."

—Joann Bell, Chair of Black Women's Leadership Council of Pennsylvania

"Blondell's unique blend of political savvy and intellectual curiosity sets her apart. Her deep dive into Philadelphia's education policy, driven by a genuine desire to improve public service, has had a lasting impact. This book offers a valuable glimpse into her journey and the lessons learned, making it essential reading for anyone interested in effective public policy."

—Karen A. Robinson, MPA, Senior Advisor, Equity Research and Innovation Center Yale School of Medicine

"Blondell Reynolds-Brown's new book, *Walking a Tightrope Backward in High Heels*, offers a nurturing tale of her private and public life and how they intersect. Blondell is brave enough to share her story, with its ups and downs, which will surely help demystify what life is like for women in politics and help some women get off the fence and jump into public life."

—Dana M. Brown, Ph.D., Executive Director, Pennsylvania Center for Women in Politics at Chatham University

"My helicopter Mom is my everyday heroine. I watched her in action through the highs and the disappointments, never complaining, never ceasing to make things happen for her family . . . even while helping to run America's fifth-largest city. She has shown me what it means to be a fearless and devoted friend, a diligent activist, and resilient in my pursuits. My strong work ethic and character are attributed to my mom."

—Brielle Autumn Brown, Esq.

FOREWORD

I met Blondell Reynolds in 1983 while working on an election campaign. I was about to return to Philadelphia after graduating from law school in Washington, DC, and I looked for a group of politically active young professionals with whom I could volunteer and form friendships. Blondell welcomed me into the political family she had been affiliated with for many years with a big smile, open arms, and shared personal and professional values.

After many years of getting other people elected while also advancing in her professional pursuits, Blondell decided that it was finally her turn to run for office. She drew on the goodwill of her fellow graduates of the Philadelphia High School for Girls and Pennsylvania State University and on the many people she had worked with and served as a dancer at one of Philadelphia's premier dance companies; as an administrator who opened up the door to so many at Penn State; as a staffer for other elected officials, delivering constituent services while honing her political skills; as well as the sage, down-home, and faith-filled wisdom from her mother, Sadie, a southerner who moved to Philadelphia in her thirties, and who overcame racism and sexism to successfully raise Blondell and six other children.

After an unsuccessful first try, Blondell was elected as councilwoman at-large to the Philadelphia City Council in 1999, representing all Philadelphians. While Blondell distinguished herself in many areas, from her first day in City Council, she set out to and never apologized for carrying the torch to advance opportunities for women in all walks of life and for steadfastly walking the tightrope of career woman and mother, even as she had to learn forgiveness of self after a campaign career blunder.

Blondell put all that she learned from twenty years as a member of the Philadelphia City Council, as an active and influential member of a successful and tight-knit political family, as a married woman who then experienced the pain of divorce, and as a mother who unapologetically put her daughter first, into a book that shows in captivating, unvarnished, and emotionally vulnerable detail, how she accomplished what she did. Her book reveals that none of her accomplishments came by chance. She prepared for her success by absorbing her mother's never-say-die attitude, reading and absorbing biographies of successful people and self-help and inspirational books, including writing down and posting reminders of the many quotes that resonated with her, and participating in professional and community leadership programs in Philadelphia, all the while leaning on an unshakable faith in God. She outlined her paths in this book so that others can learn from and follow them.

Councilwoman Blondell Reynolds-Brown improved Philadelphia by authoring legislation to create the Philadelphia Children's Fund, which requires the Eagles and Phillies to donate $1 million per team, per year, for thirty years; to require restaurants to institute the practice of labeling their menus with calories and sodium content information; to create the Philadelphia Women's Commission; the LGBTQ Commission; the Youth Commission and the Office of Sustainability; to require corporations to appoint women to their boards of directors; and to mandate universal lead testing of rental properties. Blondell also brought together and celebrated the accomplishments of thousands of women from all over the Philadelphia area with her many annual Women's History Month luncheon events.

As good friends with shared values and experiences, Blondell supported my career as an attorney, author, and publisher. She featured me as an author at her annual luncheons, while remarking that she always wanted to write a book one day. For years, I invited her to join me at the Book Expo in New York City, the then-annual gathering of the book publishing industry, where publishers showcased their authors and upcoming books. Once she finally had time to accept my invitation some five years ago, she saw the possibilities and was more determined than ever to write the children's book that she had envisioned. Luckily, I, and her daughter, Brielle, convinced Blondell that her remarkable accomplishments and path to get there should be her first book.

I was honored to work with Blondell to shape the book and edit the early versions of it. I knew a lot about Blondell before since we shared our political activities, personal and professional accomplishments, marriages and divorces, experiences raising children, and faith in God. However, after reading her book, I learned so much more about how Blondell got to where she is today. She inspired me even more. There is no doubt that this book will, in some way, inspire everyone who reads it, and it will increase or establish admiration for this woman who overcame the obstacles and achieved success in her unsinkable way.

—Sheilah Vance, Esq., President and CEO, The Elevator Group
Author, *Chasing the 400*, *Land Mines*,
Becoming Valley Forge, and
Threshold to Valley Forge: The Six Days Encampment in Gulph Mills

A WORD ABOUT THE USE OF QUOTES.

"A good book should leave you slightly exhausted at the end. You live several lives while reading it." —William Styron.

A very careful effort has been made to trace the ownership of the quotations cited in this memoir and to get permission to use them. All were researched and selected carefully, lovingly but unscientifically. All were chosen with the themes central to my career journey that resonate with courage, perseverance, challenge, controversy, strength, generosity, gumption, disappointment, trials, and endurance. To the original sources, if any error or omission has occurred, it is completely accidental, without malice, and with sincere apologies. Please notify me of all corrections as I will happily receive them at moxiewomenenterprises@gmail.com and correct them in a manner appropriate in the publishing industry.

TABLE OF CONTENTS

Introduction xvii
Chapter One: The Backstory 3
Chapter Two: The Moxie Woman. 6
Chapter Three: Motherhood. 21
Chapter Four: The Reinventor: The Dancer In City Hall 32
Chapter Five: Excellence Matters And Fearlessness Is Required . . 39
Chapter Six: Fundraising: Gas With A Flair 50
Chapter Seven: Cultivate Allies, Cultivate Relationships, Cultivate Votes 66
Chapter Eight: Reckon With The Naysayers Anyway. 75
Chapter Nine: Embrace The Good Times. 81
Chapter Ten: Women, Our Voice, And Our Leadership Matters . 93
Chapter Eleven: Victories And A Few Losses 119
Chapter Twelve: When You Are The News, Face The Music . .132
Chapter Thirteen: The Lion, The Gazelle, And The Caterpillar . .177
Chapter Fourteen: The Exit Strategy 182

Chapter Fifteen: Regrets 196

Chapter Sixteen: Passing The Baton a.k.a. Legacy 206

Chapter Seventeen: Dear Past, Thank You For The Lessons Learned 223

Chapter Eighteen: Recovery. 238

Chapter Nineteen: Self-Care Matters 249

Chapter Twenty: Wake Up Runnin'. 259

The Playlist Compendium. 274

Gratitude and Acknowledgments 277

About The Author. 281

INTRODUCTION

"The act of writing is an act of optimism. You would not take the trouble to do it if you felt that it didn't matter."
—Edward Albee.

Walking a Tightrope Backward in High Heels is a mélange of political stories, guidance for political hopefuls, part autobiography, and part manifesto told through the lens of one of the most popular, yet unpopular, minefields of all professions, the field of electoral politics. Most of my adult life has been as an elected official and for the most part, it has been a fulfilling journey. This book will recount those blissful and not-so-blissful years and my cherished times as a daughter, sister, friend, Village mother, and wife.

What I know for sure after twenty years in the ring is that electoral politics is not for everyone. It certainly is not for those wishing to use it for all the wrong reasons; those easily distracted by glitz and power, or those with selfish and ulterior motives to use the office as a stepping stone to power brokering. Although you'll find those who will get blemished, seduced, and sometimes even diseased by power, they are not the majority who enter the political arena.

People who usually enter politics have a heart for and a motivation to make life better for humanity. Their efforts are often laser-focused on making good things happen for the disenfranchised and the voiceless who can offer little in return. When done right, politicians represent society's best interests and believe wholeheartedly in their work, on behalf of those who voted them into office. Thus, they are consistently responsive to their constituents' needs even when they cannot move the needle on a point of desired community interest.

So, yes, the world of politics can be a constant struggle between cynicism and hope, but like it or not, political decisions—from marriage licenses to death certificates, from infrastructure to the preservation of our environment—make a difference in our daily lives. In all the cases above, a representative from the political world, or their designee, is a part of the process. Political decisions have become one of the foundations of our society.

If making a difference in people's lives is where your heart lies and politics is calling your name, I urge you to read on. My greatest hope is that as you turn the pages of the book, you'll become curious enough to read to the end. I chose to open my soul, expose my blunder and vulnerabilities, and celebrate my achievements and victories. Why? as a way to share with the next generation of women climbing the political hill, the rewards, and the pitfalls of electoral politics. *Walking A Tightrope Backward in High Heels* is no easy feat or cake walk, a popular celebratory dance performed by enslaved Black people on plantations before the Civil War. Disappointed at times, but never a broken woman, life, and especially politics, underscored what my Mom taught me, lived by, and repeated often: *"Nothing good or bad lasts forever."* Keeping my balance with style, humility, strength, and God's grace, sometimes in the face of pain, adversity, and disappointment was emotionally hard. But so many people along the way provided a bridge as I journeyed, and I am eternally grateful for that.

One last thing. Throughout this book are dozens of my favorite inspirational passages collected from an abundance of self-help, motivational, inspirational books, journals, and slips of paper. I have kept them for over forty years as they were helpful on my journey.

They fueled my spirit during moments of joy, happiness, and sadness in my City Council career. Additionally, some of the books were my tools for fighting my way back to personal restoration during those unforgettable, troubling, and awkward events throughout my twenty years in the Philadelphia City Council.

In addition to quotes interspersed in the book, you'll find a playlist at the end of the book, as music was a powerful motivator for me as I went about my days. Besides dancing and politics, music is a deep love. In the end, my battered soul survived all, and I praise God. And one more thing, I adopted the motto of my Girls' High School...*Carpe Diem*.

> *"People have a copyright of their own life."* —Hilton Als
> *Walking On A Tightrope Backward In High Heels* is mine.

Carpe Diem
Blondell Reynolds-Brown

THE MEMOIR

CHAPTER ONE

THE BACKSTORY

"Just when the caterpillar thinks the world is over, it becomes a butterfly." —Chuang Tzu

When I entered politics, it was not only to win elections but to do something bigger than myself. Once victorious, my goal was to uplift marginalized citizens in the communities they reside. I ran on the pledge to be an unapologetic voice and advocate for women, children, and families who live, work, and play in the City of Philadelphia.

My tenure was filled with highs and lows. What follows is a compilation of personal and professional experiences that were multidisciplinary, richly diverse, layered, and complex. This is an account, and, at times, a confessional of milestones reached, of cathartic and emblematic personal and professional turmoil and triumphs. The challenges were instructive, and the wins were satisfying. Telling the story you are about to read was not my initial starting point.

Sixty or so days after my official retirement from City Council, like a squirrel who had gathered her nuts for winter, I pulled out dozens and dozens of children's storybooks to reread, preparing to tackle a deferred dream, to become a children's book author. My daughter, Brielle, then a proud graduate from Syracuse University, class of 2018, curious about my next self-imposed assignment, questioned my move. We talked and reminisced about all the colorful children's books I had read to her as a child that now surrounded me. Stunned that I had kept them all and acutely aware of my long-held desire to pursue my aspiration to write a children's book series, she understood but queried anyway.

Brielle felt I would misstep if I didn't document my journey as an elected official for women who are fired to follow in my footsteps. She challenged me and my rationale for the timing of my new project. We bantered for weeks, far too long for my liking, but her reasoning and logic ultimately pierced my thinking and my heart, and it made sense. At her urging, instead of Monday morning quarterbacking to her about my public service career in the Philadelphia City Council, to her annoyance, she persuaded me to pivot and devote my time and focus on writing my storied journey as the only at-large (members who are elected or appointed to represent an entire city) African-American woman democrat of the Philadelphia City Council for sixteen of my twenty years of service.

Now a lawyer, Brielle used her early legal savvy as a first-year law student to convince me to tell my story while it was still fresh and relevant. A legacy memoir, she felt, would bookend my career and was one way of giving a clear-eyed view of the world of electoral politics to those who wish to follow.

She had witnessed, up close and within earshot, the dozens of phone calls I fielded during morning school drop-offs where I provided advice and counsel to women, men, colleagues, staff, and constituents seeking help or guidance about a legislative issue or personal worry. Brielle also passionately believed that the nonconformity of Donald Trump's (a.k.a. number 45) presidency and his unpresidential stance resulted in pushback from women, and these women needed what I had to offer. The time she argued, was right and ripe for me to tell my story.

Women unarguably lead with different values, and their voices are what is needed in electoral politics in a world struggling on so many fronts. Indeed, Number 45 had triggered and ignited the huge surge of women elected in the 2018 midterm elections, determined to stop him in his tracks. Most notable among them was Brielle's favorite member of Congress, Alexandria Ocasio-Cortez, known in our circle as AOC, who has represented New York's Fourteenth Congressional District since 2019. I heard and received my daughter's compelling case for why me and why now. So I tabled, once again, my long overdue dream of finally finishing my children's book series, *The Amazing Adventures of Autumn*. Brielle's "make it make sense and make it matter" debate won the day.

Therefore, herein is my journey of the lessons learned as an African American female elected official and mother providing public service in the political ring nine days a week, thirty-two hours a day for twenty years. You are wondering, is that right? Did she make an editorial error? No. The reality is when you are a working mother who ends up a single parent working in public service, and you are unapologetically devoted to your work and the mission of service to others in a city that never sleeps, twenty-four hours can seem, and feel like thirty-two.

It is with some consternation but with great satisfaction that I share with you my pilgrimages, sometimes adventure, at other times the firestorm I faced in the world of electoral politics. These anecdotes include amusing experiences and moments touched by history (like the election of President Barack Obama), some more significant than others, but all captured much of what I've often talked about on the floor of City Council chambers.

Carpe Diem.

CHAPTER TWO

THE MOXIE WOMAN

"There is no limit to what a woman can accomplish."
— Michelle Obama

As an elected official, I sounded like a broken record. For twenty years, I repeated my core message of community empowerment or a facsimile thereof at community neighborhood meetings, churches, small and large gatherings, in homes of neighbors and supporters, at veteran clubs, and at meetings hosted by members of the National Pan-Hellenic Council, a collaborative umbrella national and international organization made up of nine historically African American collegiate, Greek-lettered fraternities and sororities. Add to that list sports events, supermarkets, college campuses, birthday parties, and baby showers—whoever invited me and wherever two people were gathered, I was there. I reveled in settings and gatherings filled with women and working mothers. Campaigning while female and speaking before women audiences, most notably my sorority, Delta Theta Sigma Sorority, Inc., always calmed my spirit and put me in a comfort zone cushioned by their warmth, priceless sisterhood, unwavering support, and collective vows of fidelity toward public service. They were always inspiring.

When I signed up for this kind of work, I was agreeing to and accepting the long hours of public service expectations. My absence caused members of my immediate family to suffer. I had to come to grips with the fact that some members of my family did not care one bit about my decision to be of service to others and, worse, did not even try to understand. While saddened by the lack of unanimous validation that I longed for from my siblings, keeping my own counsel, as moxie women must, entering the world of politics is a decision I do not regret. I developed the mental muscle to move on.

Beyond my faith and family, I love music and the arts. I am disciplined and committed, which I believe was from the seeding of my parents, who hailed from Sumter, South Carolina. Like many, they moved North in the times of the Great Migration but still planted good old-fashioned Southern values in their offspring. They sowed grit, a necessary trait for Black people in the South during America's most heinous Jim Crow period, which allowed them to straighten their backs, often bent over from picking cotton.

My mother was the epitome of a moxie woman. Women with what she called gumption. They bring energy, verve, pep, guts, courage, skill, and know-how, to get things done with style and grace even under the most trying of circumstances. When they fall and suffer disappointments, they never allow a fall to define who they are. Moxie women realize that a fall is a setup for a comeback for the next opportunity yet to be revealed. These women, however, pay keen attention during a fall, recognizing the breakthroughs can become "aha" moments later.

Certainly, in our lives, my Mom was an oak tree. When she lost her husband at the young age of thirty-seven, with seven children to care for, her true moxie-self came into full view. Born September 5, 1927, in Elliott, Lee County, South Carolina, my mom, Sadie Toney Reynolds, was the eldest daughter and the third of eleven children of the late Walter and Estelle Toney. My grandparents were two hardworking farmers who instilled in their children the values of hard work, diligence, and perseverance. Reared in a Christian home, Mom's family, although limited in material wealth, possessed a strong faith in God, impeccable integrity, and a firm belief in hard, honest work. Following high school, Mom, a natural-born leader, was one of two siblings who pursued college studies at Allen University in Columbia, South Carolina, graduating with a bachelor's degree in education, and becoming an educator. Now that's gumption for the times.

With their eyes toward what we would call today generational wealth; the Toney heirs own the one hundred acres of farmland where my mom and her siblings worked tilling the soil and harvesting the crops. Years later, Mom was fond of saying that their kitchen table was filled with organic foods from their labor, way before "organic" farming became popular in modern-day societies. Often, I have shared the story of the day my mom came to visit us when Brielle was a toddler. She came into my kitchen looking for fresh vegetables and was mortified when she discovered vegetables in a can. Not fresh and not frozen. From that day until now, you will not find canned vegetables in my kitchen. To create a habit of eating healthy, she pointed to her library of books on topics like nutrition, herbs, and food for the brain.

My mom worshipped her father, Walter Toney. Grandpa had a fifth-grade education but was girded with an entrepreneurial spirit and an unwavering work ethic. It was his vision that guided his sons and daughters to acquire one hundred acres of farmland. So influenced by her stalwart father, up to her last day of life on June 22, 2017, my mom talked about how "I can't wait to see my daddy." Likewise, my admiration for my mother was endless, and the values she passed on were invaluable.

In 1984, long before I entered electoral politics and the City Council was even a thought, I saw an opportunity to tell my mom's story. The *Philadelphia Tribune* newspaper ran a contest for Mother's Day. The requirement was to write a one-hundred-word essay celebrating your mom. I submitted my essay, and behold, it won the 1984 *Philadelphia Tribune's* Mother of the Year contest. My mom was treated to a performance of *The Gospelers* at the New Freedom Theatre and dinner with her children.

Twenty-one years later, in 2005, another young lady and former staffer who marveled at my mom's extraordinary story, nominated her to receive the Odunde Festival Award founded by one of Philadelphia's cultural icons and activists, Ms. Lois Fernandez. A leader and unapologetic arts activist of Philly's African American cultural community, Lois grew Odunde to become the largest African American street festival in the country, her legacy now managed by her beautiful daughter, Bumi. This accolade and recognition were big and special. I clearly remember my mom's sheer joy that her only son, my brother, Angelo, flew in from Chicago and stood with us to witness this once-in-a-lifetime moment of happiness and pride before thousands of Odunde onlookers.

My sister Yvonne always had the best description of our Mom. "As a former baseball and basketball player, our mom was a sports enthusiast who enjoyed going to the gym, bowling, and sitting screen-side with her children during the annual March Madness. She possessed admirable culinary skills, and her delectable sweet potato pies and aromatic bread rolls prepared with no recipes were a hit." As a single mother and head of household, Mom was even a handywoman able to tackle big and small household repairs. During festive family gatherings, my mom took immense joy in learning the latest "moves" from her grandchildren, and she never allowed her health challenges to get in the way of her joy when they were present. In fact, she became the life of the party. Mom had a spiritually rich life and required the same of her children and for that, I am grateful. One of my favorite memories while we were all still living at home and before we began to leave for college was our annual New Year's Day ritual. My mom would require all seven of us to kneel at her bed and listen while she said a prayer for her children at the start of a new year. Anytime and every time I had the chance to lift up and celebrate my mom and her legacy, privately and publicly, I did.

There was always something moxie-ish about me even as a kid. To say I am my mother's child is an understatement. Still, it wasn't until during my political career that I would come to fully understand what it meant to be a moxie woman. I was born in Sumter, South Carolina, but I have called Philadelphia home since I was five years old. Philly is where I hung my hat and manifested my heart's dreams. My youthful years were filled with joy and wholesome experiences at the West Philadelphia Boys and Girls Club and at Girl Scouts housed in the New Bethlehem Baptist Church. After graduating from Penn State University, I signed up for the Peace Corps, only to rescind that decision once my mother reminded me of the importance of paying it forward. I was the oldest and expected to lead by example, which was my mom's requirement, so I returned home to do my part and help my siblings go to college. As the oldest who was given lots of responsibilities, I never heard my mother complain, and neither did I. However, I often heard her say out loud, "Lord, have mercy!" Still, we all graduated from college and thereby honored my Mom's number one demand, to educate her children. She was so proud that we collectively rewarded her for her many sacrifices.

The silver lining to my dream deferred was my high school classmate, Marion DeBerry. Knowing of my love for dancing, she suggested I visit the Philadelphia School of Dance Arts, home of the legendary Philadelphia Dance Company. I spent the next eight years with a dance bag over my shoulder, traveling by subway to classes, rehearsals, and performances.

Even with my passion and the fact that I was willing to wake up runnin', circumstances impacted my dreams that were out of my control. So next came gut check time. Was this my world? My sisters helped me reckon with the fact that opportunities to dance at age twenty-eight would not be knocking down my door much longer. The opportunity was like planting a cactus in water. I had to face reality and segue. I landed me a "good city job with health benefits," my mom's description of a real career. I was hired by Willie Johnson, Executive Director for the Youth Services Coordinating Office during Mayor Frank Rizzo's administration. Mr. Johnson assigned me to the Youth Programs Evaluation Unit. This was a perfect placement given my training as an educator and strong interest in youth development and programming. In the eyes of some, it was a dream job. But certain dreams die hard. For me, I was ready to explore every rationale for why it was possible to be a dancer before capitulating and letting it go.

A couple of dancer friends and members of Philadanco (Danco), called me after I landed my "real" job. They shared that a Broadway executive producer was looking for dancers who were five feet, six inches. I am five feet, three inches. The audition was on Flag Day, June 14, 1983, a holiday for the City of Philadelphia employees, and perfect for me. Not risk-averse, with my dance bag on my back, as was customary, I traveled to NYC and found my way to the dance studio for the audition. Dance auditions in NYC were what we described as "cattle calls." Dozens, and sometimes hundreds, of dancers would arrive, fabulously lean, which was never my body type. They would elbow their way to the front or center of the dance floor ready to audition. Hated it! I hated all dance auditions. I was weak in ballet, and I was short for a dancer so by the end of the cattle call, I'd already heard the refrain for the fiftieth time, "Thank you very much, this group is dismissed," from choreographers. This announcement always included me. I had a city job with a good starting salary, so nothing risked, nothing gained. I would just trundle back home, ready to try again.

In August, ninety days later, the executive producer of the show convened all the dancers at the Brighton Hotel and Casino in Atlantic City to commence dance rehearsals. I again got a call from a dancer, informing me that all of the dancers did not show up. The show was eight dancers short. While there was a need for eight more dancers was music to my ears, I had one irrefutable challenge. Their height requirement did not change. The producers required dancers who were five feet and six inches tall. Again, I reckoned with the fact and answered my question, what do I have to lose? The answer, nothing, except the gas for the car to travel, this time to Atlantic City, the location for the next round of auditions and the ultimate location for the Vegas-style dance show production and performances. I packed my dance bag with my four-inch pumps and made the trip to Atlantic City.

In the end, I survived all the rounds of the dance audition. With my five feet, three inches in height, and my four-inch pumps, I met the height requirement and got the job. I won the opportunity to live my once-in-a-lifetime dream. In today's vernacular, one would say, OMG! There is no word in the English vocabulary to adequately explain or express the immense, indescribable, absolute joy I felt. I was about to live a dream come true, as a professional dancer at the ripe old age of twenty-eight. It did not matter to me that I was the oldest dancer in the show. I wore this badge with pride. The feeling of winning a spot in the show *Hello Broadway* was simply indescribable. There are no words. The next assignment was to announce this great news to my mom.

There was a lot I was willing to give up to fulfill my dream despite the boulders ahead. While I did not meet the height requirement, was too old, was no triple threat, and was better at jazz than ballet dancing, I woke up running for many months. I was hungry. When the knock came at the door, i.e., that call from one of my Danco buddies with little contemplation, I seized the moment and was not deterred. I'd figured out a way to meet the five-foot-six-inch height requirement, passed the dance audition, and got the job. Now, imagine if I had not looked fear in its face. Imagine if I had allowed the ghost of doubt to paralyze me. Imagine if I had not pursued my dream even when afraid. I would never have been a dancer even at the age of twenty-eight! In the end, reality would trump my career as a dancer. I was good. In fact, I was great because I had fulfilled my dream of dancing professionally.

After seven years at Danco and a year at the casino, I had to face reality ... my natural ability had taken me as far as I could go at my age. I was too old to pursue a career in dancing, so with fortitude, I satisfied my passion for dance by embarking on a sixteen-year career teaching dance at Philadelphia recreation centers and Philadanco. I also became an elementary school teacher in the Philadelphia public schools. The only thing that took me away from these passions was my calling to public service. Helping people was a natural proclivity for me and one that allowed this Philly girl to rise to great heights despite jumping on the political bandwagon late in the game.

By the time I arrived at city hall, I had come a long way from that dressing room floor, but the one thing I learned about commitment and discipline regardless of career choice, is that nothing one does in life is ever wasted. There are lessons learned that carry over to whatever comes next. My rule—in my case, when I could no longer dance or teach—was to find a way to continue to feed my interests. Fundraising, lobbying, volunteering, or drafting public policy were intellectual substitutes that appealed to me. I sustained my engagement and remained active with Philadanco serving on its board for many years, attending all performances twice a year since my departure in 1982, and selling fifty-plus tickets twice a year during my twenty-plus years with the Philadelphia City Council up to the writing of this memoir. After testing the waters in a few career spaces, all of which prepared me for my new steps, I settled into the world of electoral politics.

The background on how I got started in electoral politics found its way to the desk of the leadership of the Pennsylvania Commission for Women. After my stint as a dancer and educator, in 1982

I served as a committee person for the Third Division of Philadelphia's Twenty-Fourth Ward, which kickstarted my interest in politics. In 1991, I was hired as legislative director for the Pennsylvania State Senator Chaka Fattah, and would later go on to serve as Community Affairs Director for State Senator Vincent Hughes. My name, my reputation, and my work product were submitted to a committee at the Pennsylvania Commission for Women. After an extensive interview and a fabulous photo shoot orchestrated by the Pennsylvania Commission for Women, I was selected for publication in the book *Voices*, a collection of stories about successful African American and Latinx women. It pretty much sums up my journey, and I present an unedited excerpt of my story from the interview:

> Graffiti spray-painted on her new house spelled action for Blondell Reynolds-Brown and led her to where she is today. It's a thread that runs through the fabric of her life. "This was not a part of my plan, a life in politics. I'd planned to become a teacher and later a principal. I had many detours along the way," she states.
>
> The oldest of seven, Blondell comes from a materially poor but spiritually rich background in West Philadelphia. It might have been poor economically but rich with books and love. True to her original dream, she did become a teacher for a while and later an Associate Director of Admissions at her alma mater, Penn State.
>
> In her last year of graduate school at Penn State, she walked through the graduate student's lounge and noted a sign that read, Students Wanted: US Peace Corps, earn a salary. "The opportunity to now take my academic training in education to a region in Africa and teach children was awe-inspiring and instantly struck my interest. I went

to orientation and left deeply inspired. I signed up and became a recruit," she said.

The next step was to inform her mom. She called home and told her mom that she had signed up for the Peace Corps. Crickets! There was a deadpan silence on the phone. If you know my mom, Reynolds, then you'd know that silence always meant disapproval. Calmly, my mother reminded me that I had three sisters still in college and three siblings preparing to go. Never raising her consoling voice, she replied, "Your Peace Corps will be right here in Philadelphia." My mom made it exceedingly clear. Family is and will always be, first. So as an obedient twenty-two-year-old, I packed my bags and moved back home to Philadelphia.

Filled with love, strength, and the gumption I learned from my mother, on February 11, 1995, I announced my formal candidacy to run for City Council at a standing-room-only gathering at the office of one of Philadelphia's influential unions, District Council 1199C, in Center City Philadelphia. *Your Real Voice* newspaper reprinted my campaign kick-off remarks, "I am standing here today on the shoulders of giants . . . my horizons have been expanded. I will be your voice for a responsive government and will put people first. I believe those who have a special commitment to children, the unemployed, marginalized men and women, and struggling small businesspeople, have a special role in public life. Public policy downtown works best when it connects solidly with community leaders uptown in the neighborhoods. When given the necessary resources and support, good public policy can change the lives and life chances of the weakest among us. I will bring an uncommon sense to city hall. Our campaign will be the start. I am standing on the shoulders of many giants; therefore, my horizons have been expanded. We need your time, talents, and treasury. And WE WILL WIN. Will you help me?"

Power brokers and political heavyweights with stature signed onto my campaign's masterful literature. It read "Service-Demonstrated Leadership. Don't take our word for it." I was awestruck by the response and indeed as *Your Real Voice* stated, "Her campaign filed five times more names than required for the 1995 primary." The petition organizers, Wilhelmina Moore and Marcella Daniels Gibson, led our campaign securing more than 5,500 signatures. Thanks to these noble petition captains and an army of volunteers we far surpassed the legal requirement for just one thousand signatures, and on May 16, my name was placed on the ballot for City Council at-large.

On May 16, 1995, despite roaming 142.6 square miles of Philadelphia and garnering 48,995 votes, I was close but not close enough. Of the twelve candidates for only five ballot slots, as a non-endorsed candidate, I lost by 3,200 votes citywide—only 1.6 votes per division. Placing a close sixth did not count. My number two ballot position, the significant powerful endorsements I had secured, the well-oiled campaign operations run by members of The Fattah Organization who had previous professional and public service experiences, and my seasoned understanding of campaign strategies did not carry me across the finish line. I was defeated. I lost.

My ego was bruised, and my spirit was knocked down and out. I was despondent for months. My husband was angry and annoyed with the 1995 campaign leadership, some of whom he believed became ghosts and were nowhere to be found at the campaign headquarters on election night when the polls closed as we watched the election returns. For many months after the results, I was in quiet solitude. Comforted by a husband who felt helpless and watched my sadness daily, I ached. Finally, I grasped the profound message of the author and women's political activist Helen Keller: *"Only through the experience of trial, error, and suffering can the soul be strengthened, vision cleared, ambition inspired, and fight restored."*

During the summer of 1995, I pondered again the unavoidable question, what will I be when I grow up? What did I want to do? I would figure that out eventually, but first, I wanted to become what I had longed for the most: a mom.

Inspired by the elected leaders making a difference in our challenging world, with buoyant optimism, and a three-year-old toddler on my hip, in 1999, I again decided to run for public office. Early in my career, decades before I won my first election to the Philadelphia City Council in 1999, I adopted a mantra that became my stamped handprint for every position and opportunity on my career ladder. The slogan was captured in a poster I discovered in a bookstore during my twenties that I had framed, memorized, and referenced in my many speeches as I traveled around the City of Philadelphia and the southeastern Pennsylvania region. I was never able to find the author of this profound definition of "*COMMITMENT*," and I had never seen the message quoted anywhere since I'd started my career. It was not until I had to do a search for my memoir that I finally found it. Well, here is the quote from one of the ultimate notable politicians of our time.

> *"Commitment is what transforms a promise into reality. It is the words that speak boldly of your intentions, and your actions that speak louder than your words. It is making the time when there is none, coming through time after time after time. Commitment is the stuff a character is made of. Commitment is the power to change the face of things. Commitment is the daily triumph of integrity over skepticism."*
>
> —President Abraham Lincoln

Commitment is the secret sauce of moxie women. Over a decade before, a married couple and dear friends, she a Cuban Republican lawyer and he, a Jewish Democratic lawyer, (go figure), knew that I love anything moxie. They gifted me a delightful 3x5 hardback orange book by Kobi Yamada, titled *MOXIE*. The author had curated fifty pages of quotations defining this often intangible quality called moxie. Years later this charm of a book was a repeat gift from Loree Jones, a young woman among several dozen whom my staff and I had celebrated as one of Philadelphia's young moxie women representing the city's next generation of leadership.

Moxie women savor achievements, the good, and the delightful, and become resilient as they manage the bad and the ugly. They learn to face each day, weather the storms, hold their heads up, accept the harsh lessons learned, and then, with benevolence, share the lessons when they pass the baton. Moxie women feel empowered when they turn the page and close that chapter of their careers . . . because they have delivered and feel liberated and emancipated when they decide to live not just the length of their career, but the width of their career as well.

Driven and confident, these women are clear about the fact that dreams are the seedlings of reality. They do not fret about doing the work to make their dreams come true. These women fully understand two beliefs: First, as stated by American author Napoleon Hill and then requoted by author Diana Scharf-Hunt, *"Goals are dreams with deadlines."* Second, moxie women with grit as their middle name embrace one of my teacher's mantras, *"The only place where success comes before work is in the dictionary."*

Moxie women dare to walk the tightrope in careers like politics, not traditionally embraced by women. They care about the world they live in and choose to be active participants. Never do they complain, make benign judgments, or become spectators on the sidelines of issues that require cheerleaders and champions. These are ordinary women of all backgrounds and from all walks of life with or without wealth, mostly the latter, who have chosen to make a positive contribution in their chosen professional endeavor or to advance special interests or issues that burn in their souls. Driven to shift the paradigm in a way that makes a difference for others, they intentionally and unapologetically commit and figuratively glue themselves to their causes.

Moxie women honor their word and reject giving excuses. These women believe the passage, first quoted by Vernon Brundage Jr., author of *Shoot Your Shot* and attributed to many, including President Barack Obama, *"Excuses are the tools of the incompetent used to build bridges to nowhere and monuments of nothingness."* This quote was reiterated when I pursued membership to the greatest sororities on earth, the Delta Sigma Theta Sorority, Inc. Founded on the core value of public service in 1913, the women of Sankofa, my line sisters and I, had to memorize an entire passage devoted to excuses, which discusses how in life excuses are indeed the tools of incompetence and women who use them build castles to nowhere.

Moxie women use their voices. In public service, it's good to be reminded that the only way for evil to prevail is for honest people to do and say nothing. I will tell you, without a doubt, that silence is betrayal and will always smell of duplicity. Women with character, big hearts, and unshakable philosophical beliefs about service to others must speak up and speak out for those in need of champions and advocacy. Women who relish pushing the envelope to make things better for others, and when they prevail, will win many times over.

Taking contrary positions will never be comfortable or convenient. Most times your voice of advocacy will tick others off, including family. If willingness to champion others improves the circumstances of the one or the many being diminished or treated unfairly please bring it. Ignore the bystanders. Most of those in the wings of the stage could care less and are unlikely to stretch their necks or their wallets for others, including you! While moxie women are flawed and vulnerable like every other human being, they are not paralyzed by their imperfections and failures. They understand that through experiences learned, pain is a great teacher. Every day, moxie women strive to do better so they can be better.

The chutzpah of Black and Latinx women requires moxie plus qualities and toughness to survive. The double standards that exist for women, in general, are intensified for Black and Latinx women elected officials. As a Black woman, I categorically knew that, at the majority table, double standards exist, and believe me, they are real. Experiencing inequity and being underestimated regularly was the norm. Never intimidated, I consistently prepared myself and my psyche, and I never complained when faced with America's cardinal sin—racism. Instead, I persisted and insisted. At times, bringing a chair and creating my own table was the only option.

At the table, moxie women with their invisible shields skillfully and gracefully tackle, insist, negotiate, and set agendas for matters and objectives to be accomplished. Racism and sexism are a given, so they counter the insidious, and institutionalized *isms* with thorough preparation, excellence, smarts, and unparalleled tenacity in the execution of their responsibilities. They show up daily to face the lions with courage and a spine when challenged by others.

During my campaigns, I always marveled at moxie single moms who met the demands of parenting and still reached out and showed up to help me as a candidate despite their remarkably busy lives and, maybe, uncomfortable circumstances. Devoted to making a difference for the children and families in their underserved communities they manage to carve out under-resourced time to give back to their block club, youth groups, neighborhood organizations, and youth sports teams. They recognize that the negative laws that affect their lives and the lack of services in their under-resourced communities require their action. So, moxie women show up and show out as committed citizens and volunteers, never complaining.

Carpe Diem

CHAPTER THREE

MOTHERHOOD

"Mom. One who sacrifices her body, sleep, social life, spending money, eating hot meals, patience, memory, energy, and sanity for love." —Tanya Masse

Determined never to give up, as mentioned, I ran for office a second time in 1999. After my first run for election and a close, but still embarrassing, loss, I gleaned what a real moxie woman must learn: preparation when the rest of the world is sleeping, and a visionary team is a must. It was quite the journey I shared with my stellar team, whose vision and strong work ethic matched my own. With a well-executed and well-financed strategic campaign plan, this relentless and devoted team drove hard, and it felt good to be on the right side of humanity. The second time around, we got it right. We won!

I began this campaign cycle with my three-year-old daughter on my hip. At first, people thought I was a basket case. Random stares as I walked through various doors were the norm. One of the groups I sought support from and was a member of was the Coalition of 100 Black Women, PA Chapter. I recall vividly when I walked through those doors at one of our monthly meetings as a new mother carrying my daughter, I was comfortable in my skin, the stares didn't bother me. I had already secured clearance from the leadership of the Coalition led by two dynamic women, Jackie Manns Smalley and Linda Watson, who were both mothers with demanding careers also walking the tightrope. These veteran moms were understanding of my circumstance as an inexperienced working mom who desired to remain active and engaged as a new member of this influential women's organization.

What I wasn't prepared for was the emotional tug-of-war of not being with my daughter every waking moment. Even before my political endeavor, I remember the first time I had to spend a night away from my six-month-old daughter while on a mission for Delta Sigma Theta Sorority, Inc., Philadelphia alumnae Chapter. I cried throughout the night, and every Soror on my Sankofa line understood why. During that overnight experience, I discovered that the bond between a mother and child happens before birth, and there is truth in that proverb about the strength of a mother's love for her children. It is simply unexplainable. Little did I recognize that this experience would be my first introduction to the phenomenon known as "mom guilt." It is a real thing.

Serving as a councilwoman was going to extract more than a night away from my daughter. I had to brace myself and find a solution. After multiple accidental meetings at my neighborhood church, a small group of working moms with demanding careers and I decided to intentionally organize playtime together for our children, all of whom were under the age of three. Unintentionally, we became the foundation of the core group of moms we today call The Village Moms. Three of us soon became six, then grew to nine and more. We learned to lean on each other for support and lift each other up during trying times. With our children in tow, we helped each other at birthday parties, sports events, holiday celebrations, graduations, summer camp experiences, divorces, and funerals. Carpooling. No worries. "Can you pick up my kid when you pick up your kid, after school, after dance class, after swim lessons?" "Of course."

Feelings of appreciation overwhelmed each of us working moms who held high-pressure jobs and positions. Our lives became less traumatic, less stressful, and so much fun because we knew we had each other's backs. The Village Moms all shared the value that there is no one way to raise a spiritually grounded, culturally aware, caring, and responsible child without a village. We supported and embraced our separate mom's journeys without shade or implicit silent judgment. Conversely, we were never silent about offering a friendly, neutral perspective on parent-child-rearing dilemmas. We all have them. Recognizing silence has it's tinge or smell of betrayal, we always provided a safe space to share and to seek different lenses for help, insight, and guidance. The philosophical glue then and now has been and remains our collective desire to give our children roots so that they may grow their wings. Gratefulness is stamped on my heart for the Village Moms, starting with the "home team." Our secret code to lift and encourage each other continues today even after our children have grown up and started their colleges, careers, and life journeys. The bond and affection we built remain priceless.

Motherhood is both scary and rewarding under normal circumstances, but when working in the halls of government as a woman and a mother in an elected position, there is no normal. There is no ideal formula, roadmap, or blueprint for parenting under the spotlight of the public and the sometimes annoying press. Bottom line. It is not easy being a mom at any age. So, in 2000, when I arrived at the City Council with my three-year-old toddler as the only member of the Council with a child under twelve years of age, I already understood the stares of dismay. I took Brielle everywhere I went with her Mommie-prescribed assignments before kindergarten and her school homework once she started school. Early on, Brielle learned how to complete her homework while her Mommie was completing her Council duties. The staff firmly understood that my daughter was my number one priority. My chief of staff and my office schedulers knew that all matters of my daughter's life, all activities, cross country track meets, dance classes, dance performances, church choir rehearsals, tutor sessions, and doctor and dental appointments were sacred on my calendar. Period! My presence was my required expectation. Therefore, my 100 percent attendance at all of my daughter's activities was nonnegotiable.

Sheryl Sandberg, former Facebook COO, shares in her many speeches her belief that women have the "holy trinity of fear; being a bad wife, mother, and daughter." I agree. Like me, she is among the 50 percent of the population whose marriages fell to divorce. She, too, is confessional about walking the tightrope. Unlike me, and where I depart from Ms. Sandberg's assertion is that "A woman cannot succeed without a supportive partner." Clearly, she has not met the extraordinary and ordinary women who excelled and thrived after broken marriages or the unbearable grief from the death of a spouse like my mom. Clearly, too, she has not been in the valley that Iyanla Vanzant talks about in her book, *The Value in the Valley*, wherein she makes it clear that giving up or giving into your circumstance is never an option, especially when you have a child depending on you.

I know that valley only too well as I witnessed my mother, a widow at age thirty-seven, raise seven children alone while working three jobs. My mom demanded and modeled the values of hard work, gumption, stick-to-itiveness, and drive, never giving in and never offering excuses. My siblings and I inherited those qualities, and I have brought these needed attributes into my political career. My mom was proof positive that a woman can rise to meet life's snowballs and curveballs with grace, and I would prove her right; my apple didn't fall too far from her tree. It was my mom's example that moved me to believe that I could and should fulfill my dreams and her expectations. In my opinion, moms, metaphorically, are like the sacrificial lambs in the Bible, long-suffering and triumphant in all they do for their children.

Though I do not agree with Sandburg on every point, I will admit that I drank the Kool-Aid and was one of those career women who believed you could have it all: a successful marriage, a demanding career, children, family, good friends, and more. Yes. I had the cape with the big *SW* . . . superwoman, and I wore it for a while, maybe too long. Full days for me started at 6:00 a.m. with a 7:30 a.m. drop off at Brielle's school, and most days ending after 9:00 or 10:00 p.m., and that did not allow for working at home. This schedule became a daily balancing walk on the tightrope. I had my head down at work, my head up in my marriage, and buried in Mommie mode as a mother. While navigating the daily pressures of City Council and juggling my multiple roles, I believe I can say without repudiation I succeeded as a mother and an elected official. Striking the delicate balance between my favorite roles of mom and wife, coupled with the layers of legislative duties and politics baked into most hours of every day, life as an elected public official was not a candy stroll.

Parenting magnified became less of an anomaly as I navigated my role in the world of electoral politics. As the only woman in the Council with a toddler, old-school African American women thought I had lost my mind when I entered a room for organizational meetings with Brielle. From day one, I made it clear to the organization members and the audiences where I presented that Brielle Autumn Brown was my American Express card! Much like the message in their infamous commercial, I never left home without her!

During my twenty years in City Council, I learned that if you do good work, word will travel, and when you screw up, word will travel faster. My choice to have Brielle as an integral part of my world was a good choice. Currently, there are three women in the Philadelphia City Council with young children and two with elementary school-aged children. Times have changed for working mothers, and I submit that successful examples of more and more working moms will underscore this fact: YES, we can walk on the tightrope backward in high heels, blindfolded, and succeed. The bigger, broader question is, can we do it all at the same time?

During my second term in Council, eight years later, *The Philadelphia Tribune*, America's oldest continuously published African American newspaper, in their 2008 Tribune article featured three Philadelphia moms with demanding and influential positions. Titled "The Joy of Motherhood," the article *allowed* us to share our stories of the sacred journey and the unique strategies we employed to be present with our children while meeting the demands of our careers.

My commitment to my daughter was nonnegotiable, and that spilled over into areas not directly related to politics. As a former third-grade public elementary school teacher with a master's degree in education, I had become dissatisfied with my daughter's early education from kindergarten through fourth grade in her school. Having to hire a tutor for Brielle in second grade was my first signal and red flag. The quality of her middle school and high school education, I felt, was our last chance to correct the academic ship. Changing course and steering her academic preparation in a different direction was something her father and I had to get right.

Her father was joyful that she had qualified and was accepted to Julia R. Masterman Laboratory and Demonstration School, referred to as Masterman, Philadelphia's premier magnet school that ranks as one of the top college prep schools in the Commonwealth of Pennsylvania. Brielle's acceptance into Masterman, a public school, was a good option, but its impressive academic reputation was not quite enough for me. As parents, I believed we could and should select a school that was a different and stronger fit because Brielle was also exceptionally shy and reticent. As an educator and mother with a public profile, my parental checklist drove my decision to explore an alternative educational experience.

The prospect of my daughter attending a school with thirty students in a class was not an attractive option for me to consider. As parents, you must know your child, and I knew there was no way our daughter would thrive or, at best, survive and find her voice in a class of thirty students. To use the word *shy* for Brielle as a young adolescent would be an understatement. By fourth grade, she was already being bullied by the boys because she outpaced them during track and field in gym classes. As a product of an all-girls academic experience, I became persistent with the single sex educational option. Enrollment in an all-girls school was underscored after meeting and reading the author of *The Wonder of Girls* by *The New York Times* bestselling author Michael Gurian. His book offers scientific research on the physiological and psychological development of girls and how girls shape social behavior, interests, and relationships. I am a research and data-driven kind of mom, so these types of child development science-based books not only appealed to me but guided and informed many of my parenting decisions. Family physician and psychologist Dr. Leonard Sax, M.D., Ph.D., author of *Why Gender Matters*, was another book signing I attended. His book demystifies the gender differences by dissecting the biological ways in which boys and girls learn and act differently. Dr. Sax takes a deep dive into the issues that many parents must tackle: discipline, learning, risk-taking, sex, and drugs, and illustrates how boys and girls develop and react differently.

These books affirmed my decision for my preferred school choice. Moreover, the books reiterated the importance of having a parental checklist that captures the values and attributes you desire to instill and achieve in your children. This additional knowledge, coupled with my own rich academic experience at Girls' High, hardened my parental position and decision for single-sex education for our daughter. At the most pivotal juncture in our marriage, I was reminded that *"The most difficult decision is the decision to act."* —Amelia Earhart.

For this reason and an exceptionally long list of other considerations, coupled with my strong biases toward single-sex education, Masterman School was not the best option. The direction of our daughter's education for the next eight years was our last hope to alter the course for her continued education and academic success. Consequently, my choice for the next leg of her education was non-negotiable. I was immovable. The notion that I might have to walk on water to fund her education alone became apparent. I remained steadfast in my position.

Because I grew up in a home that stressed education as an equalizer and having served as an educator, for me, there was little or no room for compromise around my vision for our daughter's education. Being a TK, teacher's kid, I was certain I knew what was best for our introverted daughter, and I could not budge. At the time, we had been married for thirteen years, successfully meeting all the challenges of any marriage. In the end, by far, the direction for our daughter's education and my decision became the unresolved wedge issue and the ultimate straw that torpedoed and eventually led to the decline of a loving marriage. In a conversation with my trusted colleagues, Council members Maria Quiñones Sánchez, Curtis Jones Jr., and Bill Green, about my decision around Brielle's education, it was clear to them I would take a political hit. And indeed, I was fiercely questioned and criticized about the political message my decision sent about the Philadelphia public schools. The Islanders, as we called ourselves, was coined because of the many years we spent sharing wonderful, sunny, blissful days at Maria's lovely hilltop home in Puerto Rico. I reiterated to anyone who dared to raise the question, and there were many, including Black women on the community meetings circuit and on the campaign trail, who felt that sending my daughter to private school was not a smart political decision. My retort to those who questioned my parental decision was that sending Brielle to a private school was not a political decision. It was a personal decision. Period. Whatever the backlash from voters, I was poised to accept the consequences. The unresolved disagreement about how to approach the provision of our daughter's education hardened on all sides. This wedge issue consequently magnified other issues. The possibility of walking the path of resolution alone was daunting. Our other shared core values and fundamental beliefs around religion, shared goals, equality, and lifestyle were not strong enough to withstand the unresolved conflict around the core issue of education. As co-parents, Brielle's father was joyful about covering all costs and expenses for her lacrosse and cross-country activities. Daddy-daughter routine visits to the golf course and gym together, this Girl Dad never missed one game. He was the ultimate recognizable cheerleader for Brielle and all of her AIS classmates. Despite the sacrifice, I handled the private school costs for academics, school uniforms, meals, tokens, extracurricular fees, community service trips to foreign lands, and student conferences on cultural diversity. Coming to grips with the reality that her father and I were not aligned philosophically and financially hit a dark, long tunnel. Emotionally conquering this chapter of parenting while metaphorically walking the tightrope took a toll. I lost my balance, which proved fatal. Today, I have no regrets about my choice for our daughter's education, even though, sadly, this includes the loss of my marriage and a new life as a single parent. In the end, I made a unilateral decision with conviction that came with marital consequences.

Yes. I can affirm. After a painful divorce, you learn to live a new norm—you grapple with the unresolved conflict of your difficult choices, tolerate sleepless nights, examine and reexamine your soul, decide how much that specific core value matters to you, pray a lot, reconcile the price to pay, and then walk the cliff, albeit, alone. As you wrestle with the "what-ifs," ultimately, you must choose, act, and seek to be at peace with your tough decisions. Unapologetically.

In an attempt to level the playing field in America, education was and remains an equalizing force for people of color. I saw its impact on my family from the insistence and example of my mother, the daughter of a fourth-grade-educated sharecropper, who defied the odds and changed the trajectory of her and the lives of her children through education. I lived and witnessed my mother's sacrifice to provide a college education for me and my six siblings. Consider the six million African Americans from the rural South who had the courage, gumption, and audacity to travel to the urban Northeast and Midwest in search of a better life and education for themselves and their offspring. If you need a reminder of their story, I recommend the brilliantly written, research-driven Pulitzer Prize masterpiece, *The Warmth of Other Suns*, by Isabel Wilkerson. It's a comprehensive, all-encompassing picture of their journeys, this history, and the impact of these forward-thinking people on generations. While economic, educational exploitation and political disenfranchisement were the impetus for the Great Migration, my mom's fire was rooted in a firm conviction that education was and remains the strongest predictable ticket to a better life.

Not acting as a harmonious team around the most critical, and to me, a key area of our daughter's life revealed my husband and my biggest value difference. Marriage is an amazing idea, and when it works, it's astonishing. One thing for certain, and two for sure, marriage requires friendship and an enormous amount of forgiveness and communication every little bitty step of the way. Starry-eyed like many, I would soon learn the lesson that romance and passion will not carry you through the journey to a lasting, harmonious marriage. Communication and alignment are key. I am in no way an expert, but my limited experience in a sixteen-year marriage compels me to advise strong-willed, career-driven women to insist on pre-marital counseling because life will throw marriage curveballs. When the hardballs come, an unwavering commitment on both parents' part is essential to reinforce the foundation as you fight for the survival of your marriage. Seeking couples therapy at the 11th hour could not save us. Don't wait for trouble to come to seek marital counseling, as you may never be able to peel back the layers of stuff. I can testify. The bottom line is that it will take two to salvage your dreams as a couple "till death do you part." I can now agree with Martha Bolton. *"If you think marriage is going to be perfect, then you are probably still at the reception."* —Martha Bolton.

Village Mom, Dr. Loretta Sweet Jemmott, R.N., PhD trained Family Mental Health Specialist and Researcher, always asked the Village Moms, "What role did you play in the mess-up"? Well. With the benefit of hindsight, I could have and should have done a far better job sharing the mental load of coordinating and communicating our daughter's schedule with her father. Her Girl Dad, who loves and adores her dearly, might have been persuaded and would have benefited greatly from, been enlightened by, or even influenced had I asked him to attend some edifying school events with me. Not including my husband in every aspect of our daughter's childhood development was a mistake, a severe and consequential action on my part. If granted a rewind or a do-over, I would have approached i.e., communicated, and handled matters regarding our daughter quite differently, starting with couples counseling earlier with Pastor Terry Davis. As parents, we do learn early when we make a good decision, we reap the rewards, and when we make a tough decision, we must accept the consequences, good and bad. Today, I can say without any contradiction that our daughter and her father are both pleased with the outcome of the decision "I" made to enroll her in the Agnes Irwin School, a leader in all-girls education since 1869. However, as stated before, with consternation, you practice strengthening the mental muscle to move on. With the benefit of hindsight, like an invisible backpack on my shoulders, I weathered the emotional storm of my decision. Grief therapy provided me with the tools to better cope with the death of my marriage. It took me three rounds of therapy over ten years to learn how to pull myself up, reposition my footing on the tightrope, stand tall, walk with grace, and forgive myself.

Carpe Diem

CHAPTER FOUR

THE REINVENTOR: THE DANCER IN CITY HALL

My love for dance taught me that you must "be very careful how you live—not as unwise but as wise, making the most of every opportunity." —Ephesians 5:15

Dreams may change throughout a lifetime, but pay attention to your dreams that appear, especially the ones disguised. Recognizing them when they present may be the only time they show up and your only chance to act. Women who dream are prepared to walk the tightrope while seeking to maintain a healthy balance between their professional demands and their personal happiness. They reckon with the fact that a successful career does not always equal a successful life. In fact, the two are not equal, not even synonymous. Their journey and, therefore, their learning is never linear or stagnant but fluid, dynamic, and never finished. To the husbands, fathers, mothers, and mentors of these audacious women—I ask you to challenge and encourage girls to chase the dreams inside of them. Claim them. Let them fly. As a woman, I can tell you we are prepared to do the work to live out those dreams and eager to do the work to make those dreams come true.

So it was with my dream of dancing. Dance, which allows those talented in the craft to be creative in amazing physical and mental ways, was a perfect fit for me. Whenever I was in the dance studio, it wasn't hard to get lost in hours of dance routines and movements in front of the mirror, time becoming a blur. Dance, a creative expression that brings like-minded people from all walks of life together, also satisfied my social side. Dancers who share a commitment to their craft develop bonds unlike any other. I have built lifelong friendships from the hundreds of dance classes and dance rehearsals I attended during my twenties. In ballet class, I stood behind the prima ballerina, Jamilla Toombs, who would become, is, and remains my BFF from an endearing friendship of 47 years, birthed at Philadanco. Working together with her and other members of the company, you learn that movement in synchrony is analogous to athletes of a team sport, members of a theatrical production, or the volunteers of a campaign organization. The discipline of dance, as I would find out, was a building block for my political career and underscored that everything you do in life has additive value. I continue to this day to learn so much from Joan Myers Brown, a.k.a. JB and Aunt Joan, founder and Executive Artistic Advisor of The Philadelphia Dance Company, affectionately known as Philadanco and founder and honorary chairperson of the International Association of Blacks in Dance. At age ninety-three, JB remains the keeper of all things dance and still goes to the studio offices every, I repeat, every single day.

There was nothing like arriving at the Philadanco Studios to join dancers in tights, black leotards, and pink ballet slippers and rushing through the front doors to arrive on time (a life lesson), ready to take class, work at the ballet barre or rehearse for a performance. The foundation of readiness was instilled in me and thousands of other dancers who came through the doors at #9 North Preston Street; you must show up in life ready and always prepared. In other words, no one waits if you are late to the decision-making table. I learned quickly how true a statement that was in my political career. Decisions, small and large, significant or inconsequential, are previewed, debated, and decided upon by those who show up. Indeed, the rigor of dance prepared me well for my life's career path as a public official.

Upon my arrival at the City Council, multiple media outlets profiled my remarkable transition of how I reinvented myself from a dancer to becoming "*The Dancer in City Hall.*" Temple University journalist and dancer, Cary Carr penned the April 22, 2009, article, "One Singular Sensation." In it, she spoke about my early lessons and my approach to life that I learned while I was a student at Girls' High and framed it this way:

> Her road to City Council, she stated, was living proof that it's never too late to chase a dream and that there's always time left to make a difference. Inspired as a young girl by the Lawrence Welk Show, the Philly-bred spitfire didn't start taking dance lessons until she was sixteen. A quick study with natural ability, she auditioned in college and made the Jazz Dance Theatre troupe. That's no small feat, considering most dancers have been taking instruction since they could walk. During her senior year at Penn State, she turned down a chance to study abroad, opting to accept the invitation to perform with Penn State's Jazz Dance Theatre.

She went on to ask me during the interview.

How did you get involved in the dance world?

At age sixteen, I got a job at Gino's (the now defunct fast food chain, not the Philly cheesesteak shop). Now able to pay for my dance classes, I started my formal training. I went on to Penn State, University Park campus, and found a dance studio. During my junior year, I was invited to audition for the Penn State Jazz Dance Theatre. With my limited training of four years, it was a dream come true.

I returned to Philadelphia and was invited by a Girl's High School classmate who also loved dance to take classes at the Philadelphia School of Dance Arts, home of the Philadelphia Dance Company, affectionately known as Philadanco. Joan Myers Brown, a.k.a. Aunt Joan or JB, had just started this budding company, giving her dancing school students a place to further hone, perfect, and perform their craft. While weak in ballet, JB observed my potential as a chorus member and invited me to audition for the company. That audition invitation changed my life forever. The chance to dance professionally, which was unusual for a twenty-two-year-old, is unheard of. Rare.

What was your favorite genre of dance?

Jazz. Jazz. Jazz. I love the jazz form, the jazz dance body lines, and the symmetrical aspects of jazz music.

Who are some of your favorite jazz artists?

My favorite is Billie Holiday. George Benson. Joe Sample. I have a black-and-white photograph that I purchased forty years ago of Billie Holiday.

How did you transition from dance to politics?

As an elementary school teacher training with undergraduate and graduate degrees in education, dance was always my avocation. As a dancer with late training, I knew I could not sustain my living on a dancer's salary for the long haul with college loans due and a quietly hovering mom wondering if I had lost my mind. These two things prompted my career revision move. I had to reckon with the harsh reality that I couldn't build a career in the dance performing arts. Furthermore, my dream was realized when the once-in-a-lifetime miracle to travel with an emerging dance company as a member of the chorus to dance at the famed Club Harlem in Atlantic City during the summers materialized. It was more than I could ever have imagined. I also clearly remember the day at age twenty-nine and only a chorus dancer, I wrote JB a formal letter of resignation, hand-delivered it to her, got in my car, and took the long ride to Atlanta. Being alone on the highway allowed me space to think, reflect, and figure out how I was going to reboot my young career.

The truth is my curiosity about politics was ignited when I watched the 1980 Democratic National Convention. I was awestruck by the diverse crowd countrywide in attendance to nominate the next president of the United States. Fast forward a couple of years, after leaving a job that broke my spirit, I placed a call to the then-State Senator Chaka Fattah and told him I was thinking of going to law school and was looking for work. Serendipity made its mark. Fattah responded, "I have a legislative aide position open on my staff. Are you interested?" There was only one hitch. The position required the daily two-hour commute to Harrisburg, the Pennsylvania state capital. I accepted the position, not understanding this career move would change my professional career trajectory forever. It bookended my political career.

When I arrived at the City Council, President Anna Verna knew of my strong interest, background, and profile in the arts. Asking me to serve as chair of the City Council Committee on Arts and Culture was a no-brainer. I was ready to use my love for the arts to champion the value of arts and culture which was on the decline in legislative public policy as my carrot and my stick. Ready to make my point loud and clear, I did so through publications around the city.

What do you think are the similarities and differences between dance and politics?

Some may view politics as a dance. You can visualize images, movement, forms, and montages in your head and then figure out how to translate those images to the bodies of others. We all can look at one piece of art. You will get as many interpretations of that art piece as there are those looking at it. In politics, we all have our point of view. We all have our perspective. The challenge is in getting nine uniquely different Council members to agree that a particular course of action will be most beneficial for the common good.

What do you think the government can do to help support the arts?

Philadelphia's number one industry from 2000 to 2019 was hospitality and tourism. It was the 250-plus arts and culture organizations that fed tourism. With so many competing strains and strings on the city budget, the delicate and tough balancing act to manage and fund basic city services while bargaining for the inclusion of the arts in itself is an art and science.

With schools having their art programs cut because of the budget, how do you think they can manage to keep the arts alive and keep children interested?

Schools must use their budgets to pay for reading, writing, and arithmetic. Therein lies the opportunity for larger cultural institutions to play a key role by partnering with neighborhood schools to ensure that some form of the arts maintains a presence in our schools. Higher educational institutions have a role and responsibility as well. Their PILOT, payments instead of taxes, should not exempt them from this obligation.

Does music inspire you when it comes to your work in politics?

No doubt. There is nothing that makes my soul happier than listening to music. I work out with music. Brush my teeth to music. Cook and clean to music. Always after a round of KYW News Radio, I turn to music to get my spirit ready for the workday. Marvin Gaye. Barry White. Luther Vandross.

Do you think dance can empower women?

Absolutely. Dance teaches self-discipline, a belief that one can soar and can accomplish anything. When you are in a dance studio you are taught to learn and execute a movement 1,500 times to get it perfect. That's life. You are going to be faced with countless challenges and hurdles. When you do, face them and do what is required as many times as necessary until you get it right.

What do you think is more exciting, dance or politics?

Dance is politics. To have the chance to be an advocate for a part of my life that gave me much joy is a blessing.

Wendy Ginsberg of the *Philadelphia Business Journal* cleverly articulated the parallel between dance and politics remarking in her article, "As a former Philadanco dancer, Reynolds-Brown—whom everyone calls Blondie—feels the give and take in political cha-cha."

As I purported, no experience is ever wasted.

Carpe Diem

CHAPTER FIVE

EXCELLENCE MATTERS AND FEARLESSNESS IS REQUIRED

"The only sin is mediocrity."
—Martha Graham, world-renowned dance choreographer

Perfection can lead down a rabbit hole, but excellence is mandatory. Fearlessness is the secret sauce of excellence. During my career, I forgot the harsh fact that perfection, which may be attainable for a moment, is not sustainable. Forty years later, it took one of my cherished former employees and public relations staffer, Jason, who sent me a note after I had edited his press release for the tenth time. Jason handed me the note written in a flier format that said "Councilwoman, excellence is knowing when very good is good enough." In other words, cease editing. Let's release the [expletive] press statement. I later took his flyer and pinned it to my office dream board which I maintained and updated regularly. From then on, I adhered to Jason's suggestion. Excellence, not perfection, is our goal.

I had met this phenom before. It is much like the insatiable yearning of the seriously trained dancer. Once you have mastered a double piqué turn and learned to stop on a dime, you raise the bar. You practice and practice and practice and practice in the mirror, analyzing your body's form and forcing your body, tummy tight, bottom under, to execute triple piqué turns. The renowned Spanish artist Salvador Dali would remind us to *"have no fear of perfection—you'll never reach it."* The audacity of the dancer says try me, test me, please. Now let me show you that I can. I had brought this attitude into my political career as well and it was one I had to unlearn. I harkened back to my graduate experience when I first heard this new phenomenon called "becoming your best self."

A required graduate school reading was Hugh Prather's first book, *Notes to Myself*. Prather, a self-help author, discussed perfection.

> *Perfection is a slow death. If everything were to turn out just like I want it to, just like I planned for it to, then I would never experience anything new; my life would be an endless repetition of stale successes. When I make a mistake, I experience something unexpected. I sometimes react to making a mistake as if I have betrayed myself. My fear of making a mistake seems to be based on the hidden assumption that I am potentially perfect and that if I can just be very careful, I will not fall from heaven. But a "mistake" is a declaration of the way I am, a jolt to the way I intend, a reminder I am not dealing with the facts. When I have listened to my mistakes I have grown.*

I reread this book, and it spoke to me anew. Seeking perfection in my endeavors was quite frankly a daunting sometimes self-defeating exercise. I am guessing I am not the only one it spoke to because *Notes to Myself* has sold over five million copies and has been translated into ten languages.

A 2007 column, "Politics Double Standard Still Firmly in Place," written by *The Inquirer's* Karen Heller aptly captured my reality. Why do female politicians who worked for the Children's Defense Fund and an expert in health care, former presidential Democratic nominee Secretary Hillary Clinton, and the historic ascendance to House Speaker, Hon. Nancy Pelosi, respectively have to be subject to 40,000 Google searches about their suits and possible use of Botox? She writes, "When female politicians aspire to higher office, it is like laundry. It's all about a soft, clean, smooth, spring fresh uplifting experience." The perfect look! Layer this reality with being an African or Latinx female in electoral politics and the pressure is compounded. The last thing you want to be is shabby. You must be pulled together every minute of every day of the year; nails groomed, hair coiffed, make-up perfect, and attire immaculate. It does not matter where you are, the supermarket, your child's school track meet, church, or the office, you must be 100 %. You must be perfect! Looking your best is relative, but not optional. It is required that you be flawless in the long corridors of city hall. The same, of course, does not hold for men, think former British Prime Minister Boris Johnson. So, what is a female politician? A fabulous oxymoron!

Excellence comes from habits honed to the highest level. In the end, *"we are what we repeatedly do. Excellence, therefore, is not an act but a habit."* —Aristotle. Practices and habits become essential when seeking to win campaigns. Inconsistent performance, which suggests a lack of goal-directed discipline, will land one in the loser's column. Campaigns require an inordinate amount of energy, stick-to-itiveness, and dogmatic, laser beam focus. For women of color leaning into perfection is what will be considered excellent. Go with it.

My Fattah training taught me that individuals do not win campaigns. Organizations win. Therefore, I attempted to answer the tough questions. Do I have an organization? Do I have a rich network of family, friends, affiliations, and associations to build on? Do I have the right stuff to persuade this network to be a part of my enterprise? Can I build a coalition of believers from these groups to help construct a winning campaign? A coalition is needed and essential when capturing the attention of the power structure, moving the needle, shifting the paradigm, and changing the trajectory to one that advances the rights of our causes.

Winning Campaigns

There are a few common denominators for all winning campaigns. They begin and end with an understanding that excellence is never an option, but a requirement. The recipe that worked for me for five consecutive winning elections was an understanding of and execution of the myriad details directed by the firecracker campaign managers I was blessed to have. My team and I started with a sense of purpose. We homed in regularly during our weekly meetings, and repeated our vision and mission until it became a mantra. Over and over we tested our will, which is one of the most powerful weapons for the campaign trail. Believing I could make a difference, fueled by a goal-oriented campaign plan with key milestones, and disciplined behaviors when married to a strategic plan was a winning formula. Once I had set my sights on a potential elected position opportunity, campaign team members and I learned all there was to know about it. That included but was not limited to learning about current and former officeholders' positioning. How much money did they raise? From what sources? We reviewed voter demographics, and voter returns and carefully scoured candidate's campaign filings. We analyzed voter trends, studied policy papers and did the research and homework necessary to be armed with the knowledge to execute at the highest level.

I asked and investigated what I had to do to raise funds at the current rate of inflation to better outperform the competition. Relying on a seasoned campaign manager who shares your ideals you become committed to a plan of action. My cardinal rule: if it is not in writing, for me, it did not exist. A written campaign plan is mandatory. Discipline is then essential in the follow-through of the written plan. Like the bodybuilder's consistent devotion to the daily laborious exercises targeting specific muscle groups, you laser focus one session at a time with as many weeks as necessary to strategize, review, edit, and tweak your written plan before the bell rings to launch your campaign.

Excellence, which equals winning campaigns, starts with the candidate. Trust that there will be obstacles, hiccups, and new surprise variables, all inevitable, during the running of every campaign. Know going in this one FACT. There is no smooth runway if you are an African American or Latinx woman. Tenacity and attitude become the qualities to neutralize the obstacles. Strength in attitude is acquired as you tackle the campaign obstacles and disappointments. Even with excellence, mistakes are imminent. Be real and sincere in your language when you acknowledge those errors. Once again, the accomplished writer Maya Angelou assures us that if we are privileged to live long enough, we are guaranteed to make missteps and mistakes. We will screw up. So be kind to yourself. Give yourself grace. Give yourself peace. Scripture, Philippians 3:7, tells us to strive to be the best, forgetting those things that are behind, and pressing forward to those things which are ahead. Reinforce, recalibrate, and reboot your courage meter. Remember, *"courage doesn't always roar. Sometimes courage is the whisper at the end of the day that says I will try again tomorrow."* —Mary Anne Radmacher.

British podcaster, author, and life coach, Jay Shetty defines six types of courage. Physical courage is about being resilient. Social courage is the guts to be unapologetically yourself. Moral courage is about doing the right thing even when others do wrong, or when no one is looking. It is an internal compass of right and wrong. Bold courage is confidence in your intellectual prowess and ability to have an open mind, and spiritual courage is knowing your purpose here on this earth. Every form of courage is needed at the political table. Boldness and resilience, I contend, however, are first cousins to excellence. They are required and essential to take risks. Risks are never comfortable, but they are necessary. Venturing into rooms where you know you are not wanted but hold the promise of achieving your objective requires a strong back and a broad smile. Women who don't quite believe they can win but are confident about their abilities are driven by the fire in their belly. This true grit will always far outweigh the potential fear you carry when you enter those rooms. These women know how to model Joanne Clancy without apology. Elect to, *"Be the woman who when your feet hit the floor, the devil says, 'she's up.'"*

Hundreds of books have been written on excellence and achievement. I have many in my home library. The first book I read on achievement during my last semester in graduate school was Rev. Robert Schuller's *Move Ahead With Possibility Thinking*. This book anchored my foundational understanding that attitude is the one dominant factor among many in career success. Attitude often determines altitude. One thing everybody agrees on whether they are doctors, lawyers, teachers, salespeople, parents, Democrats, Republicans, coaches, or athletes, is attitude matters more than your aptitude.

A study by Harvard University revealed that 85 percent of the reasons for success, accomplishments, promotions, etc., were a result of our attitude and 15 percent because of technical expertise. Charles Paul Conn's book *Making It Happen*, another favorite, consistently resonated with my spirit and my professional career during my years in the City Council. Conn offers the reasons and the fundamentals of excellence shared by extraordinary men and women. In reviewing my preparation for this memoir, I discovered that I had highlighted or underlined all the pages of his book devoted to the discussion of excellence signaling to me its importance and reinforcing its value on my work ethic.

There are two passages worthy of mentioning here about great achievers. Gore Vidal, the great American novelist who was viciously criticized in the early years of his career says. *"Great men and women choose their own goals and are undaunted by criticism from unfriendly sources."* He was a young writer, still not established in his craft, and reviewers savaged his first books. Years later, after Vidal was successful and famous, an interviewer from the *New York Times* asked how he had survived those early years of his books being turned down and disparaged Vidal replied, *"I survived, by understanding that it is I who am keeping score!"*

Secondly, remember that true winners never accept any setback, obstacle, or temporary failure as a final defeat. This is not in their DNA. Great politicians lose elections. If you check the record and history books, you will discover there were many first-time candidates and notable elected officials who had to do an encore performance before they were welcomed into the halls of government of elected leadership. I recall attending a banquet after my 1995 Spring Primary loss, where Congressman Bill Gray was the featured keynote speaker. Embarrassed by my loss, I approached him at the head table to offer my congrats for his win the second time around to the United States Congress. As he reached out to shake my hands, he held my hand and with a comforting gaze, commended me on my first race and remarked, "Blondell, welcome to the club of those who did not win their first campaign the first time around." In other words, he was saying, don't stop, stay encouraged.

Tom Peters' books, *In Search of Excellence* and a *Passion for Excellence*, and Conn's book, *Making It Happen*, became my go-to references for reinforcing my spirit and intellect on the importance of wearing excellence as my badge of honor. Conn discusses in the chapter, "The Aristocracy of Excellence," the rubber band principle, that we were made to stretch and not doing so makes us complacent and mediocre. More specifically, Conn states, *"We were engineered to meet challenges. A rubber band is made to stretch. When it stretches, it is enlarged; it becomes tense and dynamic. Stretching allows us to live up to our full promise. It is only by stretching that you become better."*

If you are a Black person in the US, you've heard the phrase you have to be twice as good. When you are Black in America, being average has no place and we can see this essential quality in those people who excel. They are indeed twice as good. Stretching for an aspiring elected official means having the audacity to burn the midnight oil for at least twelve months before the official launch of your campaign. Finding time to make a gazillion calls to prospective campaign supporters asking for their time, their talent, or their treasury, aka financial contributions expecting far more no's than yeses, is an experience that becomes your daily regiment. The work necessary, leading up to all elections, is brutal. Absorbing volumes of material about campaign public policy issues, the foundation for my campaign alone was head-spinning. I had the audacity and the tenacity to continue these exercises and routines even in between campaign appearances from sunup to sundown for three years after my first campaign loss. Compound these new routines with meeting the demands of an infant, in my case, a beautiful baby girl, and an adoring husband, and you will better understand my maxim about the thirty-two-hour workweek. Knowing that victory is a road paved with excellence and perseverance feels only slightly comforting. However, there are no exceptions, no substitutes for perseverance, and definitely no shortcuts. Putting my shoulders to the wheel and pushing toward fulfilling my aspirations and goals were anchored by sheer self-confidence, discipline in my work habits, and persistence. For me, these were the keys that unlocked my success.

But here is a kicker for political hopefuls. Even after all that preparation, be advised that there is no guarantee you will accomplish your major campaign goal to win, the first time around. Be aware that a loss is a potential reality and the flip side of the coin. DO NOT, don't be daunted because remember, you, my friend, are a moxie woman. In 1995, there were only two people, Congressman Chaka Fattah and my former boss Willie Johnson, in my circle of supporters who offered me this word of caution, pulled my coattail, and mentioned this one harsh fact, "Blondell, losing is always a possibility." These words gave me great pause because I finally understood that excellence and achievement are the flip side of failure with lessons in both. Thus, in the pursuit of my dream, I refused to be afraid of failure which to me was an impetus and a motivator to up the excellence quotient. Yet failure like excellence can also be constructs dependent on each other.

While we may not remember, in reality, we have failed many times. Possibly we fell the first time we tried to walk. Did you almost drown the first time you tried to swim? I fell the first time I attempted a double ballet turn in ballet class. I fell off the high beam at Girls' High during my gymnastics training many times before I mastered it. Did you hit the basketball hoop the first time you took a shot? Heavy hitters, the ones who hit the most home runs also strike out. A lot. Failure has gotten a bad rap. We should think of failures as the training ground for success.

Consider these stories. R. H. Macy failed seven times before his store in New York caught on. English novelist John Creasy got 753 rejection slips before he published 564 books. For the sports enthusiast, Babe Ruth struck out 1,300 times, but he also hit 714 home runs. No one surpassed the history and remarkable story of the sixteenth president, Abraham Lincoln, perhaps one of America's most consequential political leaders, who lost more times than he won. Consider his many failed attempts.

> *He failed in business in 1831, was defeated for the legislature in 1832, failed in business in 1833, then elected to the legislature in 1834. In 1838 he ran for Speaker: and lost; in 1840 he ran for elector; and lost; in 1843 he ran for Congress; and lost. He tried again in 1846 and was elected but then defeated and lost his job again in 1848. In 1855 he ran for the Senate: and lost. In 1856 he tried for vice president and lost again. In 1858, he ran for a second time for the Senate; and lost again. But in 1860, only two years later, he ran for and was elected president of the United States!*
>
> —Charles Paul Conn.

Who knew? It was only after I ran and won the second time around that I learned this awe-inspiring story. President Lincoln never once allowed his losses to define him or kill his joy while pursuing his dreams. His impact on US history is undeniable from the American Civil War to the abolition of slavery. So, don't worry about failure. Worry about the chances you will miss when you don't try. Nothing ventured, nothing gained. What disbelievers and those who throw in the towel after the first failed attempt miss is the chance to *dream the impossible dream, and to fight the unbeatable foe.* Being in the game at center court, in the ring, center stage, or at the table is worth every ounce of energy the effort requires. Progress almost always happens in small, incremental steps. Accumulated, sometimes imperceptible, or even invisible steps excellence and courage is what opens the doors.

Failure is different from laziness or a lack of enthusiasm for life. There is a long list of elements that "separate the wheat from the chaff. "That's a Southern analogy I learned from my mom. Irrespective of the profession or industry, ask any notable successful person their formula for achievement, and they will have their shortlist. However, there will be, without question, a few common denominators and essential ingredients that influence excellence and success. While achievement can differ for people, success is no accident. Discipline, hard work, passion, optimism, confidence, risk-taking, patience, curiosity, and resilience will always show up on the list of successful people. Dreaming and doing the work required to make those dreams real rests on these abilities. And here is an eye-opener, for real winners, seldom are they spotlighted when they meet gold medal moments. Being able to achieve amid doubt, misunderstanding, criticism, racism, and sexism is a mark of excellence.

A last caveat. Bottomline, regardless of profession, and especially in the world of electoral politics, mediocrity is a sin and a four-letter word. Translated, being average is totally unacceptable. And for Black and Brown women, know you must walk on water and fly to be equal. So, if you want the gold charm, fly! Fly like Michael Jordan. Fly like Usain Bolt. Fly like Serena Williams, Sha'Carra Richardson, and Simone Biles. Make boss moves, like Barack Obama and, yes, Kamala Harris. Make smart boss moves like Supreme Court Justices Sonya Sotomayor and Ketanji Brown Jackson, Michelle Obama, and Malala Yousafzai. Rocket out like Mae Jemison, Kathrine Johnson, Neil deGrasse Tyson. DO it all with excellence. Your purpose is your green light, so walk, skip, and run with the wind of excellence at your back. Leave your footprint and handprint behind. Your adversaries, opponents, enemies, and others will soon discover, *"It's hard to beat a person who never gives up."* —Babe Ruth.

Carpe Diem

CHAPTER SIX

FUNDRAISING: GAS WITH A FLAIR

"Fundraising is but a tool to achieve a collaborative dream,"
— Anonoymous

Money is the mother's milk of campaigns. One of the most challenging things for a politician is raising the money to mount a campaign. I am sure you have heard the demand of many to remove money out of politics. There are arguments pro and against campaign contributions, but in today's political climate, a credible campaign of any scale needs hundreds of thousands of dollars to win a municipal citywide race.

Since I started working on political campaigns as a volunteer fundraiser in the 1980s when records of contributors were maintained on 3x5 cards (can you believe it) the fundraising methods and donor outreach processes have been revolutionized and transformed. The demand for a sustainable campaign today requires great financial, media relations, social media, and technology plans. One factor to note is that every time you contribute money to your candidate of choice, you are casting your vote for the kind of city, state, or nation you want.

Next to money, effective campaigns are built by the citizens working behind the scenes, called volunteers. Women's Way and the Forum for Executive Women did a study. In one of the chapters of *Power Skills, How Volunteerism Shapes Professional Success*, they say "A personal or familial challenge or illness can spark an interest in, a passion for, community service." Indeed, hardship and injustice in the world can inspire empathy and be a catalyst that inspires one to roll up their sleeves and contribute to a cause. Sometimes just the desire to make a small difference in the corner of the world they occupy or the satisfaction of being a part of something bigger than oneself is enough. For me, I wanted to be a part of something bigger than myself.

Volunteers are the unsung heroes and heroines of any democratic electoral process. These worker bees write campaign plans, amend them, make phone calls, walk door to door, mail campaign literature, email letters, write policy white papers, advance the candidate, drive the candidate, prepare the candidate for debates, coordinate, and manage the candidate's schedule, recruit new volunteers, train them, in addition to raising the funds needed every day, day after day after day. Grueling, commanding, and demanding campaigns that require one to be "fired up and ready to go" is not a spectator sport. There are no words to adequately express the priceless value of the God-given angels called volunteers. If time and space had permitted, an entire chapter would have been devoted to volunteers, the lifeblood of every campaign organization.

I credit my volunteerism on multiple boards and campaigns for the invaluable skills I acquired because they were training grounds for my political career. Little did I know those priceless experiences were equipping me with intangible skills, including event planning, problem-solving, political astuteness, public speaking, fundraising, leadership, teamwork, and confidence. While I brought an understanding of teamwork and commitment to my political campaigns, many of my management, organizational, and leadership skills were honed and sharpened by trial and error through active engagement in dozens of campaigns as a volunteer. I learned so much more from dedicated volunteers who performed their duties with excellence and devotion, without looking for credit. My volunteers included everyone, from family and friends who may have thought I was possessed but loved me unconditionally to retirees looking to make a difference. In between were college students looking to be productive or to build their résumé, ex-offenders who saw value in the political process, neighbors, high school classmates, college classmates, dance classmates, former teammates, the unemployed looking for an opportunity post-election, and the children of all the aforementioned who may also have been inspired by my daring to enter the political ring.

All volunteers matter but not all volunteers are as committed as a campaign requires. Time will answer the question of whom you can and cannot count on your team. Time will also reveal who is trustworthy and who has a poor relationship with honesty, who's using the opportunity as a steppingstone, who is dependable, and reliable, who has follow-through, and who follows up. Patience in dealing with and sometimes tolerating mediocrity was a hard lesson for me to learn. It took me too many years, especially when people were giving their time and resources to deal with ineptitude. Even today, I remain a work in progress at mastering patience for ineptness. It took the 2020 pandemic and the Calm app on my phone to help me develop this quality called patience. As a hard-charging volunteer back in the 1988 race of candidate Vincent Hughes for Pennsylvania State Representative, I required everyone around me to be the same. I was gently reminded by Councilman Curtis Jones Jr. once after a visible displeasure with the work of unreliable volunteers, "Blondell, you cannot fire volunteers."

In whatever I do, I want to build a hardworking team that can embrace the vision of key outcomes. The outcomes are the ultimate goals to be attained, and life becomes so much easier when each person understands their role and executes their assignments at the highest level. A wonderful byproduct of working with people with the same vision and values is that they can become friends. Because like-minded people find other like-minded people, they can extend their rich network of quality professionals across spectrums, bringing them into the fold. The value of these relationships proved unquantifiable once I decided to run for office. Many, once-strictly political relationships evolved into long-term, endearing personal friendships after my campaigns. For volunteerism, I remain grateful to those hundreds of devoted citizens in my circle who supported me before, during, and after my City Council career.

Let's address the topic of money. I do not know of one nonprofit, cause, mission, or campaign that does not need to raise money, but according to respondents of the Women's Way and Forum for Executive Women's study on campaigning, money came in third as the most important skill. The study showed that 73 percent of the respondents saw fundraising as one of the three top skills gained from volunteering, preceded by 78 percent for communication skills, and led by 87 percent for leadership skills. This makes the money argument a valid debate but not the most important one.

As a sophomore at Penn State, I was elected treasurer of the Penn State, Delaware County Campus Student Government, but never once did I believe I would end up actively involved in raising money for anyone in the world of politics. I clearly remember returning home from Penn State prepared to start my career and soon thereafter, in 1977, hearing of this young, rising star in West Philadelphia, who was running for the Pennsylvania House of Representatives.

Adrienne McKenney, a fiftieth Ward Committeeperson, approached me and asked me to purchase a ticket and contribute to the Democratic candidate for a state representative. Knowing absolutely nothing about a political fundraiser and only to support Adrienne, a devoted volunteer herself whom I admired, I attended the fundraiser. The special guest and keynote speaker was the charismatic and former mayor of Oakland, California, the late Congressman Ron Dellums. I left that event completely mesmerized and inspired. The combination of Congressman Dellums's thought-provoking and awe-inspiring speech that evening coupled with John White Jr.'s motivational campaign remarks and melodious voice stirred in my soul. Way back then I had wondered what I could do. How could I become engaged in work even on my block, in my neighborhood of West Philadelphia, then known as, "The Bottom", now called Mantua?

Over the next twenty years after that inspiring event with Ron Dellums, I went from attending fundraisers to selling tickets for others, to volunteering, assisting organizing, and hosting fundraising events. I cut my teeth on political campaign fundraising, learning everything there was to know and doing so with a trademark of excellence. During those years, before my first run for city council, few people noticed me. My reputation as a can-do, get-the-job-done kind of girl spread. Consequently, I was called on to host fundraisers for every major political player in the City of Philadelphia before I arrived at the city council. I learned that fundraising is the toughest part of all campaigns, requiring scrutiny, attention, and the involvement of the candidate. While political campaigns and fundraising campaigns are independent activities, the staff associated with each must be intimately integrated and privy to the key strategies of the campaign. There is no substitute for early aggressive, intentional, and strategic fundraising to ensure adequate cash flow once the campaign kicks off.

The central purpose for raising the money is to metaphorically put gas in the car and once gassed up, your foot on the pedal to run your campaign. Unless you can self-finance, promises of donations are not an acceptable way to fund campaign-related program activities. To communicate the candidate's winning message, conduct opposition research, canvassing, phone banking, direct mail, and campaign staffing, there needs to be money on hand and in the bank. Unfortunately, in the current political climate there also needs to be money for crisis communication to counter the distasteful mudslinging that happens way too often. Fundraising itself is not dirty, nor is it impossible, however, it is vigorous and challenging work. If you are not prepared to ask as many people, as many times, and in as many ways, for contributions, and be prepared to hear the word no, or some facsimile thereof ten times more often than a yes, then running for elected office is not for you. As they say, *"Everything ain't for everybody."*

In this age of social media, I am the last former candidate to suggest or recommend how to craft fundraising campaigns that capture old-school and new-school fundraising methodologies. Here is what I can say without contradiction, irrespective of what approach or combination of approaches and tools used to get the word out: Fundraising is a highly psychologically difficult and stressful task. Personal solicitations to advance your efforts are not optional; it's mandatory. Further, personal solicitation is the most persuasive, and I would argue, the number one approach that ensures the greatest dollar return from both small and large contributors.

While large campaign donors may respond favorably to their professional peers or someone with whom they enjoy a preexisting relationship as was the case with our highly successful Olde School Dance Party strategy, nothing and no one beats the success that comes with the candidate making the ask. You are the campaign's best fundraiser. Therefore, you must become completely confident with asking prospective contributors to invest in you, believe in you, and support your dream.

Given a candidate's limited time in the life of a campaign, it's virtually impossible to contact every prospective contributor. Thus, the campaign's fundraising director will have the tall and stress-laden responsibility to motivate all those associated with financing the campaign. During my campaigns, my Kitchen Cabinet and Finance Committee members helped me carry the weight of tackling the universe of available target lists, including, but not limited to, prospects, proven contributors, political action committees (PACs), the labor community, and special interest groups. The Finance Committee, a group of people who agreed to lend their name to events and commit to giving or raising money for your campaign, laser focus on high-level contributors. Like the candidate, the Finance Committee members recognize and accept the harsh reality that they will be turned down dozens of times more before they hear one "yes." Therefore, as the candidate, it is your responsibility to keep your Finance Committee, your campaign volunteers, friends, and family informed, motivated, and encouraged to meet the fundraising goals needed to finance the campaign.

While the Fundraising Committee and Special Events Subcommittee (the group of volunteers who played critical roles and provided the technical assistance and details for organizing events and money-raising activities for the campaign plan) augmented my fundraising efforts and exposure, all roads lead back to me, you, the candidate. My Kitchen Cabinet and Finance Committee, made up of the most trustworthy professionals on my team were given the highest clearance on campaign developments on the political side of the campaign ledger. This was required for their good judgment and keen discretion to ensure the strategy to be implemented remained sacrosanct and undisclosed.

Not all levels of the campaign organization are entitled to sensitive information about the moving parts of a dynamic campaign. Sadly, I had to exercise caution and be very circumspect in sharing campaign updates because of potential moles, a not-so-uncommon phenom. A mole is a spy who earns a prominent position within your organization. Self-servingly, they speak with a forked tongue and their unfavorable or selfish ulterior motives are never in the best interest of the candidate. In such a case, it is imperative that you, as your best salespeople, your Kitchen Cabinet and Finance Committee, know your campaign strategy and tactics inside and out never seeking advice beyond the approved list of in-the-know individuals.

Allies and adversaries can be surprising and at times hard to decipher. And believe me, I had my share of adversaries. One pleasant and welcomed surprise was that a couple of my most devoted allies started as archenemies, adversaries, or opponents, but ended up as my biggest cheerleaders and defenders, while known allies didn't think twice about betraying my trust. Of the former, adversary-to-ally standouts two come to mind. They were Ms. Mary Mason, radio host and Queen of WHAT 1340 on the AM Dial, and Jerome Whyatt Mondesire, a.k.a. Jerry Mondesire, former *Philadelphia Inquirer* newspaper reporter who was then chief of staff for Congressman William (Bill) H. Gray III, and later President of the NAACP, Philadelphia Chapter, and founder and editor of the *Philadelphia Sunday Sun* newspaper.

In old-school language, these two were opinion-makers. In the vernacular of millennials, they are "Influencers with a capital *I*." Long before the advent of social media, Ms. Mason and Jerry both had access to and control of their airwaves and printed media. Candidates longed for access to their devoted listening audience because it could sway the outcome of an elected official, an invitation to speak on the radio to their audience was coveted. Their support and ultimately their endorsement was epic.

My mother was a devoted listener and fan of Ms. Mason. Not unlike thousands of people in Ms. Mason's listening audience, my mom paid careful attention to the interviews she conducted with candidates and people of influence and power (a word I use with discrimination) on her daily morning "drive time" talk show. Ms. Mason was masterful at teasing her listeners about who her special guests would be. She was equally skillful in diminishing a candidate and everything about them if she did not like them, or worse, if she supported their opposition. What your public policy platform entailed was immaterial and seldom a factor for Ms. Mason. She wielded a lot of power and every candidate, or wanna-be candidate, came to kiss her ring, without exception. This included gubernatorial, US Senate candidates, statewide, mayoral candidates, and every other office that appeared on the ballot. To be blunt, the woman scared me to death.

Ms. Mason was a bully with a microphone who did her political homework. She fully understood the political landscape and thereby garnered much respect from her listeners and would-be candidates alike. Like it or not, an unfavored candidate was forced to hold their nose, kiss the ring, and figure out how to reckon with her.

With Ms. Mason, I learned how to put on my protective mental armor and prepared for her intimidating tone and, possibly, insults during an interview. Since winning was my goal, I subordinated everything else to my number one objective: a request to appear on her show. I followed her instructions carefully, registered my request with her staff, then crossed my fingers and toes, and hoped that she said yes. Even though I knew she did not support me, appearing on her show during morning drive time was not optional, it was required. For a candidate, Ms. Mason was scary. In a word, fearless. She was one of those individuals for whom I had to practice and learn how to look the lion in the mouth and prepare not to be eaten. During my entire first term, for four years in City Council, she was less than cordial and every Thursday morning during the Committee of the Whole she was consistently rude and crude towards me for no good reason. Her rudeness was just unnecessary.

I would often discuss this with my mom, her diehard fan. Mom would simply remind me of the scripture, Psalms 110, in short, God will make your enemy your stepping stool. My question was when, God, when? I observed and discovered that Ms. Mason appreciated and adored adulation and applause. Not a surprise as most human beings do. So, with that in mind, Sylvia Purnell Muldrow, my former chief of staff and event specialist guru, and I explored an idea. But before I move on, let me say a word about my soror, Sylvia. What a superlative manager! She always understood and captured my vision, engaging the appropriate expertise needed to fully execute my vision. We were bold and effective as a team. While Sylvia could not fully grasp why I worked in the minefields of government, she supported me unconditionally. Following a discussion of multiple candidates we agreed that Ms. Mason met the criterion for selection as one of the Women Making A Difference awardees. We invited Ms. Mason to our annual Women Making A Difference luncheon and celebrated the profound difference she had made over decades using her *Mornings with Mary* platform to uplift and empower the African American community. The icing on the cake was at that luncheon, she met my eight-year-old daughter and embraced Brielle in ways I never imagined. From that day forward, when we spoke on or off the radio, it was never about me and my work in City Council. Her line of questioning was always only about one thing. "How's my girl, your daughter, Brielle?"

Later that term my campaign steering committee decided to make Ms. Mason the centerpiece and Mistress of Ceremonies for my 2003 campaign announcement. Going forward, Ms. Mason became my biggest cheerleader, advocate, defender, and spokesperson. This particular campaign event remains extra special to me as it memorialized the first and last time my daughter, my mom, and I were all dressed in shades of blue and white in a photo together. The lesson of treating Ms. Mason with respect and dignity, despite her disapproval of my candidacy, rightly saluting her decades of service to the African American Philadelphia community and acknowledging her value as a player in the political arena paid me back in dividends. I never regretted being kind to Ms. Mason who, by all accounts, was a challenging personality. In the end, I won by honoring my mom's values. Turn the other cheek and seek to treat people the way you want to be treated. I miss and thank Ms. Mason, the personality who challenged me to meet her moments. She made me a stronger person and better at my work.

My other known adversary, Jerome Wyatt Mondesire (Jerry), was a force to be reckoned with starting with his days at the *Philadelphia*

Inquirer. I met Jerry when he was appointed to the powerful, and I use that word with intention, chief of staff position for the newly minted Congressman William H. Gray III. Jerry, an often-controversial public figure, was known by many for his cowboy hats, funky boots, and his in-your-face outspoken activism. He was a tall, intimidating figure in the political circles who ruled with a heavy hand, and therefore, he too had to be reckoned with. He was also a formidable, brilliant reporter and editor, a little-known fact to me at the time. What I discovered was that underneath his seemingly callous exterior was a man, a public servant with a soft and sometimes fragile heart.

I became a cause of disagreement for Jerry. His dissatisfaction with me had nothing to do with my performance as a member of the City Council but with my proud affiliation with The Fattah Organization, the powerful and successful political organization that was built by activist Chaka Fattah. From being a community organizer, and after having served in the Pennsylvania Senate and the Pennsylvania House of Representatives, Fattah successfully became a Democratic member of the US House for Pennsylvania's second congressional district from 1995 to 2016. Fattah prided himself on grooming young leaders from the rank and file, out of which came several Philadelphia elected officials: State Senator Vincent Hughes, Councilman Curtis Jones Jr., Councilwoman Cindy Bass, Ward Leader Willie Jordan, and others. Jerry always believed I did not have a brain between my ears and that I blindly followed Congressman Chaka Fattah and State Senator Vincent Hughes with my nose closed. Parlaying his buoyant activism, in 1991, he was named president of the NAACP, Philadelphia Branch, where he was able to continue to use his activism in meaningful ways to advance issues impacting the African American community.

During my second term in City Council, Jerry heard me speak at a major women's event and discovered that I really could put two sentences together that made sense and inspired people. It was like a light bulb went off in his head. From that point forward, Jerry emerged as one of my biggest supporters, advocating for and promoting my work in every circle he traveled. We became silent partners frequently addressing the intractable issue of minority and women-owned business enterprise participation on city contracts. Ultimately, along with the love of his life, Cathy Hicks, in the purest sense of the word, we became friends. I am forever grateful for that friendship.

Six years after arriving at the City Council, I was truly honored to be included among that list of fifty remarkable women from across the Commonwealth. They included extraordinary professionals and leaders representing and engaged in professions from politics to medicine, the arts, science, technology, media, the corporate, and nonprofit standouts. What was this early lesson for me as a newbie in City Council? A person or committee of influencers is always watching silently in the wings. In this case, it was Leslie Stiles, one of the Commonwealth of Pennsylvania's biggest cheerleaders for empowering and celebrating women, who also served as the Executive Director of the Pennsylvania Commission for Women.

As an at-large candidate, I discovered that sponsoring or hosting themed events tied to my legislative platform gave me significant mileage, raised my credibility, and gave me the support of that specific constituency. I also stumbled upon the revelation that I was more motivated by themed events linked to public policy issues I cared about. Themed events elevated and expanded my fundraising base during the last eight years of my City Council tenure.

While not always the most financially lucrative, I thoroughly enjoyed making fundraising calls for my themed events. These planned gatherings enabled me to discuss the associated public policy issues with prospective like-minded contributors. Touching a constituency interest group member at a visceral level and seizing the opportunity to discuss mutual points of interest and disagreement around that issue gave me much satisfaction and joy. It played well into my wheelhouse. As a self proclaimed pack-rat. I have kept many of the fancy invitations from these themed events as souvenirs. I remain one who treasures handwritten notes that capture memories, sometimes far too long. A little-known BRB fact! Those dated invitations also came in as handy memory joggers during my writing of this memoir.

For example, in my stash is an invitation featuring Philadelphia's music writer, producer, and legend Kenny Gamble. I have warm memories of Jason Lewis, an exceptional volunteer who eventually joined my staff as my Public Relations Manager, and became my stalker sidekick intent on pinning down Mr. Kenny Gamble. As you can imagine, everyone wanted Mr. Gamble's time, attention, presence, and invaluable support, and Jason and I were no exception. Eventually after adjusting our schedules multiple times to meet his, we finally landed the opportunity to meet Mr. Gamble's availability, and yes, we succeeded. Kenny Gamble consented to be the headliner at the event for Philadelphia's arts and culture community. His presence elevated my campaign. I felt deep gratitude during his remarks when he applauded my efforts as an ambassador and champion for the arts.

Four years later, he and his elegant wife, Fatimah Gamble, joined us at another arts and culture event at the Performing Arts Garage. Jason and I were so grateful. To this day, I still thank Mr. Kenny Gamble, Fatimah Gamble, the late Sande Webster, art gallery owner and champion of Black artists, and Victor Keen, Esq., owner of the Performing Arts Garage for believing in the authenticity I brought to the arts and culture scene of Philadelphia. With each of these success stories, my wingspan for the arts got bigger and broader because of people like them who much like my staff, truly believed in our mission. These arts enthusiasts indeed gave Jason, my staff, and me confidence and wings!

In the spirit of this book as part coach to future generations of women public officials, my advice is to enroll in a campaign training institute for women somewhere along the way to becoming a full-fledged candidate. Ready To Run, a program affiliated with Chatham University's Pennsylvania Center for Women & Politics, is a standout. Yale University has another comprehensive program that provides in-depth training in all aspects of campaign and candidate training. As a former educator, I believe this type of specialized training is essential and gives the edge and needed knowledge to become an effective candidate. Apart from gaining knowledge and tools, these experiences will put you in the milieu of prominent elected and appointed leaders, campaign consultants, party officials, and policy experts who are sharing their expertise in these courses. The time invested in campaign training and development will pay dividends and return immeasurable benefits. You will walk away with enhanced expertise and skills on the "how to."

My playbook for a winning campaign strategy:

1. I harnessed and mustered every ounce of energy I could. Trust me, this bounty of energy will be needed for the 14-hour days on the way to a victorious campaign.
2. I braced myself and prepared for the sacrifices and disappointments which would be unavoidable. Expect surprises.
3. I got busy using my point-and-go approach!
4. I developed a campaign mission statement with specific measurable objectives and fundraising goals with critical milestones as these are the first steps to keeping any campaign on track and required for achievement, i.e., a WIN! Footnote: Remember the importance of cash flow for critical benchmarks in the campaign, such as setting up campaign offices, tech and computer equipment needs, phone banks, campaign announcement, and petition signing events, buying ads, literature for field and Election Day

operations, etc. Make the campaign calendar, both the internal and external calendar your friend.
5. I learned how to make my cell phone my best friend and an appendage to my being. I answered every call!
6. Knowing my victory would be a road paved with stick-to-itiveness and perseverance, I considered no substitute.

This next point stands on its own, and yes, I know that something written in all capital letters is bad form because, according to my daughter, it is like shouting. But if you would allow me, I will shout this one critical warning to every potential candidate and elected official.

- CHOOSE YOUR TREASURER WITH GREAT CARE. I REPEAT:
- CHOOSE YOUR TREASURER WITH GREAT CARE.

From the get-go, before day one, hire a CPA or a lawyer well-versed in current campaign finance and reporting laws. This will serve you best as there are ever-changing rules that govern campaign expense reporting. Each new world order has the power to make new requests that govern candidates' expense reporting, and this can make your head spin. Learn the ethics rules, crafted by ethic boards composed of mostly white men (during my tenure and my experience) who sit high and have no clue about campaigns. Too often, they "interpret" the rules with double standards and triple standards for Black and brown women (my experience). FACTS! Search for and identify your best ally against ill-informed, interpreted decisions, a licensed CPA and an experienced campaign finance lawyer. My sister and CPA, Angelina, who tracks illicit offshore accounts for the IRS in her career, embraced the role of watching all income for all Olde School Dance Party fundraisers. Never were there any irregularities with this event because of her watchful trained eye.

One last word about fundraising for women who are drawn to a public policy or a career in electoral politics, your future could depend on it. Do a brutal, honest self-assessment as a candidate. Do you have what it takes to demonstrate early in the game your financial viability to succeed? Early money is like the yeast that raises the dough, no pun intended. EMILYs List, an acronym for Early Money Is Like Yeast, is all about how money makes the dough rise. It is a full-service organization founded by women who provide a menu of technical assistance to pro-choice Democratic women candidates running for office. Founded in 1985 by Ellen Malcolm, it is viewed as one of the largest and most influential political action committees in the country. EMILYs List has transformed the face of the US government forever, putting and promoting women to the forefront of politics. Becoming affiliated with similar organizations devoted to advancing the presence of women in politics and campaigns is positively essential. View your time and involvement with these affiliations and organizations as a part of your professional political network and development. All offer a unique opportunity to cultivate new allies and a significant means to deepen your fundraising base and pool of prospective supporters. Do your S.W.A.T. analysis.

Carpe Diem

CHAPTER SEVEN

CULTIVATE ALLIES, CULTIVATE RELATIONSHIPS, CULTIVATE VOTES

Transformational thought leader Barbara Sunden challenges us, *"Choose not to be the pawn of negative emotions. Queens choose their moves. Choose their thoughts which guide their actions."*

There is little question that race, integral to the American psyche, plays a role in every aspect of American life, and politics is no exception. We have seen it rise front and center over several political cycles. Yet, for America to realize its full potential, it must reckon with its race problem. Countries that value collectivism and their citizens are stepping into realms we have yet to imagine. A country such as America, built on immigration, lends itself to diverse cultural thought that can be leveraged to true superpower-dom. More than its financial might, America could truly become not only what the founding fathers envisioned, one nation under God, but a might to be reckoned with in every way.

For this to happen, enlightened leaders must drive innovation and economic progress directly tied to the health of our country, socially, politically and psychologically. The risk of maintaining separatism is far too great and must cease. We must cultivate allies and relationships inside and outside of our country which far outweighs the decline associated with internal division. Inherent in this multicultural nation that belongs to us all is the diversity of thought amongst and from a diversity of people that has been shown to yield borderless solutions for humanity despite rhetoric otherwise. Running a country from a bully pulpit portends a country's demise. My opinion!

Aligning around a singular goal, united people can accomplish whatever they set out to do, and my 1999 campaign when I again ran for the at-large seat in Philly proved it. My strong showing, coming in a close sixth among thirteen candidates, was because of the many relationships I had sown in 1995 across all strata of people across the 142 square miles of Philadelphia. For four years, I continued to foster staunch supporters and made new contacts. Though my 1995 loss was a sobering moment, it benefited me greatly because it gave me four years to sow and nurture the seeds I had planted. Like business, campaigns are personal. Once people get to know you, barriers become less and less of an issue for those genuinely in your camp.

On a micro-level, the following story illustrates this point. In 2000, the election of my comrade, the brilliant, W. Wilson Goode Jr., a known campaign analytical wizard was also elected to City Council. Wilson, Councilman Darrell Clark, and I were in the 2000 City Council freshman class. The *Philadelphia Daily News* featured Wilson and me with the headline "Cultivating Relationships Gained Her a Council Seat." I believed and stated then, and indeed my council experience highlights that as a Black person in the world of electoral politics, a candidate gains little in legislative achievements being a bully. As a Black woman understanding the unconscious bias that would play a role in my success was key, and like Goode Jr., I cultivated allies and relationships across all divisions of people. I clearly understood that success in my neighborhoods of Mantua and Wynnefield impacted my potential success throughout Philadelphia.

It was important for me to carefully focus on the goals I aspired to bring to life which were key to running a successful campaign. By diplomatically pushing the envelope on public policy issues I cared about, my chances of succeeding with impactful legislation increased exponentially. Daily I focused on making the small things that mattered happen while resisting and avoiding the stupid stuff that might pluck at my emotions. Being a pawn to emotions was a death trap I avoided at all costs.

My success strategy was simple. There wasn't a race, social class, or economic level I did not touch. I started at home. I garnered my family's support. I tapped my child's high school classmates' parents. I engaged African American women's organizations, labor union support, women's groups, colleges, classmates, Penn State alumni, churches, arts and cultural groups, small businesses, environmental groups, women's homeless shelters and the list goes on. Everyone mattered. Special interest groups were helpful and became essential with many members becoming much-needed volunteers. I reciprocated and I listened authentically to their causes for four years. In 1999, my second time around, they repaid me in dividends.

During my time in the City Council, allies and partnerships on multiple occasions proved to be of terrific value. Alliances with the Forum for Executive Women, the Coalition of 100 Black Women, and the Urban League of Philadelphia proved priceless. Their leadership and membership support provided the reinforcement I needed during the many years it took to successfully move multiple pieces of legislation designed to advance the status of women. Their support and activism included providing testimony, writing editorials, spreading the word and the advocacy all welcomed and required during the legislative process. My affiliation with these organizations illustrated anthropologist Margaret Meade's view of public outreach. *"Never doubt that a small group of thoughtful committed people (volunteers) can change the world. Indeed, it is the only thing that ever has."*

If you cannot build a coalition of support from your life's personal, professional, and vocational experiences, you will want to rethink your choice. Relationships, networks, affiliations, and coalitions are the base of volunteers across all groups, which when cultivated and handled with care, authenticity, humility, and grace, pay dividends you might not have expected.

Touching People

As humans we are tribal but one remarkable discovery that always surprised me during all my campaigns was every voter's need to belong. People needed to connect; they wanted me to not just hear what was on their heart but to truly listen to their concerns. Those I met on the campaign trail remembered me for truly seeing and hearing them. Listening with your heart is not an innate quality. It is learned.

I am convinced my mother was the kindest person on earth. I can think of no one else in my sixty-five years who had never made a disparaging comment about someone's character. When I look at the many greeting cards she gave me while growing up (remember I am a pack rat), her message consistently spoke of two qualities: the value of doing your best in all tasks and being kind to others. Often, she would remind my siblings and me to "be careful what you say and how you treat people, because you never know what that person's journey has been and, unless you have walked and traveled in their shoes for ten seconds, be mindful of judgement," Further, when you have a generosity of spirit, resist the need to remind people what you have done for them. It is disgraceful and it stings.

My family foundation and training armed me to be keenly tuned in to empathy when I greeted voters. As a candidate, I met voters from every social class imaginable, and every citizen, every voter had a story. So, I made the effort to *"Be kind, for everyone you meet is fighting a hard battle."* —Plato. When I met my voters, I looked them in the eye and listened to those who agreed with my vision and those who didn't. Listening attentively and authentically broke down more barriers, even with those who disagreed. The opinions of all voters matter and because of my mom, I was always especially drawn to meeting seniors letting them know that someone in government cared about their needs. Hugging is the most basic form of nonverbal communication that says to the receiver, I care. Seniors love hugs, and I loved giving them.

I learned from voters and from watching candidates who made me wonder if they had a soul and what not to do. Genuineness ultimately reveals itself in deeds and in actions, Unfortunately, sometimes disingenuous behaviors are not fully revealed until after a candidate wins their election. There were a few personalities I encountered during my tenure, but the most glaring example was a former councilwoman who did good work and should have been credited for raising the bar on the issues she spearheaded, yet her time in City Council was brief due to the choice made by voters. The way she treated her staff, and I am quoting one of her former staff members was "shameful" which naturally trickled down to her constituents. One too many times, too, I saw the sadness in her staff and unsolicited, heard the whispers speaking privately and publicly about how she treated people in general. Witnessing her story, I made sure when building my team and legacy that my treatment of people was unquestionably respectful, and kind. I also heeded my mom's spiritual teachings. Be careful, be mindful about how I treated people because the circle always loops. Said best, "Karma is a patient gangster." I wish I could meet the brilliant wordsmith of this warning. So, check in to see if you are your worst enemy and cleave to the adage that attitude impacts altitude.

When traveling across the city, county, state, or nation in my appeal for support, I reminded voters at every bus stop, corner bar, church, and veterans club that the single most important freedom we enjoy as American citizens is the right to vote. When I hear voters' broken refrain, "I'm just one person, my vote won't make a difference," I seize the opportunity to remind them of what the author of one of my favorite books, *The Measure of Our Success: A Letter to My Children and Yours*, had to say. In her book, Marian Wright Edelman offers vintage advice in her no-nonsense voice. *"People who do not vote have no line of credit with people who are elected and thus pose no threat to those who act against our interests."* Further, President Barack Obama reminded us in his run for the presidency that *"there is no such thing as a vote that does not matter."* Our vote affects our families, our community, the block where we live, our military, and ultimately, our children's future. The Philadelphia Citizens for Children and Youth had an expression. *"Vote as if your children's future depends on it—because it does."*

We saw this phenomenon of people voting against their own and, therefore, their children's interests play out in the 2024 elections. People, caught up in rhetoric and emotional gerrymandering, voted against their welfare. Donald Trump tried desperately but unsuccessfully to disenfranchise hundreds of thousands of voters in Pennsylvania during the 2020 general election. Upping his rhetoric in the 2024 election, he carried and won Pennsylvania. However, Pennsylvania is one of the states with significant farming concerns. If he deports immigrants, who will become the migrant workers to work the farms? Time will answer that question.

One of the hardest things to do is help voters understand that they cannot hide behind the false truth that their singular vote doesn't count. Historical evidence and examples are abundant on how one vote made the difference in the win or loss of an election. Consider the following few examples. In 1878, the right for women to vote amendment was introduced in Congress. Champions and activists for women's voting rights worked strategically and tirelessly to achieve this goal. In 1920, women finally won the right to vote when Tennessee ratified the nineteenth amendment by one vote, changing the face of the electorate forever. President Teddy Roosevelt, the twenty-sixth president of the United States, who had served four terms, passed away six months before the passage of the nineteenth amendment, granting women the right to vote. Given his progressive stance on issues, I would like to think he would have silenced the critics and asserted his belief in gender neutrality. In any case, despite the good, the bad, and the ugly, at the end of the day, life truly is a song worth singing! It took forty-five years and the civil disobedience of the Civil Rights Movement for African Americans to earn the right to vote in 1965. Sadly, ratification did not ensure full access for everyone.

Another example is Loretta Sanchez, who was elected to Congress in California by less than four votes per precinct in 1996. Yet another, John F. Kennedy, who collected twenty-seven electoral votes in Illinois eked out wins in several key divisions. His margin of victory over Richard Nixon was less than one vote per precinct. I, too, lost my first election by less than 2,500 votes. Broken down by division or precinct, it was 1.6 votes per division. Likewise, in my election, if two more voters per division had walked to the polls in the May 1995 Primary election, I would not have come in a close sixth, which, in the end, didn't count. I failed and was not one of the top five to win a Council seat. So, I am quick to remind citizens I meet on the campaign trail that when they don't vote, they lose their right to complain about taxes, health care, housing, immigration, politics, protections for children, civil rights, women's rights, voting rights, minority business development, the environment, and more. The aftermath of every election has far-reaching implications for each of us. Avoid election spin and fatigue by not engaging with the wacky, repetitive, "approved by" commercials that start to pop up every May and November. Do the opposite. Examine the causes and issues and pay attention to what matters to you. Decide which candidate best speaks to your values, your issues, and the future of you and your children. It ALL truly matters.

Politicians work for you. It is your tax dollars that support the government's policy initiatives, and the programs implemented. Be a judge and jury and decide who wins and who loses by casting your vote.

The Power of the Vote

Noted scholar, historian, and author Dr. Henry Louis Gates Jr. released a book called *The Black Church*. From 1773 to the present, the Black Church, the oldest continuous institution in Black America, has remained the glue for the African American community. Both the PBS special and the book explored its significance from the days of slavery. The powerful influence of the church in shaping African American culture, politics, and history is undeniable. For political candidates, as far back as 1862, when during the Civil War, President Abraham Lincoln sought out the leadership of the Black Church to best learn how to use relevant language in crafting the Emancipation Proclamation. Today, the Black Church is a political calling card. Politicians, recognizing the power of the institution, have made visiting Black churches nationwide a required stop on their campaign trail.

In May 2020, the power of the Black Church was demonstrated during the Spring Primary. Joe Biden and Kamala Harris were hanging on to the election by a thread and on life support. Coming to their aid was the highest-ranking African American Congressman, Jim Clyburn, from my home state, South Carolina. On Sunday, February 23, 2020, Clyburn invited President Joe Biden and Madam Vice President Kamala Harris to the Royal Missionary Baptist Church in North Charleston, South Carolina. I and so many others were moved by Biden's remarks. *"The thing about the African American church is that it's all about hope. The African American community in South Carolina will make a judgment about who the next president will be . . . You have in your hands the power to decide, to determine who the next Democratic nominee will be . . . You can own this election."* And we did. Campaign media talking heads provided unanimous consent, affirming that it was Congressman Clyburn's coveted, glowing, and personal endorsement that helped Biden score the big comeback. The invitation to a Black Church and all of what the Black Church represents re-anchored Biden's team and helped to resurrect their campaign. The rest is history. But you may be asking, why this story? My answer is that this story demonstrates the power of the Black vote. Hard-won, any person of color who does not exercise their right to vote should reconsider the freedoms gained on their behalf, the lives taken on their behalf, and the power they hold to be the change they want to see and live.

Any good campaign manager and field director knows that touching voters in their houses of worship matters. It does not matter the faith of a voter. Baptist as I am, Methodist, Presbyterian, Pentecostal, Catholic, Jewish, Muslim, or atheist, if you are a candidate, you'll learn very quickly that churches hold sway over their constituents. Your attendance each Sunday for the entire run of your campaign is not optional. It is required. Whether you're running for a judgeship, council, mayor, row offices, state legislature, or the governor's office, going to church is imperative. If it's a Black Church, you may have to attend two services on a Sunday. Understanding the importance of the church not only in Black communities but in other communities is an important part of the psyche of electoral politics.

My mom viewed the Black Church as a refuge. Like our forebears, my mom knew that the church was a sanctuary that reinforced the values she was instilling at home. It was all she had to help her in raising her children. So, attending church was an essential activity on Sunday mornings. We would rise early as we did every other day of the week. There was no day that my siblings and I could sleep late. Never. My mother's refrain, "Get up and act like you have a job." Mondays through Fridays, we were up early for school. On Saturdays and Sundays, we were all required to be up by 6 a.m. As I reflect now, I imagine those couple of hours while we were at Sunday school were a time of peace for Mom. Speaking before members of the Divine Nine and attending church regularly were two of the campaign requirements I welcomed with glee.

Carpe Diem

CHAPTER EIGHT

RECKON WITH THE NAYSAYERS ANYWAY

"We "play" in the sandbox fairly with others"
—Councilwoman Maria Quiñones Sánchez

Most citizens running for office willingly enter the shark-infested waters of electoral politics. Their desire to help those who may never know their names outweighs the treacherous waters they will have to swim in. When the sharks start circling, candidates must remember their why.

My toughened skin and deep spiritual grounding were my aces in enduring all kinds of malignment and stupidity I encountered while campaigning. Even when candidates walk on water to do the right things, they are never enough. I accepted this reality, armored up, and refused to allow the naysayers, the distractors, or the troublemakers on social media—there would be too many to count—to pierce my spirit or raise my dander. With God's grace and mercy and the choices I made, these bullies never defined or impacted me and my work as I soldiered on. I had learned from the best how to stay focused on the big picture window, my mom, Joan Myers Brown, and Congressman Chaka Fattah.

Reckoning with naysayers is essential, and there is probably no place greater for naysayers than in politics. The bully pulpit gets stronger when there is no pushback. There must, without question, always be pushback, but there is an art to it. My team and I were always in peak performance around negotiations for legislation. I learned to develop my negotiation and conflict resolution strategies when dealing with the bully pulpit. Since there is strength in numbers, I tapped into the value of my priceless relationships, which became invaluable in strengthening my defense. This is one of the reasons to choose your relationships with discernment. It is vital that you carefully select friends, supporters, members of your family, and allies who will show by their actions that they are in your corner. Those who do not show up otherwise should not be included in your inner circle or sphere of influence.

Once I had identified my distractors, I was judicious and graceful as I distanced myself from those with ill intentions—not so much for them, but for me. It wasn't easy, but it was necessary, especially those few "age-old friends." The pain of my decision was real, but the decision to distance myself from those who sought to steal my joy and dim my light was necessary.

One of my former brilliant campaign strategists, Greg Naylor, was a soothsayer of campaigns. Aspiring candidates, Federal, state, and municipal candidates would flock to Greg for his brilliance, superior, strategic brain, and campaign expertise. As a novice candidate during my first campaign in 1995, when I lost, and again in 1999 when I won, every day as I headed home from the campaign trail, I would call Greg after a community meeting or in the evenings after a ward meeting to whine about the callous or distasteful voters and opponents I had met on the campaign trail. At the end of every one of those check-in calls, Greg would always require me to repeat and answer his questions. "Blondell, what types of voters are there?" Like a high school athlete on the field reporting to her coach, I would repeat to my campaign coach the following: "There are two types of voters: those who support you and those who you want to support you." His instruction was that simple and that complex. I adopted and practiced Greg's self-talk mantra forever going forward and I learned how to defang my opponents and the naysayers.

One sobering experience involved his "friend," who decided to carry me on his ballot for my election in my last campaign although, he silently thought my candidacy was a moot issue, following my campaign crisis. The paradox of his actions was a surprise and a big disappointment. I knew better than to belabor the point with my sounding board, my sister, Pandora, whose comment about this type of duplicity was always, "Whatever." It was a character flaw of people she had warned me of many years before when, to her surprise, I decided to jump into the ring of electoral politics. I took her advice and moved on. There was no time to dwell in that space of dismay or to allow that surprise incident to siphon off my emotional resources. It was counterproductive, would dampen my spirit, and had the potential to deplete the energy and mindset I needed for my campaign.

The second person, who was not as much of a stunner, was a White colleague. This man, like many of my colleagues, knew I had a penchant for hiring talented young professional firecrackers for my team. He poised himself, ready to poach my talent. It's not uncommon that privileged white men sometimes forget that there are men who do look like them but believe and practice the values my team and I modeled in my campaigns. Tangible qualities like loyalty, allegiance, fidelity, and fairness. This man simply assumed that because my staff looked like him, prying him away was a fait accompli. It made my heart proud when I learned from an outside third-party that this Council colleague and Democratic Ward Leader had the audacity and the arrogance to solicit one of the most sought-after professionals on Team BRB. He was flatly turned down. Jason Lewis, my public relations guru, now a senior marketing executive in corporate

America, was the real deal. Jason helped him understand how awkward it would be for him to work with former Council peers but on another squad; unintelligent and another example of foolishness.

Duplicity, dishonesty, and inauthenticity usually take care of themselves, and as they say, leopards don't change their spots. Sadly, he was forced to step down from City Council because of allegations in a federal criminal corruption case. A father of two sons, whom he loved dearly, he was rightly credited for serving his constituents with distinction, attention, and care. Regretfully, his arrogance, and white male privilege landed him with an unhappy political ending. Unfortunately, the power that politicians think they wield can be very seductive, very intoxicating, and give a false impression that which is invisible. Because of my political ethical snafu, many friends and foes alike counted me out of my last race. What they never counted on was how my substantial and impactful fifteen years of legislative work record and constituent service delivery achieved during my City Council tenure carried me across the finish line. Further, I owned my poor judgment. Elected officials and politicians are not invincible. Why? Because we are all flawed human beings.

Clearly, during my campaign career crisis, he and other naysayers underestimated my work ethic, drive, and competitiveness. He and too many others never counted on my ability to stir enough hearts and votes in his district and the other nine districts all over Philadelphia despite my painful winter season of embarrassment and personal despair. The best part of this ugly story during that "secret" meeting where the Councilman nudged Jason Lewis to leave team BRB is this. Jason, in his respectful manner, enlightened the councilman on what it means to be loyal and to have allegiance to a cause bigger than skinship. Of this kind of duplicitous relationship, Maya Angelou said it best. *"When people show you who they are, believe them."*

If you are in politics, duplicity and criticism are not an if . . . expect it. Just know you will be criticized and taken advantage of by foes and even reminded by family members, who may remark, "That's the life you chose". That comment stung, but it was truly the life I had chosen. Implicit in that statement for me, was you are on your own. However, the intangible feeling and satisfaction I experienced helping to change the lives of thousands of citizens who will never know my name far outweighed the noise from the critics or the naysayers. For those who have the resources, but opt not to stretch to be helpful, meet them where they are, practice that mental muscle, and move on. The joy and gratitude from those whose lives were touched by my efforts, and the example I set for my daughter remain frankly, absolutely, positively irreplaceable.

So, when confronted with individuals in my workspace, on the campaign trail, or in the media who prided themselves on attacking those of us in public spaces, I let my grace and my E.I., emotional intelligence prevail. I learned to lean and find solace in Mother Teresa's timeless poem, "Do it Anyway." It has been and always will be my go-to affirmation when I need to self-talk, and it has become my mantra for mental strength when under duress.

I cannot remember when I first heard the poem, but Mother Teresa, a Catholic nun who became famous for devoting her life to uplifting the poor, orphaned children and the destitute in the slums of Calcutta, India, was a person I admired. In 1979, she was awarded the Nobel Peace Prize and, after her death, was canonized as Saint Teresa. The poem was engraved on the wall of her home for the children in Kolkata (Calcutta). What I know for sure is this scripturally based passage, part of which began as "The Paradoxical Commandments" written in 1968 by Dr. Kent Keith when he was a college sophomore, armed me to endure the jealousy, envy, and stupidity I often encountered but did not understand. I learned to hold my nose, tolerate the intolerance, and give respect to the unreasonable demands some voters would throw my way. I learned to accept the harsh realities and troubling moments prevalent and inherent in the dynamics of all campaigns—without exception.

People are often unreasonable, illogical, and self-centered. Forgive them anyway. If you are kind, people may accuse you of selfish ulterior motives; Be kind anyway. If you are successful, you will win false friends and true enemies; Succeed anyway.

If you are honest, people may cheat on you; Be honest and frank anyway. What you spend years building, someone could destroy overnight; Build anyway.

If you find serenity and happiness, they may be jealous; Be happy anyway. The good you do today, people will often forget tomorrow; Do good anyway.

Give the world the best you have, and it will never be enough. Give the world the best you have anyway. You see, in the final analysis, it is between you and God; It was never between you and them anyway.

It was equally important for me to recognize and laud those who buoyed me and elevated my work. As my sister Pandora firmly believes and constantly chants, "It's all about timing." A time to let go and a time to embrace. You may not fully understand the why, but when the "aha" moment comes months and sometimes years later, appreciate the lessons learned from being tested by the naysayers. I might not have achieved the highest level of altruism when it came to dealing with the bully pulpit, but I can say, in all situations, the good, the bad, and the ugly, I conducted myself with dignity and grace, anyway.

Carpe Diem

CHAPTER NINE

EMBRACE THE GOOD TIMES

"Pause and remember every situation in life is temporary. Nothing good or bad lasts forever."
—Mom (Sadie Reynolds)

Congressman Chaka Fattah was brilliant at crafting unorthodox initiatives and programs, which always had as an underpinning the opportunity to gain votes.

Immediately following my victorious election in November 1999, during one of our regular check-in meetings, Fattah brain dumped multiple legislative and program ideas he believed would give me a jumpstart as a new council member.

Francis M. Jones, Connie Little, Lynette Brown-Sow and Wanda Bailey-Green in collaboration with a group of dynamic old school like-minded women today called Influencers, spearheaded a small campaign event to honor my community service work the spring of 1999 when I ran the second time around. The idea to recognize my early achievements as a Black woman was lovely and all inspiring. To be recognized by African-American activist women who shared the belief that we must lift as we climb was special and remains quite a positive memorable experience.

Interestingly enough Fattah was already sponsoring a spectacular annual event celebrating Men Making A Difference. This event drew notable local and national personalities and keynote speakers, like Jesse Jackson, Mayor John F. Street, and my favorite, Susan Taylor, Editor of *Essence* magazine, along with many other erudite African American leaders. Proud of his program, he mentioned, "Blondell, you should develop an event similar to my Men Making A Difference that will be your signature brand. You can call the program Women Making A Difference and select Councilwoman Augusta A. Clark, your predecessor, as your first honoree." It was a brilliant idea that resurrected my dormant thought. In consultation with my mentor and off-line advisor, who consistently offered sage advice, I decided to heed his recommendation to develop a similar type of signature program as a new member of the council focused strictly on extraordinarily accomplished women. This made complete sense to me, especially since I had recently experienced the joy of being celebrated by women earlier that spring. I adopted his suggestion, branded Fattah's idea with a friendly amendment, and decided to label the event, exactly as he had suggested, Women Making A Difference (WMAD). Separate from my legislative duties, the focus and goal of WMAD was to encourage and inspire women to work hard, work smart, and do well, but also demonstrate service that benefits others. The proceeds would benefit local nonprofit organizations dedicated to the ideals that mirrored my campaign and legislative goals: advancing the lives and life chances of women, children, and families.

Throughout my tenure in the City Council, I would pay attention to women in the news doing amazingly good work in all sectors, from nonprofits to corporations, government, and entrepreneurship. Hearing the surprise and joy from women when they were called and told they were selected to be the awardees and would be recognized by my office never got old. Sharing good news with these extraordinary women deserving of recognition was priceless.

For ten years, working with a WMAD subcommittee, my office hosted, organized, and managed the gazillion details of the awards event. It was exhausting to plan and organize, from soup to nuts, this annual initiative. Proofreading the program book, always my self-imposed prized assignment, gave me purpose beyond my legislative work. I loved it. Sylvia, who possessed helicopter skills and an eagle's eye for details, was coincidentally a Soror as well as my chief of staff. Since excellence was her handprint for four years, she served as the A-to-Z event manager guru who completed and executed the affair flawlessly. The event grew from 285 women in its first year, 2000, to over 750 women and guests by its tenth anniversary. Up to that point, it was, bar none, the most diverse cross-section of women and men in the city who gathered to celebrate the achievements of other women.

Hundreds of men and women of diverse backgrounds across Philadelphia attended WMAD annually. The one quality and requirement for honor consideration was a record of community volunteer service and devotion to a cause or activism. This blueprint, which became WMAD's cornerstone, expanded to include and celebrate women from all walks of life, cultures, and experiences who dared to make a difference while they continued to master their career aspirations and achievements. The women in attendance, irrespective of their station in life, were hungry for professional development information and career guidance. Sylvia and I recognized the importance of keeping pace with these demands from our guests and the increasingly technological-oriented society and responded accordingly with experts in these fields to lead workshops. The experience grew from just a luncheon and morphed once again into a morning forum of workshops featuring highly influential women providing a wealth of information and resources. Designed to guide and coach women to achieve their personal best, career, and financial goals, WMAD continued to transform its mission to keep pace with the changing times.

Following the inaugural launch in March 2000, during Women's History Month, the program served as a vehicle for saluting women who had attained more than exemplary success in their fields of endeavor. The gathering evolved to celebrate women who choose to make outstanding contributions of their time, their talent, and their treasure, demonstrating an interest and eagerness to tangibly uplift their communities. This new, unintended revelation gave the Event Steering Committee and me so much satisfaction.

WMAD became a win-win for all in attendance. The mix of professionals provided the opportunity for women and, because of its popularity, enlightened men the chance to network with intention. It became a think tank of sorts. Walking through a ballroom draped in purple allowed for a no-pressure opportunity to catch up with friends, nail down contacts they had been chasing on the phone, gain insights from the professional development workshops, forge new business relationships, broaden their career network potential, and acquire tools and skills required for career success. Increasingly each year, the atmosphere of optimism and inspiration to work hard with excellence as your flag was palpable. The WMAD luncheon became the must-do on a checklist during March, Women's History Month.

In its tenth year, following an unresolved dispute about who conceived the idea and branded the effort, namely Congressman Chaka Fattah, I was confronted with another difficult decision. With consultation and guidance from a Kitchen Cabinet of women with whom I conferred with and understood the backstory, I leaned on a dear friend, Vernease Herron Miller, Esq., to help me craft a carefully drafted letter and later hand delivered that letter officially informing the appropriate parties that my office and I were officially closing the books on the event known as Women Making A Difference. Further, I stated that all efforts steered by the Office of Councilwoman Blondell Reynolds-Brown would cease. Never again would Sylvia, my chief of staff, and I be the driver of such a magnificent initiative for any parties who refused to share the work and the credit for its success. Not embracing the teamwork required for its astounding success stuck in my craw. In my work, I cleave to the concept and strong belief that teamwork makes the dream work. I would be hard-press to imagine WMAD's success without my team of stellar, faithful, and committed individuals who were content to check their egos at the door. Making a leadership decision to bow out gracefully in the termination letter, I wished the "founder" well and indeed advised her to please have at it, best of luck and fly!

It took me three years to move past the heartache and heartbreak of a long time, decades-old, personal friendship that crumbled because of one's inability to share the credit and be inclusive of those who worked tirelessly, consistently, for WMAD's accomplishments. In the end, sadly, WMAD died a slow death without ceremony, never to be heard of again. Without the energy, constructive collaboration, and devotion of like-minded women who met for ten years in my office under the leadership of Sylvia Purnell Muldrow and me, the effort faded. Striving to make the experience consistently meaningful, WMAD became just an acronym with an empty shell of a name and was no longer my burden to bear. Sylvia and I acknowledged the reality, practiced building our mental muscle, and moved on.

When you have achieved a long-desired goal or hard-fought achievement, the joy you experience after crossing the finish line, torch in hand, is indescribable. The euphoria is the concoction you wish you could harness in a bottle and save for rainy days. The joy is awe-inspiring and motivates you to do more. Give yourself a standing ovation, and be mindful to salute and say thank you to others who helped you make it to the finish line. There is no greater sense of satisfaction than the feeling you experience when you see and hear the joy of others who deserve to be celebrated.

Always committed to celebrating women, my team caucused and commiserated on what's next. Witnessing my now teenage daughter growing up in the new age of the monster known as social media awakened a new purpose for my council's role in celebrating women and girls. First Lady Michele Obama, a mother of two girls, reminded her followers and readers every chance she was given that it behooves us to be smart in our approach to empowering girls. No one, no organization, no legislature, no country, no entity can grow and develop in a healthy, productive way if, with intention, it seeks to suffocate the boundless possibilities of women and girls. We rob us and them of their gifts and their limitless roles.

That summer-long pondering at my happy place, The Beach, was mentally agonizing. The new question for me was how to make a difference, not just in the lives of accomplished career women, but also how to feed and support promising girls who were poised to be the women leaders of the next generation. The answer inspired me and led to my next move. Always hearing the echo of my mom's favorite word, *gumption*, I googled its synonym, inventiveness, get-up-and-go. That's exactly what we did. The Celebration of Moxie Women: "Empowering the Potential of Girls, The Promise of Rising Stars and the Power of Women" was born. This became the new slogan for my women's new initiative with Liz Murphy, Senior Executive with the Philadelphia Electric Company (PECO), who never abandoned the effort as the lead sponsor. We turned the page on March 18, 2011.

I always felt exhilarating joy when I won an election, but following the victory of my 2015 May Primary, I was euphoric! The voters had spoken loudly despite the non-city elite suburban dwellers' roadblocks who sat on the editorial board. My campaign team, and I prevailed because of the fire inside my campaign manager, Tracy Hardy. His can-do warrior spirit coupled with the quiet counselor, cheerleader and policy wonkish Tommy Massaro burned brighter than my firestorm. Winning the most difficult of my five campaigns was my biggest prize for sure. I was excited and grateful to be granted the opportunity by the voters to return to the City Council; to continue to advocate and elevate public policy for children and families around the retractable issue of lead poisoning; to continue the fight for economic parity and equity for women and to push the envelope even further to level the playing field for women and minority owned small businesses. Given the significance of this particular campaign, this victory was embraced with the presence of ALL my sisters, The Village Moms, former and current staffers, campaign staff, volunteers, and supporters who cared about me and the re-election process.

I did the grind, faced the naysayers, and met all the demands dictated by captain and coach Tracy Hardy. I managed the unrelenting and agonizing work that comes with seventeen and eighteen-hour workdays for one hundred-plus days of our vigorous campaigning. We won, placing third in the top five among twenty-one candidates. My 2015 victory was my fifth time at the rodeo, and what a night it was. In the end, the hard work was done. I waited to exhale and celebrate with my staff. The Palm Restaurant was always an ideal go to location to let our hair down and talk shop. Here, you could pull the patience button from your gut as you continued to listen to staff and colleagues who were still conflicted, angry, or both about some Council or office dilemma. Whether it was from countless phone calls, the barrage of emails, op-eds, floor speeches, off-line meetings in colleagues' offices, or the last pitch for a vote count asked during 7:30 a.m. phone calls, something along the legislative journey process was sure to make staff crazy. Celebrating at the end of the council session or the closing of a campaign trail was never the end of the journey. The happy hour meet-ups allowed council members and staff to take a moment to pause, to celebrate and embrace moments of joy and achievement of our legislative goals.

On Thursday mornings, sitting before the Committee of the Whole, my staff waits to see if the bench sitter has decided, triple-checking to make sure soft yeses committed to you the night before have not flipped. The council president, who always had a real sense already of how the vote would fall (another attribute of his brilliance), announces the votes. Legislative staffers, perched with sheets, are waiting to hear the voice calls of the vote. With a straight back and a pen in hand, holding their breath, they mark "yes" votes as they are called. "Yes" votes heading to the number nine means you've succeeded in your efforts. Your staff texts you. "We have nine." Texts pop up from colleagues who supported your measure. "Congratulations!" Bravo. You exhale quietly. Your piece of legislation will now move to the mayor's desk. Silently, you praise God and say thank you.

I am a product of the Philadelphia High School for Girls. Celebrating traditions was embedded in us. As a member of the gold team that won the contest gymnastics competition during my senior year, I knew a celebration always followed. Thus, when you make a short step, a small step, or a seemingly insignificant step with legislation that secures nine votes, passes, and moves to the mayor's desk, celebrate! Feminist, poet, and civil rights activist Audre Lorde reminds us that *"Even the smallest victory it's never to be taken for inevitable granted. Each victory must be applauded because it is so easy not to battle at all, to just accept and call that acceptance inevitable."*

Your staff will appreciate this shared camaraderie after a job well done. Such experiences build loyalty and foster trust among your team, which is invaluable. *"No work is insignificant. All labor that uplifts humanity has dignity and importance and should be undertaken with painstaking excellence."* —Dr. Martin Luther King.

Celebrate that victory, no matter how small. Don't apologize or diminish the effort. It matters. Celebrate with your team, who all bring different talents to the legislative process, and collectively respect the fact that only you can be the quarterback. It matters more to your team who helped you bring the ball across the finish line. Make sure you and your team go to your favorite happy hour and exhale collectively. Toast to yet another small-earned victory that incrementally moved a measure that improves the life chances of those whose lives you pledge to improve and serve with fidelity.

For the first time, a year after the Primary of 2015, I felt I was on my rebound and metaphorically moving back to center. WDAS Radio's recognition of my work in 2016 came at a time when my spirit was broken, and the WDAS Woman of Excellence Award felt like my career was coming full circle. The timing of the radio station's recognition was a much-needed affirmation for my bruised ego and, by far, one of the several public memorable recognition experiences during my council career. The radio station management and radio personalities decided and chose not to punish me for my campaign debacle. On the contrary, the Woman of Excellence Award reminded me that my name is "I am" and not "I was."

It had been three years following the breaking news of my career calamity in 2012. I was reminded at this banquet hosted by one of Philly's popular local radio stations of my record of service. To be included with four dynamic African American women selected to be presented with the Woman of Excellence Award that saluted my work on behalf of women, children, families, the arts, and culture was amazing. The leadership and radio personalities of WDAS Radio chose to spotlight my work, its impact, and its value over the years. In that moment, my spirit was restored. I was reminded and so grateful that WDAS chose to examine and recognize the full spectrum of my council career and not view my work through the singular lens of my career stumble.

Women from all sides of the nonprofit, corporate, and business spectrum attended the annual Women's Way dinner that never had less than one thousand guests. Receiving their distinguished leadership award, symbolized acceptance by mainstream Philadelphia. The distinction and recognition by Philadelphia's regional premier leading women's organization unapologetically dedicated to the role to champion, advocate, and be a voice for the advancement of women and girls since 1976, Women's Way, was a WOW! Moment. Their celebration of my work was another affirmation, confirmation, and confidence booster for the acknowledgment of my extraordinary and unprecedented legislative efforts and achievements on behalf of women and girls. Thank you!

Receiving awards like the United Way's Leadership Award in 2012 was notable because Brielle was present in a room of over one thousand women and men. The view from the podium was breathtaking! The video featuring Girls' High alums, including my longtime friend and high school classmate Terry Graboyes and staffer Katherine Gilmore Richardson, was especially unforgettable. Their attendance, along with colleague and dear friend Councilwoman Maria Quiñones Sánchez, remains a wonderful memory and highlight of my council career. One thing for certain and two for sure, you can always count on your girlfriends to lift you up and encourage you during the highs and the lows. You remember those who stick and walk with you when the car breaks down. If you are in a fight, look for my former colleague Maria Quiñones-Sánchez. She is forever That Girl!

The brightest highlight of my last year in City Council was learning of the submission of my name to the nominating committee of the greatest sorority on earth, Delta Sigma Theta Sorority, Inc., Philadelphia Alumnae Chapter, for its coveted award, the Sadie T. M. Alexander Award. Soror Alexander served as the first national president of Delta Sigma Theta Sorority, Inc., and she represented the supreme symbol of excellence. Consider this. She was the first African American to earn a Ph.D. in economics in 1921 and graduated from the University of Pennsylvania Law School in 1927, again the first Black woman to do so. This award was particularly sentimental for several reasons. My mother's name was Sadie. Thus, receiving this recognition two years after my mom's passing in 2017 tugged at my fragile heartstrings. I adore my sorority and all that Delta Sigma Theta Sorority, Inc. represents. Receiving this recognition from my sisterhood, founded on three basic guiding principles—scholarship, public service, and sisterhood—made my heart sing loudly!

My daughter, a Delta Legacy, initiated at the Kappa Lambda Chapter at Syracuse University, and Linda, my very "first" dear friend, Penn State classmate, also a Soror, were present. When two of the most consequential people in your life are present for an extraordinary once-in-a-lifetime moment in a room full of Sorors to celebrate you, your heart gets the jitters! On that Saturday morning, feeling a a giddy thrill, my happy heart was no exception. I was introduced to the luncheon guests by another Soror, a Penn State College classmate, and Village Mom, Marcia Penn. Oh, what a tender moment! This is what she had to say:

> The Honorable Blondell Reynolds-Brown is currently serving her fifth and final term as a member of the Philadelphia City Council. Councilwoman Reynolds-Brown serves as Majority Whip and is the only woman serving in city leadership. I met Blondie, as our girlfriends and Penn Staters called her at Penn State, University Park. We have remained friends for the past forty-eight years. Forty-eight years' worth of stories will have to be told at another venue!
>
> Blondell clearly acknowledges the impact that her early years had on shaping her life. Being the oldest sibling of seven, serving as a teacher for the City of Philadelphia, and dedication to dance and instruction led her to mentor hundreds of women and girls. These experiences guided her to advocate for the citizens of Philadelphia by serving as a committeewoman and ultimately a legislative director before running for City Council. Blondell is a problem solver, creative thinker, and activist. Coretta Scott King said, "Women, if the soul of the nation is to be saved, I believe you must become its soul." Blondell has become its soul by passing meaningful legislation and supporting valuable community programming that accentuates and impacts her core values: children and youth, women, arts and culture, education, small business development, and the environment.
>
> Perhaps you are not aware of all her legislative accomplishments. If you have ever worked with Blondell, she would tell

you to do your homework. Check out her legislative record. Here are just a few things she accomplished that capture her commitment to her core values. Championed increased funding for the expansion of Early Childhood Education by directing the allocation to the Office of Housing and Community Development; negotiated for increased funding for Big Brothers Big Sisters of Southeastern Pennsylvania, the Greater Philadelphia Tourism Marketing Corporation, and the Philadelphia Convention and Visitors Bureau to promote the tourism industry; authored pension forfeiture requiring city employees convicted of sexual abuse of a minor to forfeit his or her pension. I believe Philadelphia is a better place to live, work, eat, and play because of Blondell's legislative focus on her core constituencies. Maya Angelou said, "We may encounter many defeats, but we must not be defeated." Just as our first national president, Dr. Sadie T. M. Alexander, Blondell surely has encountered many defeats and overcame many obstacles in her career. She has persevered and achieved despite those obstacles. Many of you have heard Blondell say, "I had to learn to walk on a tightrope with high heels backward." Thank you for staying the course in your high heels. Thank you for Mrs. Reynolds. Blondie's MOM, or Miss Sadie as we affectionately called her, is surely smiling. It is with pride and great pleasure that I introduce Philadelphia Alumnae's 2019 Sadie Tanner Mossell Alexander Award recipient, our Soror, and my friend, Blondell Reynolds-Brown.

What an indescribable, priceless, once-in-a-lifetime moment!

Carpe Diem

CHAPTER TEN

WOMEN, OUR VOICE, AND OUR LEADERSHIP MATTERS

"When we cast our bread upon the waters, we can presume that someone downstream whose face we may never see will benefit from our action." —Maya Angelou.

Often in my speeches during Women's History Month, I repeated the fact that my daughter would be at my retirement age by the time women and men were paid equally. This is a disgrace in a so-called progressive city. Then and now, women make up half of the US workforce. This will be the case forever going forward. The traditional family structure portrayed by Hollywood for decades is a relic, forever. It is past time for policymakers to stop shortchanging women. James Kristie, the editor and associate publisher of *Directors & Boards* presented a history lesson that might partially explain how modern women ended up with such disparities in the workplace.

> Early in the 1900s, there were a handful of women who, upon the death of a husband or father, came to occupy a board seat of an American corporation. Among them was Marjorie Merriweather Post, who, in 1914, joined the

board of the frozen foods and cereal company started by her father. Another was Lettie Pate Whitehead, who, after her husband's death, led Coca-Cola to remarkable success and was the first independent woman to serve on the board of a major corporation in 1934. This coincidentally was a year after President Roosevelt appointed Frances Perkins as Secretary of Labor, the first woman to hold a federal government cabinet post.

Thus begins and pretty much ended the shameful tale of women's progress, that is, the lack thereof in achieving a representative and deserving role at the highest level of business leadership: being a member of a public company board of directors. Indeed, this is a higher role than even that of a chief executive officer of a public corporation, as the preeminent role of the board is to hire and fire the CEO.

Now, let's jump ahead forty years to the mid-1970s. This was a time when the Securities and Exchange Commission began to critically eye the "old boys club" board membership in America's major companies and started a bully pulpit campaign for change. A startling statistic from 1976 indicated that women made up about 5 percent of the directors in Fortune 500 companies. A back-of-the-envelope calculation meant there were about 400 board seats held by women (some women serving in multiple directorships). That may initially sound impressive to go from 1 to 400—but over 40 years? Bear in mind that this meant that men held about 7,500 seats in the Fortune 500 in 1976, one of the greatest boom periods of American history. Under the SEC's prodding as the media began to pay attention to this issue "corporate governance" was not even a term in the common business lexicon in the 1970s, women began to be invited in greater numbers to join corporate boards.

Now, let's jump ahead another almost forty years to 2012. Women made up about 16% of the Fortune 500 Directors and 17 percent of members of Congress and earned $.77 for every $1 earned by males. In Philadelphia, women comprised the 115 executive board seats. For female board participation to go from 5 percent—which was an admittedly depressed base in 1976—to 16 percent today is deserving of the term glacial progress. Still, projections indicate that at this rate of incremental progress, it will be another 60–70 years before any semblance of parity is achieved on corporate boards. Women and minority participation does not show the same stats, but we must ensure that it is no longer optional but a requirement for boards to represent and reflect all of America's women of all perspectives and all colors.

Male CEOs and directors have reported that the presence of women in the boardroom leads to better discussion and decision-making. The publication *Directors & Boards 2015* further stated that, "Effective boards should represent the diverse thinking and different perspectives of their customers, consumers, employees, and shareholders, so to exclude women from the ranks of directors is to limit the success of the company. Women's participation on boards leads to better performance, period." The fact that women in the seventies couldn't have a credit card, to today, controlling household decisions on spending, is a testament to their prowess.

Gender and Politics
Fierce women leading change have existed since time immemorial. From the biblical times to the current day, Gro Harlem Brundtland of Norway, Mette Frederiksen, Denmark, Saara Kuugongelwa, Namibia,

and more represent a shift in the right direction. Formidable is the island of Barbados, the only country in the world where both the serving heads of state of government are women.

Still, expect that if you are a woman in office, there will come a time in your career when your beliefs about leadership and advocacy for women and the values they uphold will collide, be tested, and challenged. These moments of truth will knock at your door unsolicited.

As much as it seems progress has been made, if you survived the four years of the administration of the forty-fifth president of the United States and must face a do-over from the fallout of the 2024 election, irrespective of party affiliation, you now know that gender matters. What should also matter are facts, but, as they say, perception is greater than fact. Everyone can have an opinion, but no amount of rhetoric or denial can change the facts. These facts will elucidate why it matters now more than ever that the leadership charged with securing our democracy knows how to use these facts and has the gumption to never give up in the face of what appears to be backward trending.

Donald Trump got pretty much the same number of votes as he did in 2020. His constituency of disgruntled, racially biased people did not grow in 2024. I believe for good reason. Most Americans have long passed the stuck point of hatred for their fellow citizens and educated people disregarded his over-the-top rhetoric. But here is where other biases played into the loss of the election for the juggernaut called Kamala Harris. Given the baton to bring it home in just two months with less than 100 days before the election, this titan of a woman delivered 71 million votes to Trump's 74 million, and, in comparison to Biden's 81 million votes in 2020.

That there was no more support for Trump could mean two things for the millions of people who decided not to vote in 2024: They didn't think the country was ready for a woman president, a Black woman at that, or the messaging from the Democratic Party was unclear, ambiguous and clearly missed the mark. This doesn't surprise me as Kamala Harris had zero time to craft the perfect connecting message about her presidency while Donald Trump's messaging to his constituents pandered to their fears effectively for four years. Thus, sexism and racism clearly stood taller in the rooms across America for four years leading into the 2024 election. The prevailing big question is who will lead a future nation and what will leadership look like?

Black Women

In keeping with the role of the Black Church, the historical bedrock of our community, other organizations guarded our self-esteem and secured our children's future. Several of these organizations focused on the power inherent in women. Organizations such as the Deltas, the AKAs, the Zetas, the Sigmas, the Coalition of 100 Black Women, the Eastern Stars, the Black Women's Educational Alliance, 2000 African American Women, the Black Women's Leadership Council and others were essential for nurturing the aspirations of women seeking public office. I remain forever appreciative to these organizations for allowing me to tell my story as I sought their support, which they enthusiastically gave during those twenty years in the City Council. There was no greater sense of comfort than speaking to the hearts and minds of Mona Lake Jones', "A Room Full Of Sisters." There is nothing like belonging.

Leadership

My favorite lifestyle magazine for decades, the only magazine of its type for African American women, founded in 1970, the year I enrolled at Penn State, was *Essence*. The monthly lifestyle publication covers fashion, entertainment, and culture. Given my status as a member of the baby boomer generation and pre-internet, my method of holding on to memorable writings was to clip and file the hard paper copy of those writings filed alphabetically. I maintained files in my home office on dozens of random topics for decades.

Call the subject matter—exercise/physical fitness, the arts, women, women in politics, home decorating, leadership, family, etc.—I have a file. In addition to clippings, my home library holds dozens of books on the topic of leadership.

For more than twenty years I clipped the editorial page that was written by *Essence's* then editor-in-chief, Susan L. Taylor. Ms. Taylor later authored a book, *In the Spirit*, which was a compilation of inspirational writings from her column. Taylor had an anointed gift for expressing eloquently and gracefully topics that touched and pulled at my heartstrings, and I suspect the majority of her Black women readers. For example, on the topic of leadership, I admired her writing so much that I framed her December 1985 column entitled, "Passion for Life." I hung it in every office during my career and adopted its message for honing my professional career as a leader. The following excerpt became my reference point at different critical crossroads during my tenure in the City Council. Ms. Taylor advises, "*Lead the change. Take the leadership role in your life and your career. This is where the strategic advantage lies— in following your heart and preparing for what is nourishing to your spirit. Fashion a plan to help you boldly leap forward in this rapidly changing global economy. Hold steady your vision, and no matter what, don't give up.*" I took her message to heart and began to take imperceptible strategic career steps that might offer leadership opportunities and experience.

Although a gazillion books have been written on the topic of leadership, and I have used dozens as references throughout my career, in 1990, it was a local advertisement published by my alma mater, Penn State, that stuck with me as a young professional building my career. I was facing my first test as a fresh leader, managing and leading staff all senior to me. In the role of Director of the Philadelphia Recruitment Center and as Associate Director of Admissions, Dr. Robert Dunham, Senior Vice President of Penn State Admissions during one of our annual admission conferences taught my colleagues and me the early nuggets of leadership. He asked us the question: "What makes a great leader?" His answer: "Compassion, endurance, and personal magnetism. Truly great leaders are guided by the interests of the people and are ready to publicly assume responsibility for their actions. They have the ability to withstand pressures. Throughout the years such leaders have guided this city. Their hope for the future has paved the way for generations to come. Philadelphia's leaders, past and present, we salute you."

So, to answer Susan Taylor's question... where is leadership born? There are arguments on both sides of the table on this topic. Some believe leadership is an innate skill found in those with exceptional personalities, while others think it can be learned and improved over time. That's the debate behind natural versus learned leadership. But which one holds true? Does nature or nurture play the strongest role in developing strong leadership skills? I might argue that effective leadership is what matters, whether it's innate or learned. Women, it has been noted, are innately more capable of leadership than men yet there are so few represented in C-level roles in this country, be it politics, corporations, or business. I learned to use city council as my bully pulpit. Thus, I am a firm believer that if we are granted the chance to ascend to a leadership role women in leadership and especially African American women leadership, have a responsibility to seize the moment, leverage and use that position to stand up and speak out to advocate for those who feel voiceless. Research shows that leaders can grow the profit margins 'and' serve others simultaneously. To use Councilwoman Maria Quiñones Sánchez's dictate. The proposition can be an "and" not" or."

Later in my career, I had the good fortune of meeting Ms. Taylor in Philadelphia at a Graduate Opportunities Conference, hosted by Congressman Chaka Fattah. She was all I imagined and more. With the carriage of a beautiful Egyptian queen, dignified, gracious, and always elegant, she became a regular featured headliner and motivational speaker for college-aged conference attendees. Always provocative, always motivational, there was no question she embodied the qualities of a leader who inspired.

During one of her visits to Fattah's Graduate Opportunities Conference, Susan Taylor asked the question: And what of the leadership of women? As I stated earlier, everyone could have an opinion, but no one gets to have their facts. Let's examine the facts. During my tenure in City Council, women made up 52 percent (an average) of the population, yet female representation in elected office in Philadelphia never matched or came close to that level of representation from 2000–2019. From school boards to state legislatures, from Capitol Hill to the White House, fewer women held elected positions than our male counterparts. This is even more apparent on corporate boards. Why is that? According to *The Athena Doctrines* by John Gerzema and Michael D'Antonio, the significant traits of women such as nurturing, cooperation, communication, and sharing are qualities of superior leadership. They even proffer that femininity is the operating system of the twenty-first century. So why such a pushback on female leaders? The legislative effort and research around this topic was one my staff and I undertook to challenge the conscience of corporate Philadelphia's benign attention to advancing qualified, competent, credentialed women to leadership positions and on corporate boards.

In response to a resolution I introduced, I was shocked and stunned that one of the city's leading media outlets had paid attention to the work of this African American woman on the City Council. On Friday, March 16, 2012, during the national celebration of Women's History Month, *The Philadelphia Inquirer* printed an op-ed, "Women Aren't Treated Equally."

> Women are more than half of Philadelphia's population, so why do so few hold top leadership positions? Councilwoman Blondell Reynolds-Brown posed that question

last week to coincide with Women's History Month. Her call for public hearings to address gender inequalities is appropriate.

Women account for 53 percent of the city's 1.5 million residents, according to the latest US census data. But they are underrepresented in corporate and other boardrooms across the city. "If you're not at the table, you're on the menu," said Reynolds-Brown. She cited statistics from a recent survey by the Urban League of Philadelphia that are troubling: Women represent only 10 percent of the executive board seats in Philadelphia and only 16 percent of board seats nationally. Only 17 percent of the members of Congress are women. On top of that, the gender gap in salaries remains a reality, with women earning less than male workers for doing the same job, despite having the same skills and background.

According to the National Partnership for Women and Families, nearly 14.5 million households nationwide are headed by women who make an average of only 77 cents for every dollar paid to men. It's worse for minorities: Black women are paid only 61 cents, and Latinas only 52 cents, for every dollar paid to men. In Pennsylvania, a woman working full-time averages about $35,301 a year while a man working full-time is paid $57,738.

The outcome of my legislation was the successful passage of the Women on Boards law. With the firm proud signature of Mayor Nutter, it required contractors seeking to do business with the city to disclose specific demographic information including gender, race, and geographic data of those serving on its board and executive staff. Since it's impossible to manage what cannot be measured, the bill required companies to report the numbers of female executives at the firm publicly. Total transparency was mandatory to determine whether a contractor valued and upheld diversity in the workplace in the City of Philadelphia.

No longer did Council members have to guess about an organization's commitment to the principles of diversity and inclusion going forward. Lobbyists warned their clients of the directive and instructed them to just show up to council hearings prepared with their demographic data forms completed in their submitted documents of testimony with no excuses.

Too many times during the hundreds of hearings, we learned from witnesses seeking approval from the city that city businesses and their boards' memberships were all white men. This fact was blatant and not acceptable. Sadly, there were instances when I had to call out on council floor, on the record well known recognizable organizations in our city who had not caught up with the times. The Committee of Seventy was one of the most egregious local non-profits who thought it not robbery to function in this way. In fact, for too long the Committee of Seventy had no one of color on their board, in a majority-minority city. FACTS!! Today, the Committee of Seventy's President is a woman. Moreover, I discovered that most businesspeople who want to do business with the city will never make changes in their organizations voluntarily. Seldom is that organizational action organic. When businesspeople decide to take this long overdue action, they are motivated to act because they know it will affect their bottom line.

Little did my colleagues, supporters, and voters realize, that the mandatory annual sexual harassment training for the City of Philadelphia I introduced was just the caboose of the subsequent legislation I would introduce to further the advancement of women. Soft initial efforts were always my first step toward a longer-term legislative strategy to ultimately introduce multiple pieces of stronger, more impactful legislation designed to forever alter the paradigm and the metrics for the future of women's rights in Philadelphia. The subsequent package of bills included bill #171109, in response to the #MeToo movement, to amend the Philadelphia Home Rule Charter with a provision requiring mandatory sexual harassment training for all city officers and employees, including exempt, nonexempt, and civil service staff. Sexual harassment training is now a mandated requirement for all City of Philadelphia employees. This question was presented to the voters as a ballot question and charter change. The measure was approved by voters overwhelmingly. Enough said!

To ensure women would become and remain permanently entrenched in the government, my staff and I prepared for the next steps on behalf of women. Once again, research showed that thirty-one cities, including New York, Boston, Phoenix, Los Angeles, Atlanta, Seattle, San Francisco, and others had a Commission for Women. Philadelphia was not one of those enlightened cities.

The forty-fifth mayor of Philadelphia, Mayor W. Wilson Goode Sr., had the foresight and gumption to create a Commission for Women by executive order. Its first executive director, my Soror, an audacious leader with true grit, and one of my very first women career coaches Barbara Daniel Cox, led the Commission with aplomb. Instituting unprecedented programming for women and enlightened men, Barbara was an amazing giant of a woman who always pushed the envelope on behalf of women and was a pioneer with an audacity for uplifting Black women. She placed the celebration of women on the radar long before it was "a thing." Barbara Daniel Cox was a *shero* for so many women.

The Mayor's Commission for Women was not an established department in the city government or on the second floor of city hall. This fact created another major legislative opportunity for my staff and me. That said, I wrote an editorial for submission to the *Philadelphia Daily News* on March 23, 2015, justifying why "A Commission for Women is Overdue." As City Council's only female at-large representative for fifteen years in 2015, I stated the following:

Every year, Congress has designated the month of March to celebrate the contributions and accomplishments of women and to learn about the long road to gender equality paved by courageous women who came before us. Women continue to break glass ceilings. Janet Yellen (now Secretary of the Treasury) became the first woman to serve as the chair of the Federal Reserve Board in its 102-year history. Last summer, it took a thirteen-year-old girl from Philadelphia to teach the world that girls can throw just as well as boys. They can throw better!

Mo'ne Davis became the first girl to pitch a shutout in the seventy-year history of the Little League World Series. Seventeen-year-old education activist Malala Yousafzai was shot by a Taliban gunman because she believed that all girls have the right to an education. She survived and did not stop, give in, or give up. She won the Nobel Peace Prize for her efforts.

Chart-topper Taylor Swift broke records when her album *1989* sold more than 1.2 million copies. During the first week of her sales, 22 percent of all albums sold in the United States were hers.

"Queen of the Small Screen" Shonda Rhimes produces ABC's entire Thursday night line-up and dominates the ratings.

(NOTE: As of 2024, 151 Women in Congress (107 Democrats, 43 Republicans, 1 Independent), 24 women in the Senate; 127 in the House of Representatives; 4 US delegates nonvoting)

Finally, as a former teacher, when it comes to higher education, there is a gender gap: 61 percent of male high school graduates are attending college, while 71 percent of women are pursuing higher education. While we are proud of these victories for women, we are also dismayed. In 2015, women continued to earn 78 cents for each dollar earned by our male colleagues. Despite representing 52.8 percent of the city's population, women occupy 11 percent of corporate board seats in Philadelphia and women of color represent less than 1 percent.

This May we will have the opportunity to make a change by establishing a Commission for Women, offering women and girls a permanent seat at the table of city government, and creating pathways for leadership and equal employment opportunities. The Commission would be charged with promoting the civic, educational, and economic policies for and on behalf of women, providing advice and recommendations to the mayor and City Council on policies and programs that advance equal rights for women and opportunities for girls.

As a world-class city where "liberty and justice for all" was born, Philadelphia should not only have a Commission for Women; we should have the flagship Commission for Women and be considered a national thought leader on the issue of gender equality.

This is a historic opportunity to bring women to the table of city government in an official leadership capacity. Pause for a moment to think of the women who paved the way before us. Ernesta Ballard, Edwina Baker, C. Delores Tucker, Augusta A. Clark, Onah Weldon, Happy Fernandez, and countless others. We are standing on their shoulders. Think about how we can grow the next generation of women leaders . . . who can set records and change the paradigm for young women and the trajectory of girls.

On March 31, 2015, Mayor Michael Nutter signed and thereby approved my bill to place the question on the May 19 ballot to amend the Home Rule Charter to establish the Commission for Women.

Finally, the city would have an entity of twenty-seven members: ten appointed by the mayor and one appointed by each of the seventeen members of the City Council, all devoted to addressing the structural inequities that leave women and, therefore, their families at a socioeconomic disadvantage that always threatens any city's potential. Mission accomplished! The May 19 ballot passed overwhelmingly. One year later, the Office of Public Engagement and I officially announced the appointments to the new Philadelphia Commission for Women. The Forum of Executive Women and I firmly agreed on the one disputable fact: women with ambition, drive, grit, smarts, and moxie must always seek to achieve and grab the gold charms in all places including the board rooms.

My devoted comrade, W. Wilson Goode Jr., as was his custom, challenged all matters related to increasing opportunities that advanced the ball toward a more equitable playing field for minority and women-owned businesses (MBE/WBEs). During his tenure in the City Council, he authored more than 160 bills, 145 enacted into law, with more than two dozen pieces of legislation focused on diversity, equity, and inclusion. From responsible banking to diversity in contracting, Councilman Goode was dogmatic, unapologetic, and in-your-face about bringing corporate Philadelphia to the witness table. Exposing corporate Philadelphia's sometimes silent racist and sexist practices that too often blocked equity business opportunities for businesses owned by women and people of color continues to be a battle. During my tenure, Councilman W. Wilson Goode Jr. remains the GOAT on this public policy issue.

Regretfully, the correction of too many injustices must be mandated legislatively for there to be minimal change. The Women on Boards law was the result of my coalition work that had to be mandated for there to be effective change on corporate boards. On tough nontraditional, hard-fought legislative issues, those you work with soon learn that *"Every difference of opinion is not a difference of principle."* —Thomas Jefferson.

On May 24, 2018, I again presented remarks from the floor at the City Council Committee of the Whole meeting on this topic of women's rights. My staff believed this was one of my shining moments of advocacy on behalf of women. The difference my staff and I made in the women's rights space will have everlasting long-term implications and benefits. One of the initial reasons I ran for office was because of the scarcity of women representation in the halls of the Pennsylvania State Senate. After learning of the progressive measures that Great Britain and Australia had successfully undertaken to advance women's roles in management and board directorships, I was determined to push the envelope for Philadelphia to do better with the city government leading by example. In such a case, a coalition is essential to capture the attention of the power structure, to move the needle, to shift the paradigm, and to change the trajectory to one that advances women's rights.

Despite the long and uneven road to women's progress and equality, this hearing showed a bright spotlight on the issue, which is always compounded for Black and brown women. My strong convictions about women's rights had been amplified after about a year's worth of deep study of national trends and research on the topic during my third term. I doubled down on my commitment to do more. My homework led to what Soror and Congresswoman Shirley Chisholm noted, *"The emotional, sexual, and psychological stereotyping of females begins when the doctor says: 'It's a girl.'"*

Regardless of the current environment that still seeks to keep women in their places, women whose aim is to join the political ranks must show themselves approved at every turn. Sign up for your neighborhood block clubs, neighborhood town watch, volunteer on a campaign, organize a fundraiser for the woman candidate who inspires you, become a Big Brother or Big Sister, lead an effort that changes the outcome of an issue, volunteer at your local church, engage in an interest or a cause that burns in your soul. Start where your neighbors are. Meet with them, get to know their concerns, identify your target issue to change for the better, show mutual respect and appreciation, get busy, and move the needle forward. Then, do the work and earn your stripes. Ultimately, to inspire your circle of friends and potential supporters, you must win their respect and attention, which will come from the work that you do that benefits others.

My opportunity to openly support a Black woman came during my last term at the tail end of my career in the City Council. I became privy to a circumstance where one of the only two African American women in the mayor's administration was being diminished, used, and pointed to as a scapegoat. On its face, with little detail and background information, this scenario was potentially a concern for my staff and me. Subsequent phone calls and emails substantiated and affirmed that hallway and water cooler whispers were true. Additional information received signaled that on the horizon, there was going to be a smear campaign about this African American female professional who was about to take the fall for a problem in her department that did not occur on her watch. After double and triple-checking the facts, I was not having it. Customary to my practice, and Girl Scouts training, my chief of staff, Katherine Gilmore Richardson and I prepared for show time.

As we gathered more facts and the more I learned about the case, it became exceedingly clear that I could not and would not give the elite and privileged few, none of whom looked like me, a pass. My staff and I, armed with verified facts and data, drafted my remarks and response from our illuminating discovery. I was not a happy camper during the week as I prepared to present my "Remarks From the Majority Whip" on May 24, 2018. Customarily, at the end of all Thursday City Council sessions, I was perched to push my speaker button to alert President Clarke that I had much to say. When the council president recognized me, I presented my argument.

Thank you, council president.

Thank you to the mayor for recruiting and identifying women with impeccable credentials, competence, and exceptional experience. Our city treasurer is not an exception.

My mom's name was Sadie Reynolds. She raised my five sisters and only brother on pearls of wisdom we now call *Sadieisms*. Recently, I was reminded of one of those Sadieisms. *"When you care deeply about an issue or an injustice, when a subject matter taps or tugs at your heart in a visceral way, DO NOT be silent."* Recognize that silence is betrayal.

Today, I rise to raise my voice because I will not allow any woman to be thrown under the bus and blamed for years of mistakes, inefficiencies, mishandlings, missteps, and/or lack of oversight caused by others when she, an African American woman, has finally been given a seat at the table.

Our city treasurer has served as an investment banker, financial advisor, and bond issuer in her stellar twenty-year career. She has also worked in the municipal finance department at Loop Capital Markets in Philadelphia and most recently served as the assistant to the director of finance in debt management. Throughout her career, our city treasurer, Rashia Johnson, has managed over $7 billion in transactions with complex technical and analytical experience. Therefore, she has a proven record of leadership and excellence working in both the government and private sector. The record will reflect that she has earned her stripes.

I commend our city treasurer for her commitment to complete transparency in our government. We thank her for not only bringing the issue of the unreconciled bank accounts to our attention but also for releasing an RFP to find a third party to resolve the problems that were present years before she was appointed to her post. To be clear and to ensure that there is no interpretation or misinterpretation of my intent, I have chosen to speak up and speak out as an advocate for a highly qualified woman with an unblemished record of performance who decided to accept the Mayor's appointment as city treasurer and the unique opportunity to serve the citizens of this city.

I went on to innumerate the facts and timetable of the case, which clearly showed the folly and implicit racism of the accusation before concluding.

I stand today to say I am not weary. I will stand up and advocate for women, most especially competent and qualified women with unblemished careers when they have been unjustly belittled (in this chamber and in the press) and accused of oversights, mistakes, and nondisclosures created on someone else's watch. Further, I will holler from city hall's rooftops when the career of a woman who looks like me falls prey to critics who pride themselves on imposing double standards.

Mr. President, we can all have an opinion. However, no one gets to argue the facts. Thank you, Mr. President.

I was proud of the moment that reminded me that a true leader never abandons their people. I had seen this happen one too many times, and I always considered it shameful. Like in the case above, I remember a former devoted managing director who walked the plank for the administration during the George Floyd Black Lives Matter movement and was never given a net by his former boss. I have watched as people have made blunders approved by their bosses only to be abandoned. I was particularly disappointed in one of our former members and verbalized this to his staffer shortly after I retired, "one would never believe your boss was a member of the Philadelphia City Council. Never have I witnessed a mayor who allowed major city-appointed officials, and most especially the police commissioner, in this case, a Black woman, to stand alone during a press conference for any crisis." I felt this inaction was reprehensible, but as Martin Luther King so aptly said, "*The measure of a person's character is not where they stand during times of comfort and convenience. The true measure of one's character is best revealed during times of challenge and controversy.*" Governor Rendell's book, *A Nation of Wusses*, speaks most directly and honestly about elected officials who lack the spine to make tough decisions and further lack the moxie to stand by their team members or allies when the going gets tough.

During my preparation and drafting of my remarks and after extended discussions with my staff, it became evident that subtle racism was again at play in ousting a perfectly fit professional in the Mayor's administration. Ultimately, as the elected official and the leader of the team, I made the critical decisions and wrestled with the question of whose toes I was willing to step on or not. The question for me was, do I skirt the obvious or ignore the issue of race and hope listeners would read between the lines? After a couple of sleepless nights, I decided to call out the facts, including the race factor, and decided to let the chips fall where they may. I went through the intellectual exercise of weighing risks and landed on the side of taking a calculated risk. I raised my voice in support of a woman who looked like me, and I left that Thursday council session with no regrets. I was at peace and pleased that I did not allow my unsteadiness in courage to tempt me and win the internal struggle to edit my remarks and thereby silence me. I looked the lion in the mouth, vowed I would not be eaten, and opted to meet the moment.

Subsequently, stating the facts as seen through my lens on race opened an unexpected door. Councilman Allan Domb called me later that afternoon. We had an in-depth, sensitive, and uncomfortable discussion about racism, how pervasive insidious double standards were, and its ugly, quiet prevalence across the government. We started with the demographics of staff in our individual council offices. Who knew? From that candid, no-holds-barred conversation about the four-letter word, race, a new friendship took root. Getting to know a colleague's experiences and lens of reality were diametrically polar opposite to my own inspired more fascinating conversations and discoveries about the different worlds we come from and live in. Over time, we became friends, meaning he is one of the few in this business I elected to have a glass of wine with after hours. The important decision to follow my heart, call out my rage, and present the facts unvarnished was affirmed. Two days later, that Saturday, I received a text from my leader, Council President Clarke. His text read, "My hero." One thing for certain, and two for sure, leadership is not for those with weak spines, including those with bravado who boast, but when called upon and tested to solve complex societal problems, fold.

There are over fifty thousand books on leadership on Amazon, and approximately one thousand books on leadership are published every year. Can you imagine? There are a million more workshops, academic programs, and now TED Talks that provide the tools and strategies for cultivating one's leadership skills. Pick one!

The theories about what leadership looks like, what leadership styles you can apply, which leadership strategies to implement, and the pros and cons of each leadership style are not my academic expertise. However, I remain grateful for the Urban League's Institute Leadership Program, which selected me for its 1988 Charter Class. I credit the Board Chair, A. Bruce Crawley, and President Robert W. Sorrell, who called me to chastise me for not applying to the newly minted one-year leadership program. They recognized my potential and convinced me that my enrollment and participation would become a vital building block in my professional development. They were right.

My participation proved to be an essential cornerstone of my career. This leadership training opportunity was neatly aligned with a major assignment in a middle management leadership position with my alma mater, Penn State, leading their Philadelphia Recruitment Center. I remember feeling and believing, quite frankly, that I did not have the confidence or "the right stuff" to enroll in such a prestigious program. This signature initiative with intention, structure, and an enormous amount of homework assignments was designed to sharpen the potential leadership skills of mid-level professionals and provide tools and strategies to foster extraordinarily professional and sustainable relationships. The goal was to graduate with a defined or refined personal brand that I and members of the class would market with the central purpose of applying those newly acquired skills to uplift and empower the African American community.

The Charter Class was filled with aspiring young women and men, firecrackers who moved on to do exceptional work, including notables like Senator Vincent Hughes; Donna Frisby-Greenwood, now with the Pew Foundation; Steven Scott Bradley, successful businessman and Chairman of the African American Chamber of Commerce; Pastor David Brown; and Mayor Michael A. Nutter, just to name a few.

Leadership is never comfortable. Hard decisions are fraught with splinters, which suggest you will annoy those not in agreement with your vision. This simply means that you must have the desire to work diligently and honestly with your opponents, skeptics, and disbelievers. Find the middle ground by applying the tools and strategies in the nonfiction best-selling book, *Getting to Yes, Negotiating Without Giving In* by Roger Fisher and William Ury, one of my favorite go-to books. As a leader, you will be called on through texts, emails, letters, notes left in your council office, stopped in the corridors of city hall, in the hallways during your child's school visits, walking to your car, in your car, in the supermarket, and on Kelly Drive during your power walk. You will hear the sadness, the desperation, and the despair of those seeking support and in need of your lens, ears, advice, and help. All who pull on you will ask and yearn for your compassion, interest, and leadership. Choose to rise and meet the moment. Advocate for those with no voice and little hope. Lend your voice. Exercise your influence. While serving as the legislative aide for then-State Senator Chaka Fattah, I first heard the former Governor Bob Casey of Pennsylvania, US Senator Bob Casey's father ask in one of his annual speeches to the State legislature, "What did you do with the power, (i.e., your voice) when you had it?" Trust that at some point in your career, you will be asked this one piercing question.

Bottom line. When you are in leadership, choose to be loud, and at all times, be graceful, intentional, and respectful about policy issues that are important to you and those constituencies you care about. Your delivery, especially in the presence of others, matters. You never have to diminish anyone, most especially your colleagues, and never the doorman, in the presence of others. You will be remembered for how you handle those tense situations. Trust that fact. Compassionate leaders opt to bring and draw in others around them to become believers in their vision even when they, the followers, are kicking and screaming. When you arrive to speak at those ward meetings, community meetings, barbershop gatherings, Divine Nine Chapter meetings, or the 7:30 a.m. Sunday morning church worship services, use your voice. Roar! Don't be the echo. Choose to be the girl on fire.

I had the benefit of working with many great leaders who accomplished enormous wins for their constituents, and I can attest that what Notre Dame football player and later Notre Dame coach, Knute Rockne stated in his short life of thirty-five years fit Mayor John F. Street to a T. *"Leaders are like eagles. They don't flock. You have to find them one at a time."*

Mayor Street possessed one important quality of leadership that I admired greatly. His ability to galvanize the masses to embrace his vision was infectious. He took immense pride in teaching and bringing others along to embrace his vision, and if you chose not to, he was cool with that, too. His attitude was always, so be it. John Street was the kind of leader that people would follow voluntarily long before he had a title and was elected to represent the residents of the Fifth Councilmanic District. He, along with his boisterous brother, Milton, were formidable champions and built a reputation fighting for food truck vendors, men and women alike who just wanted to feed their families long before it was fashionable. John F. Street, the street activist, was no punk!

I greatly admired his insatiable energy and his commitment to guiding and coaching the new city council members of the Class of 2000. He made it a practice to offer nuggets of advice essential for us to achieve success in our legislative endeavors. So, what makes a great leader? For me, it's compassion, endurance, personal magnetism, and the ability to withstand pressures. I truly believe that inspirational leaders are guided by the earnestness, the needs, and the interests of the people they represent. Most importantly, great leaders are ready to face the lions and publicly assume responsibility for their actions, popular or unpopular. They don't run and hide. They meet the moments even when it's awkward, hard, threatening, and downright uncomfortable. John Street's leadership style embodied these qualities.

His big, bold, visionary Neighborhood Transformation Initiative (NTI), while rocky and controversial at its rollout, was the first real effort by any mayor before or after him to remove blight across the city. This was an unprecedented mega public policy and financial initiative that incorporated a sustainable housing development plan designed to revitalize Philadelphia's poor and distressed neighborhoods. The transformation of neighborhoods and the related work continued well into my last term on the City Council. While he was viewed as unorthodox by the naysayers, this did not deter him from making a difference in controversial winds. With his inner circle and his firecracker A-Team, Mayor Street forged ahead, making a difference in several areas that mattered to him and his base of support, voters in distressed neighborhoods, which at times was not popular with the "establishment." I had the privilege and the unique opportunity to serve with three mayors. Mayor Street remains my favorite chiefly because of his authentic, consistent, intentional interest and tangible support for his cabinet members who cared about the success of other first-year students, aka freshman legislators, namely W. Wilson Goode, Jr., Darrell L. Clarke, and me. Mayor Street gets my five stars.

There are so many people in public service who should read Ukrainian President Volodymyr Zelenskyy's forthcoming book on leadership. President Zelenskyy epitomizes leadership. His compassion, conviction, endurance, and personal magnetism during the Ukrainian crisis have been epic, admirable, heroic, and sure to become legendary. He has been unapologetic in his quest to rumble with the warmonger, zealot, and tyrant President Putin. It remains clear to the world that President Zelenskyy was and is deeply and genuinely guided by the interests of the Ukrainian people. Zelenskyy did not pander, telling America and leaders around the world, "I don't need your goodwill. I need weapons." The entire world witnessed up close a leader, a champion for the Ukrainian people who never for a nano-second wavered. President Zelenskyy is neither a pimp nor a punk, a lesson many in public service could learn.

A Note on Leadership to My Fellow Black Women

I have been and continue to be inspired by the remarkable stories of courageous Black women who, amid overwhelming adversity and the ugly monster known as racism, persevered with resilience. I have been energized by the stories of Black women who have been fearless and who, with ferocity, faced down multiple lions at the same time. Rebel women such as Harriet Tubman, Fannie Lou Hammer, Rosa Parks, Paula Murray, Ella Baker, and Shirley Chisholm, et al., have moved the pendulum for Black folks. One of my favorites was the educator, orator, lawyer, and the first African American woman elected to the Texas State Senate, and then the first Congress-woman in the twenty-first century, Soror, Congresswoman Barbara Jordan. Her book, *Barbara Jordan: A Self-Portrait*, tells her truth with "eloquent thunder."

Black women of thunder are in and have been in every field. My third love, after my God and my daughter, is music. I still own, fifty years later, my first purchase of a black-and-white art photo of the first African American female vocalist to work with a white orchestra, one of the greatest jazz singers of the twentieth century, Billie Holiday. If you have not seen *United States vs. Billie Holiday*, a fictionalized view of the life of this complex and extraordinary artist, directed by another Philadanco alum, Lee Daniels, make a point to see it. Having been familiar with her story while at Penn State, this movie made me weep and infuriated me once again because of the insidious racism prevalent in our society. Despite the duplicity and fraudulence of the federal government, Billie Holiday was no pushover. She valiantly continued to expose racism for what it was.

One of my brightest highlights and revered memories while at City Council was the day I received a call from Karen Warrington, a former dancer. Karen was calling from Congressman Bob Brady's office with a request that I present a City Council citation to the dancer, choreographer, and change agent of American dance in the 1930s, the incomparable Katherine Dunham. Having studied the

Dunham dance technique at Philadanco for many years, my admiration was of the highest. This session was going to be topped by meeting and presenting *the* founder of the Dunham technique an overdue citation. Does it get any better? In my book, it does not!

While sitting in her wheelchair, Ms. Dunham delivered stirring remarks I shall never forget. With unrestrained humility and ineffable grace, she shared with council members and guests that she had had the rare privilege as a Black woman to have traveled the world teaching her artistry. Gazing at the City Council chambers ceiling, she drew us in with her nonverbal gestures and her remark that she had never been in a room with such majesty and architecture as our City Council chambers. Council members, mesmerized by her grace, were riveted. What a moment it was! You can only imagine what she endured in a field that, even today, is reticent to welcome talented people of color.

Another of my standouts is America's first Black female self-made millionaire entrepreneur, philanthropist, and political activist, Madam C. J. Walker. The daughter of former slaves, one hundred years later, a vision of her prowess still shines brilliantly as a standard bearer of excellence. Literally. This bold Black woman dared to use her platform of wealth boldly, with no fear of reprisal, and with the utmost pride, she chose to engage her political and social activism through hair. For my entire twenty years in office, above the conference table in my office, Room 588 City Hall, hung a black-and-white photo of Madam C. J. Walker. Another must-see is the Netflix miniseries, *Self Made: Inspired by the Life of Madam C.J. Walker*, if you are not familiar with her remarkable and unparalleled story.

So, Black women, brown women, all women leaders, to be leaders, wannabe leaders pull up a chair for a Sistah.

Carpe Diem

CHAPTER ELEVEN

VICTORIES AND A FEW LOSSES

"In management as in legislation, 2 percent of the problem is making a decision, 98 percent is persuading others to accept the decision." —Elliot Richardson, Former US Attorney General.

Typically, those who enter politics, regardless of color and whether they know it or not, believe in the African-based Kwanzaa principle: *Ujima* (oo-GEE-mah). This principle is an understanding that collective work and responsibility are embraced as an obligation to the past, present, and future and a belief that one has a role to play in their community.

In 1968, Shirley Chisolm, an original warrior woman, was the first Black woman ever to be elected to Congress representing New York's 12th congressional district. A trailblazer and change agent, her accomplishments while serving Brooklyn Bed-Stuy for seven terms were notable. She was the ultimate community builder. Potent and relevant, Chisolm became the first Black candidate of a major party nomination for President of the United States and the first woman to run for the Democratic Party's presidential nomination. Congresswoman and Soror, the Honorable Shirley Chisolm, challenged and chastised those in her community who sat on the sidelines. *"We have to show up to move the ball of progress and to help execute ideas that benefit the others, including our rights".*

Politics is not for the dancer who stands in the wings longing for the day when they are no longer the understudy, nor is it for the basketball player sitting on the bench waiting for the coach to call their number to the floor. It is for those who find a way to win or improve their chances of winning. Chisholm encouraged bystanders to get on the stage and break a leg; to get on the court and get busy!

Getting into the legislative arena means bringing ideas and ideals that can be crafted into laws and policies which will benefit the lies of those longing without hope. The true win for politicians comes from the outcome of the causes championed. My first year in Council was mired in what would become the most controversial public finance debate of my freshman term. The funding of our city's new sports stadiums became the centerpiece of our legislative calendar languished for two years. It was during my freshman year, too, that I learned whom to trust, which Council members would take advantage of novice legislators, and of the few who genuinely cared about legislative success. It was common that a Councilperson would bring firewood, douse it with gasoline, and then retreat when the house was ablaze. Because they didn't strike the match, they could hide behind an issue. Just as it takes all types of people to make the world go around, there were all types in the Philadelphia City Council. I learned that consensus-building was my style. It was the approach I used when I introduced my very first and probably one of the most impactful pieces of legislation that remains relevant and in full effect today. I remain grateful to Council member Darrell Clarke, who would rise to the top of the Council leadership circle as council president and who would always be my go-to peer trusted advisor, along with the brilliant Councilman at-large W. Wilson Goode, Jr. With their support, coupled with the guidance and coaching from George R. Burrell,

Esq., special advisor to Mayor Street, we strategically negotiated and convinced the leadership and ownership of the Philadelphia Eagles and the Phillies that they had to do something big and tangible for Philadelphia's children and youth. The alternative was my no-vote for the building of the new stadiums. While young in my tenure, the muscle in my corner, Mayor John F. Street, helped make my conviction exceedingly clear. Given the benefit of hefty tax breaks the teams were slated to receive, I believed strongly that the teams should provide a lasting benefit for our city's children and youth, as well. Ultimately, the owners agreed that contributing in a substantial, financial, and impactful manner was in their best interest if they wanted to seal the deal.

After a long year of protracted negotiations, in the end, both the Phillies and the Eagles agreed to donate $1 million per team per year for thirty years. YES! The board of managers at the Philadelphia Foundation adopted a resolution to create the fund consistent with City Council Bills 721-A and 722-A on February 21, 2001. The first round of grants was made in 2004. This has yielded $40 million to date since Philly's initial contribution in 2004 and will continue for another ten years, up to 2034.

This legislative victory was achieved for multiple reasons. Separate from the brilliant strategic thinking of Mayor Street and his attorney, George R. Burrell, I also realized early on one of the elements for legislative success. That element and skill is called collaboration. There is value in pulling together like-minded citizens who share a philosophy around a prevailing issue. In this case, carving a benefit for our city's children in this mega, unprecedented public finance deal was essential. Meeting with people smarter than me who specialized in an issue or skill always carried unpredictable guaranteed rewards. In the case of the Children's Fund, for many months, I met with a Kitchen Cabinet of women who each had a special advocacy perspective, lens, and expertise and carried a critical role in the city around protecting and advancing the safety and well-being of our city's children. The common threads were a) we all cared about children and b) these were women leaders willing to lobby and be on the hit squad to help me secure the required nine Council votes. Checking egos, leaving hard-earned titles at the door, and leaning on like-minded professionals for their expertise and perspective are strengths and trademarks of an effective legislator. This coalition of believers helped me refine the language for the Children's Fund provision of the stadium legislation and later helped me tell the story on the way to securing the nine-plus votes. This Kitchen Cabinet included Shelly Yanoff, executive director of the Philadelphia Citizens for Children and Youth; Christine James Brown, the CEO of the United Way SE Region; and Sandra Dungee Glenn, a nonprofit executive and Philadelphia School District board member. Our coalition and the collaborative efforts took a year and, like sausage, had several checkpoints on the Legislative Assembly line before the final vote count and before the bill arrived at the mayor's desk.

The Fund for Children, now managed by the Philadelphia Foundation is a legislative win that will stand for the next twenty years. The outcome of that successful policy allowed any Philadelphia nonprofit 501(c)(3) providing services to children and youth to apply for grant funds to make tangible differences in communities. The rolling grant remains popular and in full effect today.

Getting to a win for me was elevated to a new art form. How do I get a meeting of the minds around duplicitous shenanigans? When tackling complex public policy issues, look to lean on and draw upon the insights of the experts and advice of the community that will have a keen sensitivity, experience, and knowledge base on the issue. The powerful testimony and storytelling from an expert in the field of Board development, who did not look like me, resonated and brought credibility to the discussion of the inequities against women. Yes. Even on this issue, it took an enlightened white man to add legitimacy to the discussion on the imperative for more women on boards.

Opposition is a natural part of the legislative process. Expect it. Embrace it. Strategize around it, and then craft a plan to garner your nine votes. Long before I arrived at the Philadelphia City Council, Senator Vincent Hughes gifted me my go-to tool and weapon, the book *Getting to Yes, Negotiating Without Giving In* by Roger Fisher and William Ury. For formidable debates, which were many, I read and reread the yellow highlighted parts of that book throughout my twenty-year career at major touchpoints. When I had to prepare for a tug-of-war or intellectual gymnastics with tough opponents on a prospective piece of legislation, it became my bible. I can say with confidence that I learned to navigate the rocky waters of irate constituents who were ready to call me out using street corner language to demand their way or the highway. With love and attention, I gave those unnecessarily ugly citizens words of comfort in a way they may not have fully understood and worked to become the ultimate diplomat as I shepherded my bill to the finish line. In every negotiating session, I intimately understood my goal as well as I understood my BATNA (Best Alternative to Negotiated Agreement) position, my walkaway position if my optimum negotiation failed. It is like asking for an investment ... you need $1 million, but you ask for $1.5 million, and you'll take nine hundred thousand if offered.

When seeking agreements and win-win scenarios on complex matters layered with nuances impacting multiple constituencies, disagreement does not instinctively mean disrespect. Your opponents should be valued, and their views on each issue respected. Even if their perspective doesn't matter to you, they are vested in that position, therefore acknowledge that their view matters to them.

When tackling controversial issues, former councilwoman and my predecessor to the City Council, the late Councilwoman Augusta A. Clark, always stated with a calm demeanor, "*We can disagree without being disagreeable.*" The one exception is knowing the heart of those with whom you are seeking to reach a mutual consensus. You must be tuned in to that rare colleague who consistently operates from a place of self-interest and what's in it for them. This includes sacrificing you, misrepresenting you, at worst, pimping you as a Black woman, and sometimes just being an outright liar speaking with a forked tongue about what they bring to the table. The golden rule for people cut from that cloth is always to listen to what they say, and then watch what they do. Pay attention or have a staffer who works with you keep their antenna and radar up. It will always be what that colleague does and how they treat your staff that reveals who they are at their core. Be like the teacher who is always paying attention to the student least likely to surprise you. Pay attention.

I credit and give big applause to another great leader, Mayor Michael Nutter, for signing multiple bills my staff and I crafted into law. One I am proud of my landmark menu-labeling bill and the measure of establishing a new department of government, the Office of Sustainability. Mayor Nutter was the torchbearer for the hospitality and tourism community, which emerged as the number two industry in Philadelphia during his tenure. His strong leadership and focus on this industry were substantial and impactful because the domino effect of hospitality and tourism energized the arts and culture community, among others. Mayor Nutter and I shared our enthusiasm and respect for the hospitality and tourism sector, and we championed their vital work as was evident in me serving on the Philadelphia Convention & Visitors Bureau Board of Directors. His advocacy in this space was indeed meritorious.

By Resolution 120187, the City Council's Committee on Commerce and Economic Development authorized hearings examining the level of female participation on executive boards in companies that do business with the City of Philadelphia. The resulting hearing, which included five panels held on May 29, 2012, provided startling findings and formed the basis for a 2013 report outlining recommendations addressing how to tackle the lack of female representation in executive positions and on corporate boards.

The legislative process requires good judgment in knowing when to follow the sage advice sung in Kenny Rogers's song, "The Gambler," *"You've got to know when to hold 'em, Know when to fold 'em, Know when to walk away."* Councilwoman Maria Quiñones Sánchez best described my legislative style. "I've seen when Blondell must be feisty and when she must be the consensus builder. I've seen her when she's taken the role of facilitator."

A new policy issue that seeks to climb the mountain to approval quickly shows that the legislative process is not linear and is in no way predictable. Newbies or even more seasoned legislators must be prepared for the unexpected detours and hiccups that require pivoting left and right on the way to securing the nine votes, and twelve, if there is any hint of a mayor's veto. Persuasive negotiating skills on all sides can highlight and focus the commonality of the group and with intentional deliberation on the problems that unify both sides, consensus can be reached. In other words, strip away the opposing issues and begin negotiations by reading from one sheet of music. Gracefully and selectively reject the retractable, difficult, nuanced issues that divide. This judicious approach and subsequent action can become your legislative style and anthem cry.

Another top priority legislative policy issue that mattered most to me was advancing business opportunities for minority and women-owned businesses. No one on the Philadelphia City Council or in the mayor's office deserves more credit for this policy area than the Honorable W. Wilson Goode Jr. This issue intersected all topical policy areas and involved all city departments. With smarts, intention, insistence, and, oftentimes, in-your-face indignation, Wilson elevated this policy area, giving it unprecedented prominence on the council calendar during his entire tenure of sixteen years in City Council. The battle cry for our city leadership was to be unapologetically aggressive. Moving the needle in demonstrative ways and advancing business opportunities for minority and women-owned businesses (MBE/WBEs) never made Wilson weary. He marched to his own drum as he tackled the historic and systemic practices that have locked out this business sector for decades. These businesses remain the backbones of neighborhoods and are vital to the city's economy. Providing MBE/WBEs with benefits to help level the playing field, and offering technical assistance for access to government contracts, business financing, and loans, has not yet found its natural place in government. Ensuring fairness and equity in the processes that facilitate equitable business opportunities will never be organic because doing so requires challenging rooted, arcane systems laced with bureaucratic and interstitial racism. Consequently, holding government bureaucrats and mayoral-appointed administrators accountable will never go away.

While the numbers of minorities in professional services and commodities rose for MBE/WBEs during the Street, Nutter, and Kenney administrations, government leaders must be committed at all levels (the executive branch and the legislative branch) to continue to push the envelope on this issue and hold department heads accountable. W. Wilson Goode Jr., who has been recognized nationally by the National Community Reinvestment Coalition for his laser beam focus on this issue, is unmatched. Goode Jr. remains my hero in this legislative policy area.

The menu-labeling bill was another high-water mark in my growth and development as a legislator. This measure, which was harshly treated (in my opinion) by many with great suspicion, tested my ability to build alliances and forced me to practice and master the art of persuasion. The restaurant and fast food industries and their affiliated PACs of the state and national restaurant associations were vehemently opposed to this public health measure. Unfortunately for me, they had unlimited political action committee dollars to spend promoting their opposition and lobbying my colleagues. As a legislator, I found I had to repeatedly edit my delivery for strategic and carefully worded language to support my arguments to secure one vote at a time. It was my approach to practice what was first stated by Winston Churchill to tell disbelievers, "*To go to hell in such a way that they look forward to the trip.*"

This major, highly controversial legislation I was spearheading took me two long years to secure nine solid votes. I employed every tactic discussed in the book to achieve my goal. What was the outcome? Today, when you go into any chain restaurant within Philadelphia County limits, you will find menu labeling, described by Monica Yant Kinney, a *Philadelphia Inquirer* reporter, as a "sort of a GPS for the dieter" that includes caloric and nutritional information. More importantly, this bill, "thought to fall into the foie gras ban category, had a surprisingly positive impact," remarked the *Philadelphia Daily News*, and helped me seal their endorsement for the 2011 May Primary election. Later, my staff and I augmented and updated the law to require chain restaurants to provide and disclose menu warning symbols for sodium, a contributor to the deadly killer hypertension, a health condition most prevalent in the African American community.

Contrary to widespread belief, most of the sodium we eat comes from packaged, processed, and restaurant foods and not from the saltshaker. Given the high blood pressure among too many of Philadelphia's residents, this policy had relevance and deserved to reflect this public health dilemma as well. Test your knowledge of caloric information by taking the pop quiz found on my website. See if you know the difference between a Big Mac and a Whopper Jr. See if you can get an A on the quiz! Good luck!

Lastly, remember my signature legislative priority established in my first term was to be an advocate for children. Sticking with that goal, my staff and I rendered one final tweak to the menu labeling legislation during my fifth and last term. Our last effort required restaurants to list healthy beverage options for children on their menus. Food service establishments that offer a children's menu now must make their default beverage options water, milk, or 100 percent fruit juice with no added natural or artificial sweeteners. The measure passed with ease, thus encouraging children and parents to make smarter, healthier choices when dining out. While Philadelphia was not at the forefront on this matter, we did get in step with more progressive municipalities like Seattle, which first passed menu-labeling legislation over a decade before Philadelphia. Nutritional information on menus is a growing phenomenon and increasingly becoming the expected norm when dining out locally and nationally.

Our effort on this legislation underscored one of the most important lessons to be learned in politics. It resonates for all the daredevils who long to make a difference despite the naysayers, the roadblocks, the boulders, the hurdles, and the outspoken discouragement. American attorney and thirtieth president of the United States, Calvin Coolidge, says it best why the roadblocks, the boulders, the benign doomsday thinkers become immaterial and insignificant. *"Nothing in the world can take the place of persistence. Talent will not: nothing is more common than unsuccessful men with talent. Genius will not: unrewarded genius is almost a proverb. Education will not: the world is full of educated derelicts. Persistence and determination alone are omnipotent."*

Walking the tightrope required me to sustain the delicate intellectual balance between the persuasive arguments of the state and national restaurant associations stacked against the science and views of the public health child national data and advocates with whom I agreed. The competing, compelling childhood obesity health metrics, data, mapping, and trends occurring around the country carried little weight in the face of the well-financed business lobbying conglomerate networks. This debate required regular weekly briefing sessions and an exhaustive list of meetings with a cross section of stakeholders that lasted close to two years. The fact that other major cities like Seattle and NYC had successfully instituted new menu-labeling measures was immaterial.

The legislation garnered much press coverage on both sides of the issue. I was always impressed by young college students who were paying attention to City Council legislation. Jamie France of *The Daily Pennsylvanian* titled her article "Nutritional Tough Love." France stated:

> Nutritional facts are exactly the kind of in-your-face action needed to combat obesity. Philadelphia's local politicians are not only reinforcing the age-old philosophy, you are what you eat, they're rubbing it in our faces. Overall, this proposal has so much promise that it has spurred my ideas. This isn't merely the request of a spoiled private school student; a display of nutrition information in Penn's dining facilities would do wonders. If we were provided with basic nutrition information for meals offered on campus, we would probably feel more comfortable eating them, and much less food would be thrown away with the money that we fork over for our meal plans. No pun intended.

If there are losses to be acknowledged, which there are, my flip flop on DROP, the City of Philadelphia's Deferred Retirement Option Plan, was the worst. DROP is the City Council-approved plan that allows municipal employees, including elected officials, to freeze and collect both their salaries and their pensions at the end of their final twelve to forty-eight–months on the job. A veteran Councilwoman, Marion B. Tasco, stated that DROP is "earned retirement income" and is a legal option available for all city employees. I was against DROP initially but changed my position on this measure once I was debriefed about its legitimate value. DROP was not illegal or unethical. With the benefit of hindsight, which we know is always 20/20, I should have been a yes vote at the door. After I left office to work in another city department, I exercised my rights under DROP and caught major negative press. Devoured by the press, the lack of support and silence from the shadow on the second floor of city hall killed my opportunity to be a beneficiary of the program.

The lesson learned—take the heat and stay the course like the steel-willed magnolia of Councilwoman Tasco. The fact that I was no longer a public official didn't seem to matter. What got in my craw was that the public record did not show the men who did not look like me who had signed up for this legislatively approved measure and got it long after I had applied for the earned benefit. With the invisible assistance of the mayor, my former colleague, these long time city employees, who were also deserving of their drop benefit escaped criticism from the media and were protected albeit silently. Go figure. With a dampen spirit and no political support to neutralize the press, I accepted the loss of the earned benefit, practiced strengthening my mental muscle and moved on.

Herein lies another reminder. Women must walk on water, and women of color must walk on water and fly to be treated equally, fairly, and justly in all spaces. In the end, be prepared for the double standards, take the media hit, and prepare to walk through the fire alone because you will be criticized, anyway.

The criticism from the short list of white male journalists who needed to bolster their careers didn't realize that I come from a family legacy that achieved mightily despite insidious racism. The piercing lesson I learned from this loss was emblematic of President Teddy Roosevelt's view about the backseat driver pundits.

> *It is not the critic who counts, not the man who points out how the strong man stumbles or where the doer of deeds could have done them better. The credit belongs to the man who is actually in the arena, whose face is marred by dust and sweat and blood, who strives valiantly, who errs and comes short again and again because there is no effort without error and shortcoming but who knows the great enthusiasm, the great devotions, who spends himself in a worthy cause, who at the best, knows, in the end, the triumph of high achievement, and who, at the worst, if he fails, at least he fails while daring greatly so that his place*

shall never be with those cold and timid souls who know neither victory nor defeat.

During the last year of my last term in City Council, I felt proud of having moved the needle on many issues that improved the lives and health of children and families. In the legislative process, you will discover that a meeting of the minds and a bumping of heads are quite different things. So, savor the victories and never allow the losses to cripple or trip you. Catch yourself, pull back up on that tightrope, refocus, now walk in your high heels as you practice the mental muscle to move on.

Carpe Diem

CHAPTER TWELVE

WHEN YOU ARE THE NEWS, FACE THE MUSIC

"At any given moment, you have the power to say: this is not how the story is going to end." — Christine Mason Miller

For two decades in the City Council, I gave all I had to give to the families, citizens, and voters in the city of Philadelphia. After twenty years, I made an exceedingly difficult and painstaking decision not to run for a sixth term, opting to leave City Council on "my" terms. Upon my departure, despite some emotional bruises and a temporary career setback, I was able to declare, without hesitancy, that I had delivered on my campaign promises.

For four successful terms, I executed my job with diligence and looked forward to going to work every single day. After placing first in a campaign with thirteen other viable candidates, I was re-elected to my fourth term as an at-large City Council member. The good news was that I had carefully and quietly managed a separation from my husband. Public opinion would only have complicated things, but with the end of my sixteen-year marriage, my life was spinning out of control. My husband and I could not reconcile the decision of our daughter's future educational direction, and our marriage became the casualty. When our marriage fell apart, so many other matters did as well, including the possession of our home. Our marriage separation led to no communication, which had severe consequences. Unaware until I received a bank notice; our home was in foreclosure. When I became privy to this, fear rose like bile. Fear is ugly, and the ugly came for me in 2011. In a moment of despair and desperation, I made a bad step, a misstep that was followed by misguided action. Period.

In my turmoil, void of good judgment and lack of clarity, my blunder would tarnish my record and cause me to experience the greatest pain of my career and face the disappointment of those I served. My pristine record in politics ended abruptly. While I had not committed a criminal offense, I did cross the ethical line of campaign finance. Unless I could come up with $40,000 for the bank in 90 days plus $1,000, I would lose my home. I had been able to pull from savings and insurance policies, and with help from my family, I was left with an uncovered balance of $4,500. Desperate to save the home where my ailing mother, daughter, and I resided, I blurred the line by borrowing the balance from my campaign account money to meet the bank's requirement. While borrowing from my account was not criminal, the borrowing was unethical due to the lack of disclosure. All candidates MUST DISCLOSE. Everything in your campaign finance filings must be disclosed. NO EXCEPTIONS. PERIOD. The last thing anyone wants is to be in the news, and if the news is bad, you scream silently. In 2011, because of the lack of disclosure, I became bad news and fodder for the local news.

I was brought before the City Board of Ethics (BOE) for not recording and disclosing the loan. To make matters worse, in January 2013, the Board of Ethics decided to audit Campaign finance funds for several political candidates going back to 2010. It was at this time, to my surprise, that I discovered that my campaign manager was accused of using political donations for personal uses, which caused another firestorm that prompted an additional investigation of my campaign finance reports. The nightmare thickened when the investigators found violations in my records dating back to 2010. My campaign was charged with not reporting contributions in a timely way on finance disclosure forms and for numerous donations being over legal limits. The discovery during the investigation of my campaign manager's pilferage over four years erupted a blazing, blinding firestorm. The bad news was this fact: the buck stopped with me. It was personally gut-wrenching and deeply embarrassing to have been caught up in the drama, which made my lapse in judgment look worse. I was draped in a blanket of hurt that I carried for months. The disappointment from my marriage, coupled with my breach of ethics, was maddening. The indiscretion of my longtime campaign manager, a young man I had been mentoring since his college experience, was devastating. I was tested daily, beyond measure. Even today, I often catch myself dwelling in that head space answering questions such as: How did I get there? How did I go through it all? How did I perform my most favored duties joyfully every day in my most honored role as Mom? How did I meet the demands of my sister and the family's general requirements regarding our ailing mom? The ongoing demands of my council duties? How did I survive? Head spinning, I marveled at how life can change on a dime. It was all surreal!

As the leader of the pack, when you sign campaign expense reports, accurate or not, all roads lead to you, me, the candidate. More disappointing was that my campaign manager of twenty years and treasurer for more than twelve years was a "friend." With changing rules and hence my all-caps warning to have the most experienced lawyer well-versed with the ever-changing campaign reporting requirements it was determined that another $4,500 in fines for ethics violations would be levied, due to the BOE's decision that the campaign money was used for personal reasons. Regardless of my past exemplary campaign reporting record, the Board of Ethics made me a shining example. Never before had any elected official in the City of Philadelphia been fined at the record level of $40,000 in campaign fines and $4,500 in personal fines. All fines had to be paid within twenty-four months, two years before the start of my 2015 campaign for reelection.

This was the beginning of a bad dream, a living nightmare with high stakes. My personal and private circumstances exploded into a very public campaign crisis, including a federal investigation resulting in several dozen news stories for close to a year. I vividly recall a comment offered by one of my strongest financial campaign supporters and seasoned political wizard, Karen A. Robinson. She texted me during the beginning of the firestorm and said in her classic Karen-esc style, with encouragement, "Blondell, you are wounded, but not fatal," a needed boost for my confidence and reboot.

Sharing in the care of our eighty-five-year-old mom while sustaining my role as a helicopter mom for my sixteen-year-old daughter, meeting the ongoing demands of council, and dealing with a campaign career crisis resulted in complete chaos and a near personal meltdown. I paid for this nightmare handsomely, financially and emotionally, while in the public's eye. I learned then that no one, no one gets an exemption from the lessons to be learned after an error in judgment. Prayerfully, you learn from the aberration, take stock, get back onto the tightrope, head up, shoulders back, confidence and faith restored, and practice your mental muscle exercise so you can move on from what should never be repeated.

There was no excuse for what I had done, and I made none because my every intention was to refund the money borrowed. Unfortunately, in the hailstorm of investigating the city's officials, because of my affiliation with my former boss, now simultaneously under the microscope for inappropriate usage of finance campaign funds, I became a standout. The fallout in government and the investigation of Congressman Chaka Fattah Sr., coupled with the rumbling of many others who were also going to be brought up on charges as it got louder, engulfed me.

Still incomprehensible to me during this time was my sister Pandora, who was the captain of the oversight in the caretaking needs of our mom. She was most encouraging while I was fulfilling and meeting my commitment to Council duties, which did not cease during the storm. Pandora was a rock for me. The tolerance and the supportive spirit of those who cared about me threw me a safety net. I learned one of life's lessons often attributed to Robert Frost. *"The best way out is always through."* There was no other way. I had to woman up and face the dissonance of the music I had orchestrated. However, in the end, with the benefit of hindsight, I submit that this experience yells sheer resilience, comprehensible only to God. Because of my faith and the prayers of many, I am still standing, today.

I am forever grateful to my former husband, Howard Brown, for hearing my appeal for us to purchase a home with such an invaluable asset as a mother-in-law's suite because it made life more tolerable and delightful for all of us. My daughter's grandmother was like most endearing nanas—angels on earth, with a lot of practice providing unconditional emotional and practical support in countless predictable and unpredictable ways. Reflecting on those days, months, and years, I grew to value having my mom under the same roof and deeply appreciated the huge blessing she was for Howard, our daughter, Andrew, Howard's son before our marriage, and me. The only saving grace and blessing during this dark period was that my mom, who lived in the mother-in-law suite of our home, was also the family spy, who commiserated daily with her stalwart partner, sister Pandora. An avid news junkie, my Mom reported everything to Pandora. Mom became my pillar. I still miss her every single day, but *"Like a bird singing in the rain, I let grateful memories survive in times of sorrow."*—Robert Louis Stevenson. I learned only after my mom passed from my sister Pandora that Mom always wanted a home with a picket fence and a red brick walking path. What a joy to learn that my former husband and I were able to fulfill my mom's wish while on earth because our home fulfilled that dream. What a blessing!!!!

During this crisis period of my life, the one book I read and reread was *Learning to Trust God* by Deborah J. Kern. Along with pastoral counseling from Pastor Terry Davis, this book guided me in acknowledging God in all circumstances, including the bitter ones and the heartbreaking moments, knowing and trusting that good would come from the turmoil. Central to the message of this book was learning *"to lean not on my understanding, but in all thy ways acknowledge him and he will direct your paths."* —Proverbs 3:6.

Drowning was never an option. I was frustrated and scared, and the badgering press was cruel. There was no time for whining. I had to push through. I had to lecture myself and believe I was far bigger than the salivating lions I had to face. Every morning, as I took my daughter to school, I was keenly aware that Brielle was listening and watching and there was nothing I could do to shield her. Understanding the spiritual purpose for this career trauma was not on my mental radar while crawling through the dark tunnel. My head did not have the bandwidth for anything more than piecing together immediately the puzzle for my resurrection.

When in the news, I did not run. Don't. The press stalked me. Hounded me like a dog. To them, I acknowledged my poor judgement, accepted my mistakes and braced myself for inevitable criticism. I apologized and leaned into the scripture, *"The rain falls on the just and the unjust."* —Matthew 5:45. Relentlessly, I prepared my heart for what was ahead. The hardest was promptly delivering the bad news to my family, my inner personal circle, and my Kitchen Cabinet. It was painful but necessary. Sharing with my inner circle served as a precursor to facing the music, and it gave me good practice as a dress rehearsal for facing the bad news publicly and the *mea culpa* pleas to my broader public. The bottom line, I was an elected leader in a public position, and I would not retreat from the world during a time of crisis. I was ready to face the music, the embarrassment, and the professional instability. I reacquainted with my moxie woman, trying not to trip off the tightrope. I said my prayers daily as I put one foot in front of the other and walked through the doors of City Hall. I persisted as I faced the lions and what the day held.

Since being in the press was inevitable, I selected the news media outlets or publications that were known to be fair and objective in their reporting of "just the facts." Then, I said a prayer, beat my face (theater lingo for applying your make-up), and pulled out my navy blue business suit the night before an interview. On the way, while traveling to the press interview, I could hear my heartbeat doing the mambo. I rehearsed the possible questions I might be asked and prepared written answers on paper while I answered them in my head. I would say yet another prayer before I slid from my car, straightened my back, and held my head up. Walking like a dancer and not like a lumbering truck driver, I entered the conference room—the inquisition room. With grace, I accepted this fact—I was not on the short list of the very few people who get through life without any regrets, stumbles, or fluff-ups.

Confidently, I faced the reporters and members of the news editorial board eyeball-to-eyeball. I was ready. I was prepared to answer the tough, probing, but necessary questions to come. I provided answers, which filled in the blanks in the story. An hour later, it was over. I exhaled. Next, I waited and waited and waited for the release of the story. Prepared to read the outcome of the interview, which for sure would be an encore of bad news for those I held dear, I steeled my spine. Regardless of the content, I called back and expressed my appreciation to the editor of the publication. I said a heartfelt thanks to the tough, but always fair, Bob Bogle, of *The Philadelphia Tribune* newspaper for the chance to offer my lens and my voice in telling my side of the story.

For months I was in a funk that only a daily prayer could meter. I started my day with an inspirational reading and found journaling at the end of the day cathartic. Eventually, I began to focus on my recovery, rebuilding my campaign apparatus and reassessing the lessons that this debacle was meant to teach me. Day by day, I began to pick myself up emotionally and journaling proved invaluable. I reminded myself of one of my mom's proverbs, *"this too shall pass."* Once I began to feel some semblance of normality, indicating I was in the recovery phase of healing, I sensed the time had come for me to dust myself off. I prepared my heart and my spirit for the renewal and restart.

Going through the fire, I not only discovered a lot about myself but those around me. I had heard Oprah make this remark early in her distinguished career, paraphrased, too many of your friends will be ready to jump in your car when it's a smooth highway, free of thunderstorms, but these rides do not count. Focus instead on remembering and showing gratitude to those friends who don't step away from the car when the hailstones hit or the car breaks down and you are faced to take an Uber. True to word, those angels revealed themselves. They just showed up. And as many of the others silently disappeared. Like pouf!

Friends like my Girls' High School classmate Terry Graboyes and The Village Moms reached out to assist me financially. They hosted a needed and timely fundraiser to help me begin to raise the funds required to pay the fines levied by the Ethics Board. Sorors, like Sharmaine Matlock Turner and Judge Renee Cardwell-Hughes, who also walked tightropes in their high visibility leadership positions, offered their guidance without fanfare and judgment but with empathy and fidelity. Forever friends like Linda sent me a text reciting her favorite comforting words, "Hang in there." Colleague Councilwoman Maria Quiñones Sánchez, campaign craftsman Al Spivey, and chief of staff David Forde, Esq. met with me *ad nauseam* on long weekends over months as we combed through campaign expense reports and crafted the new strategies needed for the rebooting of my career. Kevin Greenberg, Esq., one of the few legal eagles who specializes in campaign finance law, provided pro bono legal services. John Milligan, the Managing Partner of Milligan and Company,

LLC, the largest minority-owned consulting firm headquartered in Pennsylvania assigned one of his CPA angels to lend their expertise to make sense out of the campaign bank records. None were interested in recognition. They knew my heart and had read about my track record of service in the press. They showed up with their expertise, empathy, and compassion. Their only objective was to guide and coach me successfully through this rough, humiliating ditch filled with both craters and sinking sand. Facing my rational self was the hardest. In my right mind, I would never and had never done anything so asinine. I exercised flawed judgment, and I owned it.

Much to my surprise, I received a handwritten message from another Girls' High School classmate, now a lawyer, Carolyn Gaines, whom I had not seen in decades. The message: "Dear Blondell, Be encouraged. Many people still stand with you. Things will get better and I'm praying for you. Be strong. Life is tough! Sometimes you gotta bend, but not break. You gotta roll with the punches. You gotta bounce back." It would be easier if you were made of foam rubber instead of flesh and blood.

My brother-in-law James mailed me a card with a most appropriate and sensitive message from a poem written by the poet laureate Helen Steiner Rice, "The Way To God." The passages that most resonated with me were:

> *If my days were untroubled, and my heart always light, would I seek that far land, where there is no night?*
>
> *If I never grew weary with the weight of my load,*
>
> *Would I search for God's peace at the end of the road?*
>
> *If all I desired was mine for the day,*
>
> *would I kneel before God and earnestly pray?*
>
> *I ask myself this and the answer is plain.*
>
> *If my life was all pleasure and I never knew pain.*

I'd seek God less often in times of distress.

No one knows, as those who have met him on the pathway up pain. God has a wonderful purpose for you.

James went further with his touching handwritten message.

In one of his most memorable sermons, Dr. Charles Stanley preached that the challenges in our lives are meant either for our corrections or our perfection. In other words, God is eliminating some deficit or enhancing an otherwise positive quality so that we might become more productive for working in his vineyard. No one enjoys the pain associated with having to dwell in the valley, but if you accept Dr. Stanley's teachings, it's easier to comprehend the Biblical principle outlined in Romans 8:28, which assures us that in all circumstances, the Lord is working things together for our good and his glory. Therefore, do not give up or be discouraged. Instead, Dr. Stanley suggests amid the difficulties, we should ask God to reveal whether he wants us to be moved into a different place or mindset. Although it may seem like an eternity, this too shall pass. Psalm 30:5 states in part, "weeping may endure for a night, but joy cometh in the morning." One of my favorite Christian authors expresses the same truth quite beautifully in his text, Reaching for the Invisible God*: "The crack in my house freezes over every winter. If I bend down close, though, I can hear it flowing beneath the ice, the sound muffled but unmistakable. Never does it stop. Under the frigid layers of winter lies proof of an inevitable summer. Your summer is coming. Know that we love you.* —James

Wanda of The Travel Crew was another girlfriend who was rooting for me. Her card cover stated: "If God brings you to it, He will bring you through it." Wanda's handwritten message was so reassuring and comforting.

> *While we may not understand the challenges God allows us to face, what I know for sure is that what does not kill us, simply makes us stronger. You are a woman of faith and strength who will overcome this challenge. You will come out stronger and take away all the lessons you've learned from it. I was challenged once in a very public way that set me on a course of depression. My shrink reminded me of the great person I was and told me to look at my awards and accolades over the years and to surround myself with positive people and inspirational readings. This simple advice turned my life around. I searched my life and decisions to get the lesson I could learn from that challenge. That's what I decided to take away from that incident—lessons learned that allowed me to grow and get better. I pray that you do the same. No one could convince me of anything bad about you. When you are ready, I am here. You have been a blessing in my life, and I thank God for you. Thousands in Philadelphia are thankful for all you have done for us over the years. If you need anything let me know. Love, Wanda*

I read and kept dozens of these handwritten notes which were my lifeline of hope. I left my Philadelphia City Council office on December 31, 2019, with all of my letters in tow, and dozens I still treasure to this day.

I was also pleasantly and gratefully surprised by emails I had not expected attributing my blunder to my head and not my heart. Even at this writing and during subsequent multiple reviews and edits of my transcript, I still get misty-eyed. I might not have survived without the love and kindness of these amazing friends and messengers of hope. Thank-yous will never be enough for the notes of encouragement and kindness I received from so many.

While it is hard to be down and grateful at the same time, my testimony reminds me that difficult hardships are indeed transformative. This bend in the road of my career was never going to be the end of the road of this journey. The next challenge for me was to reboot, create a renewed purpose after my recovery, which was mandatory, and boldly execute the steps to rescue, resuscitate, and rehabilitate my career.

The encouragement I received was essential as it served as an antidote to the hateful and self-righteous social media addicts. Their comments were vicious, distorted, and a distraction to my psyche. I am thankful for the devoted staff who shielded me whenever and wherever they could, allowing me to remain laser-focused on my two most important roles, mother of Brielle and the city council at-large member managing the legislative and constituency demands of my City Council office.

For twenty-four months the hailstorm did not let up. I woke up every day wondering what the prevailing question of the day would be. I prayed, Dear God, please show me. I asked for guidance on how to remain steady amid the negative news stories. I asked God to gird me as I attended the weekly scheduled meetings with my campaign lawyer, my divorce lawyer, and now my criminal defense lawyer. I prayed for preparedness and sanity to handle all the required council committee meetings with care while my council staff and I continued crafting meaningful legislation. Praise God I never lost my balance on the tightrope in my role as an attentive mom of a high school junior about to embark on the intimidating college search and admissions process.

For two years, I was vulnerable on all sides. I wanted to go and hide. My private morning weeping spells weakened my spirit, stole my joy, and made me weary. The family's other spy, my sister, a former investigative reporter in her career, was the organizer of the

Olde School Dance Party fundraiser. Almost to annoyance, but with deep gratitude on my part, she would call me often to see how I was doing. I was never honest with my sister in the answers I gave because I knew they would be reported back to my mom, who was already burdened hearing the daily barrage of negative stories about her firstborn child on KYW News Radio, Philadelphia's all-news, twenty-four hours, seven days a week, news radio.

What I didn't say to my sister was that I was alone, afraid, and lonely. That I had learned to wear the façade, and a veneer was my way of coping. Each morning, despite my sadness, I beat my face to look fabulous, dressed in the uniform outfit for the day, a suit, and proceeded to enjoy those fleeting morning rides to school with my daughter. Then I would do a reverse U-turn and head back to city hall to face another day in City Council. Daily I looked the lion in the mouth and declared with a smile that I would not be eaten by the press, the naysayers, the onlookers, or the new and old skeptics. In the words of author and gifted filmmaker, Ken Burns, each day for me for two years was, *"a negotiation between strength and weakness."*

Most painful to acknowledge was the realization that the one hundred-plus pieces of legislation I had authored over the past sixteen years were now meaningless in the face of adversity. Pursuing a career of service to others and advocacy to enact legislation that would improve the lives and life chances of Philadelphia's vulnerable women, children, and families, took a back seat to the inner turmoil, the embarrassment, the disappointment, the hate on social media, and the betrayal.

Legislation that included the strongest menu-labeling bill in the country, the creation of a new Commission for Women, and the passage of an unprecedented Women on Boards bill, the first of its type in the country, were examples, but empty achievements because of this devastating train wreck. Awards from every women's organization in the City of Philadelphia, from Girls Scouts to Women's Way, gave me no solace, no comfort, no affirmation of my proven work and track record of service. I was in a very dark valley having to face each day with a smile, grace, and sheer but quiet determination. Each morning during the storm when I walked out the front door, I knew throughout the day that I had to have a strong back and the mental constitution to adjust my sail.

The onslaught of the press's laser beam focus on the collision of my campaign and personal crises took my breath away. To arm my daughter, one morning while on the way to school, I shared with her that she needed to know that I had been on the television evening news the night before and in the morning newspaper—again. With her face in her homework binder, she never looked up. Her nonchalant unaffected response was, "Mommie, my friends don't read the paper." In that instance, she provided me with a small sigh of relief, unconditional love, and a resolve that would carry me for the rest of that day.

Bounded by this storm, I leaned into reading and re-reading a couple of books that would restore my spirit and keep me motivated. They included *Learning to Trust God* by Deborah J. Kern and *The Purpose Driven Life* by Rick Warren. Unexpectedly, in my home library, I also stumbled upon one of my favorite quotation books featuring the quotes of Dr. Martin Luther King Jr. I came upon the quote which now is a question I pose often in difficult circumstances. *"The measure of a man is not where he stands during moments of comfort and convenience, but where he stands at times of challenge and controversy."* In an aha moment of clarity during this public storm, I realized that I had to face this controversial crisis head-on and begin to take action to fight my way out of the foxhole. Only then could I move toward recovery and reclaim my professional, personal, and political career. I had to accept this ugly situation. It was time to *"Pray as if all depended on God and work as if all depended on you."*
—Brigham Young

I had played a role in this career debacle, and I had owned it, publicly. I also had to believe that I had the power to fix the spectacle, act with urgency, and proceed to change the trajectory of my career at this critical juncture, ultimately taking my life back. While I was in the political ring in a fight to restore my career and reputation, I embraced Muhammed Ali's mantra. *"Ain't nothing wrong with going down. It's staying down that's wrong."* Staying down was never an option, as I had many supporters depending on me and too many others who still believed in me. Most importantly, I had the two chief principals in my life watching me and listening daily as I navigated the press, social media, and the stares whenever I showed up—my mom and my daughter. I refused to accept the potential reality of defeat. I choose to embrace my new circumstance with the strong belief best described by author and political activist, the resilient Helen Keller, *"the bend in the road is not the end of the road unless I fail to make a turn."* It was time for me to craft a strategy and figure out what I was going to do with this negative career buster, the painful and debilitating experience that I suffered in silence.

So, I got busy. Daily, I began to use every waking minute on how best to be both tactical and intentional as I moved to restore my reputation and rebuild my career. Strategically, I crafted and practiced a new series of personal and professional routines and activities like journaling, meditation, and prayer. These new habits were all designed to bolster my confidence and counter the raw and powerful opposition of haters, the press, the pessimists, and the career prognosticators in and outside my political family, the Fattah Organization rooting for my failure. Many made their presence known on social media and in political circles around the city. Their most popular refrain was, "Her council career is finished." But this was about me, and the trailer could not end here. It was time for me to show that I was my mother's child, a.k.a. a Toney, my mom's maiden name. It was time for me to demonstrate that this career fumble was a comma in my career, it would never be the period.

While on the road to recovery, head and heart heavy for sure, my moxie woman showed up. This was the time I had to practice the advice I often gave my dance students after a dance injury. When the going gets tough, the tough get going. Therefore, no whining is allowed. During my fierce but emotionally awkward period, the emotional support I was given by my youngest sister, "Deaconess" (my words) Alesia Jacks, was priceless. Her confident affirmations and strong faith girded me, reminding me often, *"Every day is a new start. We get to make new choices."* Agreed!!!! It was time for me to make new choices and to reboot.

First, I had to take stock of who was important in my orbit and who cared enough to guide me through this crisis. Time was now the enemy. The BOE had given me a strict time limit for repayment of the fines and penalties assessed. This was one factor that required me to re-prioritize how I spent my daily Council schedule and my weekends. Careful judgment was needed to determine what was important. I had to recalibrate and determine what in my daily personal, work, and activity schedule had to be changed and what had to be placed on pause or at worst eliminated.

I made it clear to my newly formed crisis circle of love that two routine practices were nonnegotiable, driving my daughter to school daily and her evening pickups from the Overbrook train station. It mattered to me to hear about her school day while taking her home. This allowed me to also stop over to see and check on my mom who was, Praise God, one door away in the mother-in-law's suite. The ten-hour workdays became twelve, fourteen, and at times, sixteen-hour days during the firestorm. This brutal schedule continued for the three years before, during, and after the crisis leading up to the 2015 Primary reelection.

The reboot included Saturday morning meetings for weeks with colleague Councilwoman Maria Quiñones Sánchez and Councilman Curtis Jones's staffer, Al Spivey, and a young rising star, Kellan White who were consistently available and present for me for months. On weekends staffers and a short list of Fattah CORE members, Sandra and Willie would lend a hand when their schedules permitted to help me scour through the campaign expense reports name by name, every contributor, one by one, of the one-hundred-plus pages from the 2011 campaign cycle. It became painfully clear that the need to hire a campaign finance lawyer was mandatory if I was to survive the self-righteous, double standard career executioners, a.k.a. the BOE.

Managing the campaign crisis now required weekly meetings with my campaign lawyer for nearly six months. Preparing for depositions and campaign-related surprises, which were many, had to be tackled immediately throughout this period. Layer these meetings with the ongoing preparation for the emotionally tinged sessions with my divorce lawyer as he prepared for his arguments with opposing counsel. Each day required me to face the music and to do so, never throwing mud. Proverbs 17:15: *"Whitewashing bad people and throwing mud on good people are equally abhorrent to God."* I sought to avoid getting dirty hands, but the temptation was real. Forgiveness is a choice. Living through forgiveness, the healing, and the restoration of self is another. As a result of my divorce, coming to grips and forgiving my husband for our failed marriage and myself for my dogged stubbornness, and facing what was next in God's plan for my life emotionally was so much more difficult. Learning to let the past go to voicemail when it called was frickin' HARD!

However, my good sense lurked, reminding me that mudslinging would not bother the people I begrudged most, namely the campaign treasurer, the puppets in his cult, and the Philadelphia Board of Ethics (BOE). My dirty hands would be mine alone, and if I missed the mark, I would only add fuel to the smoldering embers. My energy had to be focused on the arduous work required to right the wrecked ship. I could not skip a beat to meet the daily academic and emotional needs coupled with the social and athletic schedule of our daughter. I focused and was determined not to have her life grossly impacted by my negative career fumble.

Amid this firestorm and clearly with inside intelligence about the BOE, POTUS requested an offsite meeting at a restaurant in his Councilmanic District. He stated that my situation was far bigger than I could ever imagine and because the BOE was set on not just an ethics charge but a criminal charge, he urged me to quickly find and lock down a criminal attorney to represent me because he knew I would need one. I was surprised but grateful for the advice. While that meeting was a blessing, it opened my eyes wide shut. A new set of meetings commenced immediately after another dear friend, A. Michael Pratt, Esq., referred a brilliant attorney who handled white-collar offenses strictly. My criminal lawyer, Lisa Mathewson, Esq., became another needed Godsend. As a result of her brilliant lawyering, and her keen understanding of the federal legal process, I never had to appear at Sixth and Market Street, a.k.a. The Federal Building. Praise God! Meetings with my criminal lawyer in her Center City offices were added to the weekly meetings already in play with both my divorce lawyer and campaign lawyer.

The orchestration of my time required continued assessment of what mattered. What was urgent? What was urgent and important? What was important but not urgent? This weekly reassessment was necessary as I continued to meet the daily demands of motherhood coupled with meeting the assignments given to me by the Family General, my sister Pandora. Now coordinating my mom's daily caregiving needs, services, and the coverage schedule for my siblings, Pandora showed me grace.

The outcome of my assessment was to resign from several boards of directors of agencies whose missions I deeply cared about. My remaining and now precious limited time had to be carved out and devoted to rectifying all financial and personnel matters related to the campaign crisis. With my reputation as the new target on social media the alternative, if not addressed sufficiently, would cost me my reelection twenty-four months later. When you are in a crisis, self-inflicted or external, and experiencing tough times, the words of

Albert Einstein are apropos. *"Life is like riding a bicycle. To keep your balance, you must keep moving."* Never skipping a beat each morning, I kept moving.

I discovered during the next turbulent twenty-four months that life's challenges are not supposed to paralyze. Indeed, life's hurdles are not intended to kill you but to strengthen you. They give you a glimpse of opposites so you can see the full picture of life. They are designed to, and do help, in rediscovering who we are, affirm what we are made of, and clarify for you what matters, and what matters more.

My story, laced with stumbles, is not unique. There are many examples of high achievers who fumbled and fell to the wolves savoring their inability to rise above the stumble and circumstances. They had to keep it moving. John Maxwell discusses in his book, *Roadmap for Success*, how African American civil rights leader Booker T. Washington, born into slavery, was denied access to the resources available to white society. He never let a lack of opportunity prevent him from pursuing his potential. Founder of the Tuskegee Institute and the National Black Business League, Washington said, *"I have learned that success is to be measured not so much by the position that one has reached in life as by the obstacles which one has overcome while trying to succeed."* In his book, Maxwell goes on to discuss the extraordinary story of Helen Keller, who lost her sight and hearing at sixteen months old. She triumphed over her severe disabilities graduating cum laude from the all women's college Radcliffe, as the first deaf and blind woman to earn a Bachelor of Arts College degree. She later became an author, noted lecturer, and champion for people who are blind.

People with deep self-confidence and the ability to self-talk are nonnegotiable about their dreams or vision and soldier on. Author J.K. Rowling, living on social security, was unemployed and divorced. Like me, she was raising a daughter alone when she wrote her first Harry Potter novel. *Harry Potter and the* Sorcerer's *Stone* was rejected by twelve publishing houses, but she was undaunted. Her perseverance and belief in her ability led to unbelievable success! Likewise,

Michael Jordan, one of the greatest basketball players of all time, was cut from his high school basketball team for a "lack of skill." And the incomparable Oprah, now an entrepreneurial and media mogul, the "Queen of media in all genres" had a false start in her career. She was fired from her early job as a reporter because those in power, who did not look like her, believed she was "unfit for TV." Look at her now! These stories salved my worry and knowing that for those who wished me ill, "*Karma is a patient gangster*," was reassuring.

I, who had joined a long list of the popular, both known and unknown individuals who fought back from adversity, was ready. My mistakes in judgment would become the seedlings I sowed to produce the momentum needed to move toward restoring my place and my reputation in the City Council.

After many months, my mom had the best anecdote and the most memorable punchline. The crisis was beginning to calm down in the local media and on news radio. I cherished the moments when I picked up my daughter from the Overbrook suburban train station as was my custom during her high school years. She was always seated in the popular DeBreaux's Soul Food restaurant. This African American female restaurant owner made sure my daughter was safe and fed after she arrived and started her homework at a table in the restaurant. I am eternally grateful to Frances DeBreaux and her soul food.

One day, heading home, I stopped in at my mom's mother-in-law's suite, to make my customary check, to look in to see how she was doin'. While it was late as usual, my mom was always happy to see Brielle come through her back door at the end of her school day. As we walked through her place, she remarked, "Blondell, how are you doing? I am sooooo glad I do not hear your name on KYW anymore." My mom was a news geek and a devoted daily listener to this all-news twenty-four hours, seven days a week, news radio. With the benefit of hindsight, I now believe that's when I realized that the tide of controversy was beginning to turn. All I had to do now was continue to do the hard work, keep my shoulder to the wheel, and execute the restorative, corrective actions my team and I had outlined. I needed to remain focused on adjusting the sail! As I prepared for a new campaign, amid this burst of daily negative controversy, everyone clearly understood that meeting the needs of my daughter and my mom remained my principal priorities. Period. No missteps. Despite the in-your-face career crisis, City Council business was priority number three.

So much could have been avoided had I been more vigilant. One thing for certain and two for sure, if the campaign treasurer had simply followed the rules and "disclosed", I repeat, DISCLOSED, the initial loan and a laundry list of transactions on the 2010 and 2011 Statements of Financial Interests, this memoir would not include this chapter. A lack of disclosure is a violation. It is unethical. Period. All I had to do, all he had to do, was to make sure all information and all transactions during my campaigning were disclosed. I failed in my fiduciary duties and oversight. My civil monetary penalties and fines added up to $48,834, unprecedented for any former elected official who had ever failed in their fiduciary duties. I was determined to pay it back on time. I, an African American female, elected official, became a sterling example of their interpretation of the law by the sometimes self-righteous members of the Board of Ethics whom I had to meet with on a regular basis.

The corrective action called for me to recruit new campaign personnel, starting with a Certified Public Accountant, not a makeshift bookkeeper acting as a treasurer. Seeking and finding a new CPA took a couple of trial runs made harder by the new pretenders who appeared. Smelling blood, their offering to help was made with forked tongues and flawed characters. I praised God when he blessed me with two new angels. Out of the blue, Minister Arvelle C. Jones, CPA, called me to offer his accountant services pro bono. His selflessness with his time, expertise, and his talent during this period of rehabilitation was priceless. He held my hand during the painstaking transition and cleaned up my books. His contribution was followed by the technical campaign fundraising expertise of Kristen Stoner and her team and the continued selfless legal expertise of Kevin Greenberg, Esq., who was always a phone call away. Together on a weekly basis in the office space of John Milligan, they guided me through resetting and restructuring the fundraising apparatus for my 2015 reelection campaign, successfully. Collectively, we secured a new bank account at a new bank, a new PO Box, and adopted new rigid campaign finance policies, bank and accounting procedures.

While handling the daily Council business, I worked tirelessly to meet the campaign settlement terms. For two consecutive years, every single Tuesday, like clockwork on autopilot, I met with Kristen, my new campaign finance consultant who coached me as I toiled in the arduous, unforgiving, unattractive labor-intensive duty of any candidate; campaign fundraising. You cannot fake the hard work of making those campaign calls, one after the other for hours, multiple days every week, making a case and appealing to prospective supporters and proven contributors. There is no substitute for justifying your ask for the mother's milk of campaigns, money, money, and more money.

My self-discipline required me to make a gazillion phone calls to former and new contributors during and after the crisis. President Clarke was a cheerleader pulling for me as well. I am forever grateful to Clarke, Senator Vincent Hughes, Alan Kessler, Esq., along with my always reliable angel, my Girls' High classmate Terri Graboyes, working from the wings, who led the effort and relaunched me by hosting my first fundraiser, coming out of the crisis at Larry Cohen's restaurant, Cuba Libre. This valiant effort kickstarted and refueled my campaign and provided the seedings of my campaign war chest for the 2015 reelection campaign cycle. The compassion of those who attended this first fundraising event, post the campaign career debacle with the new infrastructure, at the request of these four undaunted devoted hosts enabled me to kickstart the settlement payment requirements and meet the deadlines for the next 24 month period.

I paid in full the $48,834 on time covering all campaign fines that had been levied. I emerged as the number one fundraiser of candidates when campaign reports were filed in December 2014. To the members of the Philadelphia Board of Ethics I remind you. Yes!! *"Broken crayons still color."* —Unknown.

Pandora caught hell and ate crow from many she called to ask to support the always successful and fun event, the Olde School Dance Party. Like me, she persisted, silenced the naysayers, and told them to "write a check anyway." Under her unwavering stewardship, Pandora, along with her trusted co-pilot, Matt McDonald, all my sisters, Yvonne, Angelina, Alesia even my brother Angelo sent a contribution, and devoted Old School Dance Party Steering Committee members ramped up. Collectively, they help me raise the needed dollars for my E-Day operations, close to $30,000, thereby ultimately providing the financial foundation for a superlative victorious campaign for my 2015 reelection.

During a personal and professional crisis, you will stumble upon those who have also suffered injustice, transgression, or screw-ups in their career and survived. These cheerleaders show up and bring to the table an added layer of empathy and compassion that, quite frankly, is hard to describe and impossible to put into words. Such was the case of Tom Massaro, a brilliant policy wonk and former government official who cared about the success of selected Council members. Tommy was devoted to arming Council members with policy ideas to help them do good, meaningful, and impactful work. He cared about me, stayed present, and coached me during my fall, devoted and determined to help me reboot and repair my career. His email was one I read carefully and kept after I left City Council. His message provided instruction, objective insight, and encouragement laced in empathy.

On February 20, 2013, at 10:47 a.m., after providing the context referencing two other Council colleagues, who had faltered he said:

Unlike them, pre-freshmen, and freshmen, you have a twelve-year record on City Council being an ethical and honest person so you can make a case that your serious misjudgment was an exception. Unlike them though, your error included direct personal financial benefit via inappropriate use of campaign funds, even if it was temporary. If you are and continue to be 101% honest and fully cooperative with the Ethics Board and pay your stiff, heavy penalty, and RESUME an effort to render honest, attentive, and effective public service, your colleagues, and the public, over time, might tend to see your serious error in a wider vision that also includes all the good that you have done over thirteen years, not one mega-mistake.

You were a bad leadership example to make the mistake, you must now STAY on the path to be 101% forthright and honest and genuinely remorseful in taking responsibility for it . . . with renewed determination to get back on the right and never derail again. After having made a serious mistake, you can be a good example of leadership in how to stand up, take responsibility, accept heavy consequences, and cooperate 100% with investigators at the Ethics Board and everyone with jurisdiction. THAT'S THE PATH YOU MUST TAKE.

I'm sure the past months seem like an eternal hell that never ends. With 100% cooperation and honesty with investigators, the public and the media can tend to see that your serious mistake was an exception to your record, not reflective or characteristic of it.

KEEP DOING THE RIGHT THING! Don't even think about a future campaign, focus on dealing with the present need to cooperate 100% with the Ethics Board and focus on honest, energetic, and effective service on the City Council.

I absorbed Tommy's sage and compassionate advice and heeded it. Devoted campaign staff, big and small campaign contributors, including longtime friends from my days at Girls High School, classmates from Penn State, Sorority sisters, volunteers, family, and friends who knew my heart, helped me raise enough campaign funds to mount a vigorous, competitive, and well-financed campaign for my reelection in 2015.

For three years leading into 2015, I attended any and every event whether I was invited or not. Wherever two people were gathered, I was present. From 7:30 a.m. after school drop-off to late nights, the daily footpath was to pick up my daughter, arrive home, assist my mom and Brielle with dinner, make sure Brielle was okay with her homework assignments, and then depart for the evening schedule of multiple campaign stops across the city. My schedule ran to midnight most nights, eight days a week.

Often, I was questioned on the campaign trail about my campaign crisis. Expecting those unpleasant questions never made me comfortable. Always with a straight back and eyeball-to-eyeball contact, I reminded voters of my *mea culpa* and acknowledged my poor judgment while also trapped in an embarrassing personal crisis. Reminding voters of my proven and strong track record of public service, which was evident in our staff programming, was essential and a game changer. These programs included our Annual Warmth in Winter Children's Initiative, our Annual Moxie Women History Month Celebration, Small Business Roundtables, Step Into College High School Forums, and our Annual Fall Senior Citizens tours featuring government and nongovernmental agencies. The annual execution of these programs made a difference to the Philadelphia citizens whom we touched and helped to boost my recovery. People indeed remembered our legislative record and the breath of our constituent services. I remain convinced that our service blended with our nontraditional programming made a difference and fueled us into the victory column on Election Day May 18, 2015. Informing voters that the campaign crisis was one frame in the full video of my

City Council career and appealing to voters to examine closely my legislative record of those four previous terms, sixteen years of service, often softened the apparent, invisible tension or attack.

My campaign manager, Tracy Hardy, had skillfully executed a competitive campaign like that of a surgeon with a laser against formidable odds. Facing most notably, the heavy cloud after the storm of my campaign crisis, other well-financed candidates, and I, with no endorsement from the city's leading press outlet, were a triple negative threat. It did not matter that I prepared and studied for the newspaper endorsement meeting like it was my dissertation. Tom Massaro, one of Philadelphia's most respected housing leaders, policy-wonkish professor, and truth-teller, met with me weekly, grilling me for months leading up to the news outlet endorsement meetings. Tommy who had sent me that most encouraging email was especially considerate of the African American members. He as a white guy, had seen the underbelly of racism and believing *The Inquirer* had been unfair in their vile and loathsome coverage and attempts to brutalize my reputation, offered his support and counsel. This media outlet had plenty of ink to scar me for sure. As expected, the white suburban men who sat at the conference table of *The Inquirer* believed they could jeopardize my reelection chances to the Philadelphia City Council and therefore were emboldened. Typical!

As a political candidate of any office, an *Inquirer* endorsement is highly sought after, and it matters. In 2015, an *Inquirer* endorsement typically equaled about ten thousand votes from the liberal and progressive electorate sections of the city. Tracy's calculated formula required us to make up for those votes from other neighborhood pockets in the city. His accurate and laser beam assessment helped me to secure 62,922 votes, placing me number three of the sixteen primary candidates. How about that! I captured enough votes to be one of the top five vote-getters. As the May 19th Primary election was ending, during the evening family, Village Moms, staff, my campaign manager, his intelligence squad, campaign volunteers, Fattah

CORE members, and a host of friends and believers gathered. We watched the returns with great anticipation and fear mixed with hopefulness. At 8 p.m. that evening, eyes glued to the TV monitor, we all watched the election returns hour after hour. Like a phoenix around 10:00 p.m., I rose and moved from fourth place. Slowly the vote totals pushed me to third place among sixteen other Democratic candidates winning one of the five available at-large city council seats thereby, winning a fifth four-year term successfully! At the end of the day, Philadelphia voters, Philadelphia residents, had indeed examined and reexamined my legislative record, the quality of our services, and my visibility in places and spaces that mattered to my constituents for over sixteen years. Thankfully, these factors, coupled with my time in city hall touching voters regularly, and consistently in neighborhoods across the 142.6 square miles of the entire city through our Annual Constituent Service programming, made the difference. An enormous difference. I was so thankful!

Renaissance woman and writer, Maya Angelou, reminds me in the face of unfairness, when you are devalued and possibly dismissed, you must never, never give up. Here is why. We may encounter many defeats, but we must not be defeated. It may even be necessary to encounter defeat so that we can know who we are. So that we can see, oh, that happened, and I rose. I did get knocked down flat in front of the whole world, and I rose, right where I had been knocked down. Career falls and derailments help you get to know yourself. You say, hmm. I can get up. I have enough of life and the gumption required to face the derailment. I have so much courage in me that I have the effrontery, the incredible gall to stand up again and again.

I survived under extreme pressures from all sides that lasted for the thirty-six months leading into my 2015 primary election. For sure, I emerged from my career-altering experience stronger spiritually, better, wiser, and far more circumspect in my business dealings. My new approach and mantra when working with others in small, seemingly insignificant, or big business matters with no exceptions, has become, "trust but verify." The breaking of anyone's trust is almost irreparable. Like a puzzle of 1000 pieces with the fire, image of one of my favorite dancers, Josephine Baker, that took months and months to piece together, it gets kicked over and broken into the one thousand pieces again. Ticked off, you must decide if you want to piece together that picture once again as you know the process and sequence of the placement of the pieces will never ever be the same.

One of my biggest surprises while campaigning as I shared earlier was learning of my predatory colleagues who would vigilantly observe my hardworking and talented staff. Like wolves, they would wait for the prime opportunity to strike and prey on them. When I shared this information with the City Council president after my victorious primary win, he replied with one of his favorite words, "stunning."

My temporary career fall off the tightrope magnified my awareness of our imperfections. Yet on the flip side, it helped me rediscover a new depth of resilience and gumption within me as well. In the end, good came out of the experience. The silver lining, the people, the angels who stood by me while I was emotionally, bruised and battered; the miracle of good people with kind hearts and expertise like Terry Redmond, who helped me save my home and my awareness of the "friends" who took invisible steps backwards, distancing themselves from my problem.

Resilience is what a moxie woman learns from an experience laced with stones. The cynics should never count out a faith-filled woman until she sings. Never! I discovered that the real gift of heartache and heartbreak is who you become by facing your disappointments. With the loss of my marriage and my reputation, my faith was tested daily. For three years, I struggled to keep the threads of my career together. Every morning, I had to tilt my hand mirror, prepare to beat my face, look the lion in the mouth, and vow today I will not be eaten. Not by the hungry press or my adversaries crossing their fingers for my career demise. Moxie women never give up and never give in. We might need a good cry, and yearn for a day in bed which never comes but we understand that the sun does rise every morning. Ultimately, I had to recognize that I, too, am a flawed and fallible human being. No one is exempt from faux pas, stumbles, or failure. My renewed faith, the gumption I learned from my mom, and my relentless desire to reshape my brand drove me to push through the dark tunnel I found myself in at the end of my career. If it were to be, it was up to me to determine how this one frame of the video of my city council career would end. The weight of my personal crisis stole my joy momentarily. While fighting my way out of the ring, I learned *"It's not the load that breaks you down. It's the way you carry it."* —Lena Horne.

Abolitionist and founder of the Republican Party, Horace Greeley, declared that *"Fame is a vapor, popularity an accident, and money takes wings. The only thing that endures is character."* I will stretch that philosophy further. The one thing revealed during all this traumatic and dramatic experience was what I am made of. How I conducted myself in the face of the turmoil. I, at the core, was a person who cared deeply about my career, my duties as an elected official and my constituents. That fidelity had not changed. A lapse in judgment tested me and revealed that while my character was intact, emotionally I was crushed. In the end, during those unforgettable, soul-wrenching, and emotionally piercing memories of that winter season, overcoming adversity doesn't just build character, it reveals that *"In the midst of winter, I found in me an invincible summer."* —Camus

Yes, ultimately, I had won my 2015 reelection despite the naysayers, the duplicitous press, the doubters, and those not happy for me disguised as friends. Karma sorted out the latter. I crossed the finish line because the people I cared about had worked diligently on my behalf and the voters had spoken, convincingly. I felt a sense of gratitude, pride, and redemption in their forgiveness, but things would never again be the same.

Carpe Diem

Philadanco Dolls

PhilaDanco Dancers (L to R): Carethia Landers, Ruby Peterson-Begonia, Karin Still Pendergrass, Cassandra Joyner, BRB, Jamilla Toombs at Club Harlem, Atlantic City, NJ, 1979

Greg Naylor, Senior Campaign Strategist with BRB, 2003

Marian Anderson Awards Gala (L to R): Lana Felton Ghee, Philly's own Patti Labelle, and BRB, 2003

BRB with City Democratic Party Chairman Bob Brady, 1999

Blondell Reynolds-Brown

Tribune Cover Story
TThe Joy of Motherhood, 2008
Prominent Local Women on the
Art of Balancing Family and Career

Walking A Tightrope Backward In High Heels

Brielle at her first birthday party with BRB
and her father, Howard A. Brown, 1997

Brielle, 5, with BRB
Howard's Annual Fish Fry Campaign Fundraiser
Philadelphia, 2001

WHAT Radio Personality Ms. Mary Mason with BRB, Reelection Announcement, 2003

BRB with PA Congressman Chaka Fattah, General Election Night, 2003

BRB with City of Philadelphia Mayor John F. Street, 2003

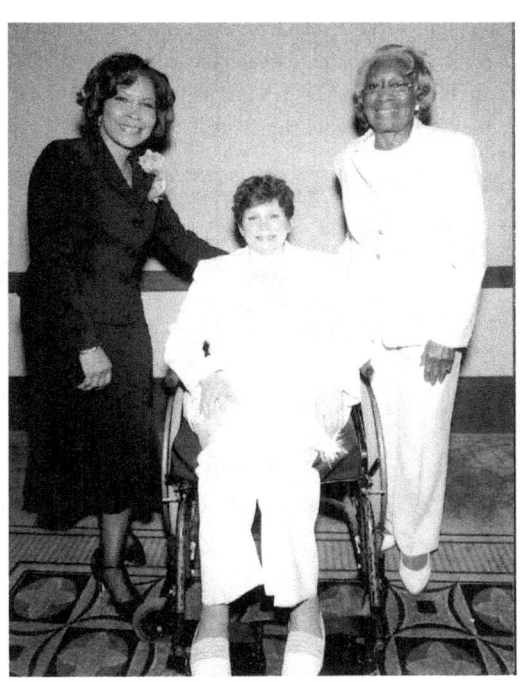

BRB, PA State Senator Tina Tartaglione with BRB's mother, Sadie Reynolds
Women Making a Difference Luncheon, 2005

(Top) Anna C. Verna, President of Philadelphia City Council
(Middle L to R) Melonease Shaw, Marcella Roane, Phoebe Coles
(At mic) Delilah Winder, Chef, Restaurateur & Author, and BRB
Celebrating Philly Businesswomen at City Council Chambers, 2003

Edwina Baker, Founder, Activist
2000 African Women with BRB, 2004

Penn State Classmates and Olde School Dance Party Committee Members
(L to R) BRB, Kenny Lesesne, Linda Burke, Linda McBride-Brock, 2007

Matthew McDonald &
Pandora Woods
Co-Captains of OSDP

BRB with
President Barack Obama
The White House, 2012

PA Governor Edward G. Rendell with BRB, 2007

(L to R): The Women of City Council
Maria Quiñones Sánchez, Cindy Bass, Marion Tasco,
BRB, Jannie Blackwell, 2012

Philadelphia Tribune: BRB acknowledging campaign finance controversy, issuing an apology to the public, 2013

BRB's Campaign Finance Committee Members
(L to R) Stephanie Kosta, Esq., Alan Kessler, Esq., with
Philadelphia City Councilwoman Maria Quiñones Sánchez, 2014

Top (L to R): Linda B. Watson and Audrey Johnson-Thornton
Bottom (L to R) BRB's Mom, Sadie Reynolds, and Ann Garrett
Belmont Mansion, Women's Heritage Society, Philadelphia Fairmount Park, 2014

BRB with her Mom, Sadie Reynolds, and her daughter, Brielle, Christmas 2016

BRB with her sisters in Holiday Red
(L to R) BRB, Alesia, Yvonne, Pandora, Angelina, December 2017

Women of City Council:
(L to R) Cherelle L. Parker, Maria Quiñones Sánchez,
TV Anchor Jim Garner, Cindy Bass, BRB, and Jannie Blackwell, 2019

Brielle and BRB, Primary Election for
Candidate Katherine Gilmore Richardson, 2019

BRB at Councilwoman Katherine Gilmore Richardson's Inauguration Ceremony, January 2020

Senator Cory Booker with BRB

Women of Delta Sigma Theta Sorority, Inc. (left to right),
Blondell Reynolds-Brown Marcia Penn
Carol Harvey, Lynn Fields, Carolyn Dawkins Valerie Christmas

Brielle Autumn Brown, Esquire, Law School Graduate, 2022

Brielle with BRB, Christmas 2023

Sheryl Lee Ralph, Actor, Author, Soror with State Senator Vincent Hughes and BRB at Delta Sigma Theta Sorority, Inc. Phila. Alumnae Chapter, May Week 2023

CHAPTER THIRTEEN

THE LION, THE GAZELLE, AND THE CATERPILLAR

"Here's to strong women. May we know them? May we be them? May we raise them?" —Amy Rees Anderson

There is an African proverb that speaks to and encourages people to press forward in all ways. The story of the lion and the gazelle are the metaphors. I went into politics as a lion, was taught and learned how to be a gazelle, became a caterpillar, and reborn as a butterfly. That feels like a full circle.

When I opted to not run again after five consecutive successful elections and chose to exit my career as an elected official I took stock of a few factors to help me see the road ahead clearly. The bumps and boulders had been diminished, crushed. Fundamentally, I assessed my immediate family circumstances. My mom had passed, my divorce was final, and Brielle had completed her Syracuse University undergraduate college experience. My future career goals, my financial status, my health, my future dreams, and aspirations yet unrealized, had to be recalibrated for the temperature of my decision viability. During my agonizing soul-searching process, I intentionally chose not to share any of my findings. My conversations, reflections, and limited discussions around this highly sensitive and now confidential topic were shared strictly with my daughter, my sisters, and my brother, Angelo. PERIOD! I had guarded my heart so well, I gave myself an A for self-discipline. Much to the chagrin and unhappiness of many, (namely the Islanders and POTUS) I chose not to share the trepidation, the conflict, and the months of anguish mired in my internal conflict. The gut check and self-assessment I needed and required regarding the next steps, the next chapter, and the width of "my" career decision was underway.

Although the dark shadowy contemplative period was exceedingly difficult, and I was tempted numerous times to reveal to a few in my most intimate political and personal circles, I resisted. I know now that President Clarke and a few select others were deeply disappointed with my silent decision-making process. Successfully, I never yielded to temptation. Under normal circumstances dealing with legislative matters, President Clarke, our very persuasive and compassionate leader would have been my go-to person. But not about this. I knew in my spirit that disclosing my anguish about this career decision would not be in my best interest. I needed to avoid being placed in a defensive position. My discipline was tested time and time again but, in the end, I was able to copy a page from President Clarke's book and successfully mimic his style of protecting sensitive consequential information. I exercised good judgment, held my indecision close to my breast, and emotionally limped until it was time for me to disclose. Consequently, I never had to deal with the domino effect of hot off-the-press information, the whispers down the lane, and the talking walls in city hall. My self-discipline won the day as I faced my choices for the fourth chapter of my career.

Preparing to tackle the realities of rebuilding for another political citywide campaign was daunting. Launching a new campaign against the backdrop of the New World order called social media and its emerging dominance in the campaign apparatus was intimidating. Hidden in the deep recesses of my heart was also the nagging aspiration to pursue my thirty-year-old unfulfilled dream of becoming a children's book author while still in good health. I had witnessed up close and personal one too many Council members who left City Council for the hospital and never made it back home in good health. The idea of staying in City Council and meeting its unyielding demands for another four years, eight days a week, 32 hours a day would never allow me the time, the bandwidth, or headspace, to move my spirit and my career in a different direction.

After my divorce and my mother's passing, I was still filled with grief from the loss of my mother and had not fully recovered from the remains of a painful public divorce. While I could quite effectively compartmentalize the elements of my life quite seamlessly, I was haunted by a passage I read, by American journalist Mary Kay Blakely, *"divorce is the psychological equivalent of a triple coronary bypass. After such a monumental assault on the heart, it takes years to amend."* No doubt. This was me. I was a living testimony of this edit.

Many in city hall were interested in my next move. While I affirmed I intended to run for reelection a sixth time, deep in my spirit and alone with my thoughts, I was filled with ambivalence and quiet sadness. I don't regret not answering questions about my candidacy. My only regret was to one person, President Darrell Clarke, for not being completely honest and transparent about my indecision and ambivalence. The last six months of self-reflection and introspection leading up to my ultimate announcement to step down reminded me of what I learned early in my career. Life presents us with choices. Life always offers up options. The challenge then becomes what we will do with the choices we have before us. To paraphrase Buckminster Fuller, when the aha moment strikes your spirit to choose to do what you need to do to live differently, that is the moment you believe and realize there can be a different kind of life. Once I made my decision, without question, I felt relieved and liberated. I began to move differently. My decision not to run but instead to step out and pursue other dreams brought much astonishment and disbelief to everyone except my chief of staff, Katherine Gilmore Richardson.

Once my decision was made, I was deliberate and intentional about leaving a pathway for the next younger African American woman who was prepared and in my humble opinion, ready to receive the baton. There are many young women in our midst willing, yearning and ready to be groomed and nurtured to accept the symbolic baton and run with it. To these young women, I would say run with the wind at your back. When it is time for us to pass the baton, and offer sage advice and counsel to these diamonds in the rough, let's be generous and do so. Remind these young diamonds that as they build their careers, *"be good to people. You will be remembered more for your kindness than any level of success you could possibly attain."* —Mandy Hale.

In one of the letters I wrote during my last year on the City Council, I stated that. "I believe that for all of us who have done the work to bring dreams to fruition, our work is not finished once those dreams are attained. I submit that we must show a willingness to develop and cultivate the potential greatness in the next generation of women leadership and commit ourselves to leaving a legacy. There are diamonds all around us." Nurturing and pushing young women forward who show stellar performances while building their budding careers will motivate them even further to raise their bar and run like the gazelle. I was confident then, and my assessment was reaffirmed, when former Chief of Staff Katherine Gilmore Richardson, was my choice to extend the baton to run with the wind.

At major milestones in my career, there was one recurring, inspirational poem that I received repeatedly from unrelated well-wishers written in 1895 by novelist and poet, Rudyard Kipling. This poem is titled, "If". It was first given to me by my mom in a greeting card after I graduated from Penn State. It is one of those universal timeless messages and teachings that illustrates the power of self-confidence, and the courage required to build a personally satisfying life and career. An excerpt is worth sharing with those you pass your baton.

> "If you can keep your head when all about you
> Are losing theirs and blaming it on you,
> If you can trust yourself when all men doubt you,
> But make allowance for their doubting too,
> If you can dream and not make dreams your master,
> If you can think and not make thoughts your aim:
> If you can meet with triumph and disaster
> And treat those two impostors just the same."

As you build your career and brand in pursuit of seemingly unattainable goals attach these mantras to your dreams. Stay focused. Amid the storm adjust your sail and never quit! Quitting is never an option.

Carpe Diem

CHAPTER FOURTEEN

THE EXIT STRATEGY

"Trust the next chapter, because you are the author."—Unknown.

Twenty years before, I arrived at City Council walking in four or five-inch-high heels, mostly pumps, wearing them all day comfortably and with complete ease. When I left twenty years later, I was carrying an extra shoe bag with flats which had become my new norm over the years. I now only pulled out my 3 inch heels for meetings and public speaking engagements.

Though I had subconsciously banked the idea of retirement after one of my city hall corridor talks with the council president, this simple sign of the passage of time reflected in now wearing lower-inched high heels was one of the many subtle signals that it was time for me to reckon with a new reality. It was time to turn the page. I had done the work I had set out to do and in my spirit, I felt it was time. I no longer wanted the increasing vitriol of the electoral process, the nine days a week, and the never-ending politics to smother, steal, or suffocate my soul. And I most certainly did not want to leave City Council with my last stop being the hospital. I was prepared and ready to pass the symbolic baton to a successor.

Time was approaching for me to face the declaration, "Someday Isle." I was also moved and stirred by the remark from the very first campaign manager I ever volunteered for. He would go on to become my, future colleague and Islander, Councilman Curtis Jones. "Blondell, you have a wonderful story about your career. You just need to read it." I decided to no longer wait or postpone long-held aspirations, hopes, and long-held dreams. The homegoing service of my mom and the graduation of my daughter from undergraduate school gave me the license to think about my deferred dreams and, more importantly, to act and tackle those things on my to-do and bucket list. I reckoned with the reality that staying in the City Council would require me to honor my council duties but also would further defer my dreams. I could not remain in the City Council handling and meeting the demanding duties of Council responsibilities half-heartedly with honor. Half-stepping is not in my DNA.

When in a position of leadership and responsibility, a part-time ghost existence will ultimately negatively impact the effectiveness of your efforts and your leadership. There is no room for dressing in an empty suit. My departure and my personal decision not to seek a sixth term was the only option available that aligned with my dreams with my longing to do something more and bigger outside the halls of government. Borrowing from the ultimate dream maker, Walt Disney, "*After we think it, believe it, and dream it, we then have to 'dare.'*" Amen!

Arriving at my career decision was one major step. Once I had decided, my fear of whispers in the halls paralyzed me. The invisible Philly political network had forced me to exercise strict discipline from discussing my ambivalence and the deep anguish that I carried for many of the following months. I hated this emotional space that at times suffocated me.

After my final seventy-two hours of reflection which included the initial writing of my announcement remarks, I said a prayer before leaving from ABC Summer Wind, Bethany Beach, Delaware.

I loaded up my car, turned on my preferred playlist and started my return trip to Philadelphia. Executing a strategic plan to delicately announce to my public without offending a lengthy list of supporters was the next hurdle. City hall has invisible walls that talk. My next hurdle was to meet personally with a short list of supporters who needed to hear my decision directly from my mouth to their ears before I officially informed my staff. Accomplishing all of this in secrecy given the world of nosy social media was going to be a monumental and, for me, an intimidating undertaking.

Before all that, I made my first call on that Sunday to my former boss and the new leader of CORE, State Senator Vincent Hughes. I was so thankful that he was in town, available, and willing to meet with me on a Sunday at 3:00 p.m. at his office. Taking a deep breath, I paused during that awkward phone call trying not to stumble over my words. I told him that I had made a major career decision, and he would be the first to know.

In his office surrounded by political mementos from his decades of public service work, including photos of Nelson Mandela, Congressman Bill Gray, Jesse Jackson, and other notables, I was caught in a moment of nostalgia. We gathered at his huge conference table, and I asked for his complete confidence in the conversation because of the sensitive, fragile nature of my topic. He committed to listening and not violating my request for confidentiality. With both consternation and utter relief, I shared with my trusted friend and former boss that for the last six months in City Council, emotionally I had been in hibernation and couldn't muster the drive I once had for my work. I spent the next two hours sharing how my mom's absence and Brielle's graduation had moved me to a state of prolonged and deep reflection which had put me on pause. I explained that still grappling with these losses, my grief was disguised, and, emotionally, I was still on the mend. Grief made getting up each morning hard and continuing the fake bravado was impeding and compromising my standards and my work. I told him that emotionally, I had been limping for months and professionally, it was time for me to do something different for my spirit and my psyche. It was time for me to get reacquainted with the other parts of Blondell.

It was all true. The wind was out of my sail, and I was no longer living authentically. Being fake sapped my energy. The need for a change punctuated my sadness, and I was in a bad mindset. When alone, it was worse. Physically, I still had the stamina, and, intellectually, I still had the passion for in-your-face debate on legislative policies, however, I no longer felt the passion for politics and the need to tackle public policy as an elected official. I could choose and be an advocate on issues I cared about from another stage or arena.

A pensive man by nature, the senator listened, never interrupting my half-memorized monologue. He leaned back, then turned around in his swivel chair, looked at me with his peering brown eyes, and with disbelief asked me, "Are you sure?" We talked further reflecting on the memories of Fattah CORE of days gone by. An hour later he posed a second series of questions, spun around in his chair again, stopped, looked up at the ceiling, then leaned forward on his conference table and asked a second time, "Blondell, are you sure?" Again, we drifted into reflections on the history of our independent political organization, how far we had come over the thirty-five years of Fattah's CORE growth, and our political success collectively and individually within the Philly Democratic political party organizational structure. I shared with the Senator that I was forced to acknowledge my loss of purpose after members of my Kitchen Cabinet challenged me to address my lingering grief during my recent quarterly meeting. The good news, following that candid session with the devoted members of my Kitchen Cabinet, I decided finally to pursue grief counseling. It was the best thing I could have done. Still in disbelief, he leaned in, looked at me with his piercing eyes, and he asked for the third time more slowly, "Blondell, ARE YOU SURE SURE?" With no hesitation and no change in my answer, I stated more affirmatively and for the last time, I answered,

"YES! I AM SURE." We switched gears and began to chart how I should execute the public relations rollout of what would be my surprise announcement to the world.

He knew, we knew, the one fact all candidates must face when entering an election cycle, be it as a first-time or veteran, you, they must be in fighter shape mentally, physically, and emotionally. The burning fire in the belly to be a change agent must be like running against the wind in a marathon vigorously. These are and will remain essential key ingredients to winning a successful campaign.

My very next meeting that same Sunday evening was with my chief of staff, Katherine Gilmore Richardson. I had called her while on the highway and asked her to come to my home as I needed to share with her eyeball-to-eyeball and not on the phone a major career decision I had made. I repeated to Katherine all that I had shared with Senator Hughes. She, too, listened carefully and never interrupted my spill. After my delivery and sharing what was on my heart, she did not attempt to dissuade me or influence me in either direction. She gave a response I never expected: "Councilwoman, good for you! You have given so much with great sacrifice. I am so happy for you." I felt and breathed a sigh of relief.

We both agreed that the next step was to figure out how to handle the pending big announcement with care and immediacy. We charted the course of action and mutually agreed that our PR guru, Jason Lewis, had to be a part of our brain dump and groupthink strategic planning process. Without contradiction, we agreed. We also knew my history with *The Philadelphia Tribune*. We revisited how the *Philly Tribune* was the only public newspaper that gave me the chance to tell my *mea culpa* story without the skewed, racially laced lens, double standards, or hidden agenda typical of its competitors. The *Philadelphia Tribune's* interest in just the facts indebted me to Bob Bogle, who allowed me to sit at their headquarters' conference table as his team of journalists peppered me with probing tough in-your-face questions. During my career debacle, Jason acknowledged that the Tribune story void of slander, opinion, judgment, and just the facts opened the door toward the long recovery of my reputation.

Our call to Mr. Bogle was both encouraging and amusing. We informed him about my decision and asked for confidentiality and an "exclusive." An exclusive in journalism occurs when the news outlet agrees to report your story and you, the subject of the story, will not offer the exclusive to any other media outlet. With my naivety, I then attempted to "tell" Mr. Bogle when to print the story. His dignified, but in-your-face, stern response was, "You can have an exclusive, but you can't tell me when to print the exclusive." His professional protocol was spot on. The best time to run the story was indeed the day of my formal announcement, Friday, January 19, 2019, and not the Sunday after. Mr. Bogle remains highly respected and sometimes feared across the professional spectrum. He is a pro in the media industry. No doubt.

The kickstart of my week was to identify the venue for the announcement. We settled on the mayor's reception room which, luckily, was available. However, one prevailing challenge remained. Keeping our plan quiet, as the mayor's office had seasoned leakers and staffers with loose lips. To ensure that our carefully crafted plan was not ruined by premature, uninformed alerts in the halls of city hall, I opted to personally complete the room reservation form, citing Senator Vincent Hughes as the user and submitted the form to the mayor's office. As expected, calls were made to my chief of staff asking about Senator Vincent Hughes and what he was doing. If we wanted anyone to know, we would have indicated the purpose on the form. We successfully blocked those leaky well-known city hall mouthpieces.

The week was marked with fever-pitch nervous impulses and sleepless nights devoted to developing my call list of financial contributors, my Kitchen Cabinet, Democratic Party leaders, and others I believed should hear my decision from my mouth to their ears and not online on social media or in the whispers down the hallways. Avoiding and strangling the rumor and political grapevine characteristic of the profession and winning against the prevailing monster known as social media, the three of us moved quietly, checking off our to-do tasks as we looked toward that big day, Friday, January 19, 2019, at 10:00 am.

I am still at a loss to remember all the responses from the people I called that Thursday night. All I called appreciated the personal touch of a phone call versus learning about my decision in the printed media or on social media. One of the more memorable and encouraging responses I do recall was from longtime no capitulating Democratic Party Boss, Chairman Bob Brady. He eased my spirit as he congratulated me on my decision and told me I had done a good job serving our city.

On Thursday, I made my rounds of city hall and then finally to the two offices I cared deeply about. I had saved them for last because I knew it would be emotionally difficult. These offices consistently, but with great affection, occupied the bulk of my long days in city hall, Room number 494, Council President Darrell L. Clarke's office, and Room 581, my staff's office. I knew from the very beginning of this self-imposed, grief-stricken reflective journey, that the *"most difficult decision was the decision to act. The rest is merely tenacity."* —Amelia Earhart.

On that Thursday afternoon, I had to dig deep as I approached the last two sessions of my tenure with feelings of anxiety. These sessions were sure to be the hardest to face and incredibly uncomfortable. I walked the fourth and fifth floors of city hall with Katherine Gilmore Richardson and pressed forward. Those two sessions were exactly what I had expected: tender, tough, uneasy, and deeply emotional. Calm was not in my repertoire for the day that lay ahead. I had to rest on the notion that *I* was the artist of my career. No one will be given my paintbrush.

My chief of staff and I tweaked my resignation speech up to fifteen minutes before show time. She reminded me that at some point that morning I said with clear affirmation, "Let's do this." In her eyes, this meant that I was resolved in my decision. I was ready. Senator Hughes, in his classic entertainment style, but appropriate genuine flair, was ready to serve as my MC. I remain thankful to the council members who stopped by that Friday morning, including Councilwoman Cherelle Parker, who insisted on a photo with my daughter, Marcia Penn, and me, all members of the greatest sorority on earth, Delta Sigma Theta Sorority, Inc. I thanked my dedicated and amazing staff, and recounted all we had accomplished together for twenty years. I was more grateful for those council members whose schedules permitted them to stay. It was time for me to step to the podium with my head up and deliver the remarks I had painstakingly started two months earlier.

> Thank you to Senator Vincent Hughes, my former boss, who serves with distinction, the constituents of the Seventh Senatorial District. Thank you to Mayor James F. Kenny, my colleague for sixteen years. Thank you to my Islanders, both of whom are present, Councilman Curtis Jones and Councilwoman Maria Quiñones Sánchez, for the special bond we built and the unforgettable experiences we share. I thank all of you for stepping away from the demands of your day and for your time to come to this announcement. I went on to thank the distinguished guests, President Clarke, my colleagues, all the elected leadership, members of the clergy, representatives of corporate Philadelphia, and officials with the administration. It gave me joy to recount being the daughter of Sadie, heeding and living by her wisdom, and being the mother of Brielle who proudly carries on our legacy of excellence. I noted with pride that all my sisters were college grads and, of course, I thanked the greatest sorority on earth, Delta Sigma Theta Sorority, Inc.
>
> I thanked my dedicated and amazing staff, and recounted all we had accomplished together for twenty years.

I learned early in my career, long before landing in City Council, that life is no dress rehearsal. As I looked with anticipation to my next act, I was approached by many friends and supporters asking the natural question, what is my next act? I made the decision to leave City Council, not having a clear vision of my next act. With lots of prayers asking God for clarity, and listening to that quiet voice that haunted me, I was crystal clear in my decision that my time had come. I had to move on, go elsewhere to learn and do something else, something more that would re-energize my spirit. They were curious about my "what next?" So was I. This included a millennial firecracker reporter from a publication I was always coaxed to be responsive to.

I had terrific public relations young professionals on my team, all of them rising stars in the PR profession. This included the young firecrackers, Haniyyah Sharpe-Brown and Jason. They helped me understand that a mutually beneficial, respectful relationship with the press matters. Jason understood my disdain and agreed that *The Philadelphia Magazine* poorly represented or covered anything positive or uplifting about the Philadelphia African American community. During my tenure in City Council, rarely did the editorial staff choose to report anything positive about Black life in inner-city Philadelphia. Their treatment of African Americans in positions of leadership and responsibility in the city became so toxic and in-your-face racist, that the city's nonpolitical and business leaders organized and finally challenged the elite magazine's blind eyes to their racism.

In 2018, The Philadelphia Magazine, after enduring much criticism for its racist, white-privileged, slanted, and skewed reporting of the Philadelphia African American community had a come-to-Jesus moment from the outcry by the city's Black leadership. This ultimately led to the hiring of a permanent, full-time African American journalist. While still unacceptable in their coverage of the African American community, Jason insisted that as an elected official, given my role as an at-large, elected member of the City Council, I needed to get over it, accept their skewed, sometimes racist, view of the world, work with them anyway, and respond to their calls for quotes about city-related matters.

The magazine's new full-time African American journalist, who represented the future, called my office in December 2019 requesting an exit interview. Coincidentally, this was the same reporter who reported that my chief of staff, Katherine Gilmore Richardson, was my most natural successor. His eagerness to cover the progress and advancement of African American women was, and remains, very reassuring.

Always with considerable thought and apprehension when dealing with the press, to his surprise, I answered all his questions. Editor-at-large, Ernest Owens, would not know that his full, unedited interview during my last month in the Philadelphia City Council was approached and completed with ambivalent indignation.

> *The five-term pol answers all our final questions—even the one about having dated a particular US Congressman.*
>
> *The start of the new year was the end of an era for Blondell Reynolds-Brown, who had stepped down from her City Council at-large seat after a twenty-year tenure. First elected to Council at the turn of the twenty-first century, Reynolds-Brown helped usher in a new wave of Philly politics. Here, she reflects on the lessons she learned, her career highs and lows, and what she hopes her legacy will be.*
>
> **What is the first thing you're going to do the moment you leave your office at city hall?**
>
> It has been said, *"Life is not measured by the number of breaths we take—life is measured by the experiences that take our breath away."*—Maya Angelou. I have had many rich

experiences in City Council that took my breath away, and for those I am grateful. After I catch my breath, I will unpack a gazillion boxes of memories from the last twenty years in City Council.

You put a specific focus on improving the outcomes of children in Philadelphia. What do you hope future Council people accomplish for our city's youth?

The City Council class of 2020 can tackle myriad issues that are still lagging behind national averages, such as graduation rates, obesity, homelessness, and housing safety. Any one of these pervasive issues impacting our children still poses challenges. Any one of these challenges will require strategic and tactical planning across multiple systems to make a small difference that shifts the paradigm.

There are now going to be two Black women holding City Council at-large seats: Katherine Gilmore Richardson and Kendra Brooks. As the longest-serving Black woman to hold this title, what is one piece of advice you have for them?

There is no one piece of advice. Personally, preserve and protect your families and choose always to be "in the present" for your children. Make no apologies for insisting that your husband and your children come first. Be humble. Do not believe the hype. Decency when disagreeing and words used do matter. Be an outspoken critic and broken record on all issues impacting women and the inequities that persist for minority and women-owned businesses. Build alliances: insist on collaboration with colleagues. Surround yourself with selfless supporters with different skill sets who care about your success—I had a Kitchen Cabinet and an honorary Kitchen Cabinet for twenty years. Expect the critics, usually uninformed critics. This reality comes with the territory. Working in silos can lead to you being viewed with skepticism. Remember that the magic number is nine.

What is the one law you regret voting for or introducing?

My staff and I have crafted and authored more than one hundred pieces of legislation passed by the City Council and dozens more have been signed into law over the last twenty years. Highlights include the Children's Fund requiring the Eagles and Phillies to donate $1 million per team per year for thirty years, menu-labeling, universal lead testing for rental properties, creation of the Women's Commission, creation of the LGBTQ Commission, the Office of Environment & Sustainability, and Women on Boards.

What I wished I had created were stronger, tougher, stricter laws that advance equity contracting opportunities for minority business enterprises and women-owned business enterprises in government or legislation that improves Philadelphia's embarrassing statistic of 2.7 percent African American small businesses—this number is a disgrace in a majority-minority city. Penalizing companies that do not honor their contracts with MBE/WBEs remains an anomaly. There are still far too many loopholes in our government. I challenge the City Council class of 2020 to do better for MBE/WBEs.

You were hit with historically high fines from the Ethics Board and allegedly investigated by the FBI. Now that you are out of the public eye, what do you—the person, not the politician—have to say about those charges and the violation of public trust?

It was a regrettable time in my career. I paid a high price and the highest was the interruption of trust I had built with my constituency over the years. In summary, I fulfilled all the deadlines and faced the double standard for the unprecedentedly high fines imposed by the Ethics Board.

You were known for your notable sense of fashion during your tenure. Why did you value bringing style and glamour to your role?

Wow!! What a compliment. Thank you! Very early in my career, I read the book, *Dress for Success*. The rules in the book became a staple and a guiding light. This book helped me frame my mindset and approach to style and how to dress in a business and professional environment as I was learning to build my career.

I learned while dancing with Philadanco (and in the theater) that red lips exude confidence and on Black skin—fabulous. I love red lipstick! Here is one thing I know for sure. Women have to walk on water to be viewed as equal. Black women must walk on water and fly to be equal, so they can never afford to half-step not even in their attire.

What is the single most important thing you want Philadelphians to remember you for on the City Council?

That I made a difference. I remain most proud of my very first legislative victory: the creation of the Children's Fund during my freshman term.

All in all, I was more than satisfied with my career and even the blemishes on my record did not diminish the joy and fulfillment I felt leaving office. My retirement celebration at the Suzanne Roberts Theatre curated by Kevin Parker, Founder of Parker Events, now an angel, and orchestrated by Sylvia Purnell Muldrow, my first chief of staff, who always understood and captured my vision for extraordinary events was epic. The sold-out theatre of 350 plus guests allowed me to express my appreciation to the many angels along my career path who were present and helped to make the night memorable as I brought my Council career to a glorious close.

Oprah is right. *"In our self-assessments and reassessments* (which took me six months), *as we gain clarity about who we are and what we are about, who we want to be at any given point in the future, we become better able to decide with affirmation what is best for ourselves, after all."* I had fully completed my duty to give Brielle a good start. I had given Philly the best I had to give and now it was time for me to no longer feel guilty about what I needed for me and my happiness going forward. I left the building with this declaration. Dear Future, I am ready. Finally!

Carpe Diem

CHAPTER FIFTEEN

REGRETS

"Action is the antidote to despair." —Joan Baez

I felt vindicated somehow when I won my reelection in a 2015 spring primary. While the past can't be changed, there are regrets. For a re-examined life, there is no way around them. Getting past and accepting regrets is necessary to write a new chapter of life. There is even one school of thought that suggests there are no regrets in life just lessons. I am clear I do not agree. I would argue that for the sincere at heart not only are there regrets, they run deep and can leave wounds. Unarguably, there are always lessons that should be learned. Fundamentally, regrets are a part of life because we cannot enjoy the rainbow or the spring flowers without the storms and the rain. Regrets allow us to grow and stretch so we don't become complacent in the comfort zones of spring and calm streams. Disappointments and regrets jump-start the moxie and the reboot in us all.

Looking back, I asked myself, would I have pursued a second City Council campaign with vigor and doggedness had I won first time out the gate as a first-time candidate? And would I have worked so tirelessly to restore my tainted reputation on my very last campaign?

The answer is yes. Though I have had a most rewarding career and there is much to look forward to in the future, I need to reconcile my regrets and forgive myself to feel whole again.

There are numerous stories about great achievers who did not get things right or meet their goals on the first attempt. I know of many extraordinary women whose scorecards fueled their fires and who became adept at managing regrets when the road got dark and lonely. These women simply face the music head-on with grit, grace, and in-your-face politeness without ever complaining. People, you, and I are all human. We all make mistakes and most often they are not intentional. The good news is wisdom comes through missteps, blunders, and failure.

Throughout my career, the lessons learned from professional experiences, sage advice received from those who cared about me and the lessons observed from the suffering and regrets of other's matters. When under duress, weigh the pros and cons, the consequences of each, make a decision, then leap. Decide how to adapt to a road that is always under construction. Does a new road need to be built or will resurfacing suffice? If success is our aim, recognize there are bumps, potholes, and boulders on the road. In every way, one must decide on the action, and then act.

In reality, the privilege to have been one of seventeen elected to lead America's fifth-largest city for twenty years is pretty rewarding. My experience included a few bumps and even a boulder along the road I traveled, but as suggested in the immortal words of one of my favorite songs, sung by Frank Sinatra, through all the doubts, regrets, and fear, and I did it, "My Way."

One of my regrets was a conversation I had in November of 2018 with the council president that I wish I had handled differently. The president, always a wise counsel to me, had a swagger that was quite attractive. I'm just saying! His commanding presence reminded me of a high school principal checking in on his faculty or a coach checking on his team ball players. Respected and well-admired by colleagues, he had learned from and trained under one of the strongest leaders and political coaches Philadelphia has known, his former boss and mayor of the City of Philadelphia, Mayor John F. Street. He was known to have the backs of the people he admired and cared about. Whenever the council president, sometimes unannounced, visited you in *your* Council office, you knew something was up. When he asked you to take a walk with him, you knew the topic would be both personally and politically sensitive. That day the walk was to an undisclosed office in city hall. I later learned its location was known only to the select Council members with whom he shared sensitive information. The location was new to me and remains undisclosed to most.

Confident there were no planted microphones, especially given the circulating rumors of the federal investigation of a couple of members of the Council in the fall of 2018, he took no chances. It was clear the president and I shared the same belief. The walls of city hall talk. To combat this ugly reality, I too had had many meetings during my midday exercise walks on the sixth floor in the halls of city hall. Highly sensitive political partisan discussions that should not be disclosed or revealed never occurred in my city hall offices. You always take a walk.

My office was on the fifth floor of the northwest corner of city hall. Not having a clue about the purpose of the long walk, with his always gentlemanly manner, calm voice, and direct eye-to-eye focus, the president asked me point-blank about my intentions for the upcoming 2019 Spring Primary election cycle. It was evident that he was preparing to circle the wagons for his team and reelection. While I understood it was his nature to look out for his core crew on the City Council, I was caught off guard by this question. I didn't know if he had a candidate to take my seat or was seeing how to best help me if my answer was affirmative. Believing the answer should be obvious, without a second thought or hesitation, I answered, "Absolutely, I am running for reelection."

With the benefit of hindsight, it was a selfish thing to do. Though I didn't know it yet, I am convinced that the brief and candid discussion that afternoon on the sixth floor of city hall was a defining moment for me and the exchange planted a seed. At this juncture of my career, it was time for me to reexamine my spirit carefully and quietly, my circumstances (divorced and still grieving about the loss of my mom in 2017, which metaphorically knocked me down), my achievements as a legislator, and my deferred dreams. It was time for me to face the hard introspective but necessary question, "Do you want to run for reelection for the seventh time?" Remember, my first election loss, campaign number one was followed by five consecutive wins. It was during this long walk, up the stairs to what seemed like a longer city hall corridor to yet another location, that I subconsciously decided.

Still, I did not face this question until months later. I had simply answered absolutely, pivoting and refocusing on the more immediate legislative and Council business that consumed my long days. Over the next few months, the seed planted by the president germinated, and I began to take an introspective assessment of my career and my life thus far which led to the difficult but careful decision not to seek a sixth term. My one regret was that I did not circle back to inform the president of my change of heart and final decision so he could activate whatever plan he had in mind. I am not sure of the full intent of his visit that day, but I do know that there were a few people who left an impression on me and positively impacted my career. President Clarke was one of them. If he were choosing my replacement, it would have been a good decision. If he were supporting my run, it would have been a good decision. He respected me enough to ask me directly. In the end, with the benefit of hindsight, I answered instinctively not really knowing for sure. My grief had disguised my true feelings.

For the entire year of 2019, President Clarke reminded me with sarcasm and tongue-in-cheek regularly, "You know I am still mad at you and Bill, right?" Councilman Bill Greenlee was the other leg of our three-legged stool in Council leadership who also decided not to seek reelection in 2019.

One of my big, big regrets, as you might have gleaned, was NOT my unapologetic decision to send my daughter to an all-girls school, but how I handled this marital issue, which turned out to be the wedge decision for our family. I had been so re-so-lute. During the robust candidate review process for Brielle's admission to the Agnes Irwin School, I was alone and lonely. The absence of my husband in the equation of our daughter's education was hard. In the interview with the middle school director, I acknowledged my sadness that my husband had not embraced my decision to send our daughter to Agnes Irwin. I was forever changed by her kind and reassuring response, which resonates even today. Whenever I find myself in a moment of reflection I remember her words. "Life is too short and has no space for regrets. If you get a chance, seize it. If it changes your life, don't look back, let it. Be grateful."

Thereafter, I quit allowing regrets to rob me of the energy I needed to make tough decisions. This, I caution, was far easier said than done.

With approximately 840,000 divorces in America in 2009, happily ever after seemed to be a challenge for a lot of people. I was thirteen years old when the word divorce became prominent in my life. It was the elephant in the room that I didn't want to notice that blocked my view from seeing anything else. My parents hadn't actually divorced but they had separated. I remember riding in the car with my mother and the song "Breakeven" by The Script was playing on the radio. The lyrics of that song made my mom very weepy. My mom knew and whispered the lyrics as the song played. At that moment I knew it was time to comfort her rather than to expect the usual tight hugs and warm smile she gave me when I was upset. I held her hand and looked into her teary eyes and said, "It's going to be okay." It was all I could seem to muster at the moment, and I questioned if it were enough. Having to comfort my mother when she cried made me feel important and needed in a way that I had never experienced before. What I remember most were our tiny jokes about irrelevant things and the moments that made her most challenging times just a little bit lighter. Mom would throw her head back in laughter, her eyes would light up, and she would smile at me for a moment. Even though it was only for a moment, I understood it was just what was needed during that time. It was a time when I needed to step up for her.

Once I understood what was happening with my parents, like a light switch, my attitude changed. I didn't believe in marriage anymore and I didn't believe in love. My optimism disappeared and pessimism took its place. I challenged my friends' ideas about love and marriage. I was rock-solid in my approach and matched my friends' arguments with equally strong points about why half of our group's future marriages would not last. I was angry, sad, and frustrated because of what I thought to be my perfect family crumbling to pieces at lightning speed.

My parent's separation allowed my relationship with my mother to grow much stronger, and I valued our relationship much more. We fought less and communicated more. This is what I came to love the most about this unhappy situation. It was difficult learning to deal with my new norm, two different homes, and who I thought to be two different people. My mother continued to be the warm and loving mother I knew, but it was clear the toll the separation took on her. She was also angry, and the mention of money would send her into a rant.

After they separated, I thought differently about my dad. It was hard to like him because I understood his faults in the marriage with my mother. However, I learned to deal with two different situations. I learned how to balance my time so that one parent didn't feel more favored than the other. Because I am a hopeless romantic, the happily ever after dream was all I ever talked about, and romantic comedies are the only movies I like, even with my change of heart after my parent's crisis, I reverted to my natural state: a hopeless romantic. This essay was just one of Brielle's catalogue of writings I maintained, collected by her pack-rat mom.

To say the school situation for Brielle was the ultimate deal-breaker for my marriage is true, but one cannot walk a tightrope backward without speaking of the unfortunate challenges it poses for marriages when the woman is an elected official. My career position caused many issues, sometimes horrific ones. The disappointment in my daughter's father and my forgiveness of him and the forgiveness of self-took way too long. When it comes to marriage, break-ups are hard to cope with. There is a sense of loss and longing, the sudden change in routine, and a whole washer full of emotions ranging from anger and betrayal to regrets and sadness. The professionals would say, it's only normal to feel this way. Even the chemicals in our brain are affected when a romantic relationship ends. The emotional pain can last for days, weeks, or months. I spent almost ten years fretting and second-guessing my decision while managing my multiple nuanced roles as mom, elected public official, daughter, sister, and friend, about what I could have and should have done differently. It is mentally brutal. As the Wizard of Oz himself explained to the Tin Man, *"Hearts will never be practical until they can be made unbreakable."*

My marriage has been over for more than ten years now, and there have been too many times when I still felt the loss. With pastoral counseling, I learned to ride the waves, suffer through those feelings of loss, and learn how not to allow memories to devour or drown me. Broken things can be fixed even if the relationship cannot be mended. Sooner or later, emerging from the dark tunnel will be the light, the knowing it's time to move on. With time as a promised healer, it only gets better. But mistakes and regrets have unforeseen consequences. It's impossible to have life-changing events that do not impact children if you have them. What is truly sitting on children's hearts when facing issues that affect them? Often the answer shows up in unexpected ways.

Enrolling Brielle in summer on-site pre-college experiences starting at age twelve was never optional. I relied on these supplemental academic programs to strengthen her social and academic skills. Thus, her participation was not a *we* decision, it was a *Mommie* decision. Over the years Pack Rat, Me kept all of Brielle's writings. Sometime after my divorce, I stumbled upon an essay, in a binder of dozens, she had written about her feelings. I also discovered that she paid attention to the one song I played "Breakeven" *ad nauseam* during my divorce, which dealt with romantic heartbreaks. At the end of a letter Brielle wrote, "I am a child of a divorced marriage, however, I also come from a family where both of my parents love me unconditionally and that is all I ever really need."

Divorce for any child isn't easy. It's emotional and frustrating having two parents who just don't work out. Everything in life is not always a happy ending. I have asked myself the question too many times. Do wounds heal? I think not. Maybe. Francis Ford Coppola summed up my view perfectly. *"We are all creatures of feelings…and when those feelings reemerge, things they trigger can break our hearts again."* So true.

In short, regrets weigh you down. It's hard not to dwell in the tears and the what-ifs headspace after a failure. Accept the fact that bad days give you experience, and the worst days give you lessons. Trials will make you strong, and stumbles keep you human and humble. So, again in the spirit of redundancy, accept the losses, embrace the lessons, and start each morning with gratitude. When your feet hit the floor, put one foot in front of the other and face the new day that is filled with unlimited possibilities. The good news is that each new morning brings the chance to start anew. Praise God or your deity and ask to be given the grace and strength to practice that mental muscle required, so you can move on until you are emotionally liberated and set free. Then move on! After months of grief counseling and later during the monster, a.k.a. COVID-19, I finally tossed a dozen boxes of files associated with my divorce. Howard, I finally said out loud using one of my treasured quotes, *"Today I decided to forgive you. Not because you apologized or because you acknowledged the pain that you caused me (our failed marriage caused us), but because my soul deserves peace."* —Najwa Zebian. No longer am I *"a prisoner of the past or a prisoner of the future,"* —Deepak Chopra, which is closed and limited.

The horrific COVID-19 had shut down the world, and in retrospect, it provided me with the space and the distraction I needed. I joined the millions of Americans who were binging on Netflix when the world was forced to stand still. During one of my TV marathons, I stumbled upon a movie that gave me the ultimate "aha" moment and breakthrough. I emotionally limped my way through *The Shack*, starring Octavia Spencer. The lessons about sadness from loss, and the forgiveness of self and others through the lens of biblical symbolism awakened in me. A loud bell rang in my heart after viewing this gut-wrenching, teary, and poignant story. The need for forgiveness which my Pastor Terry Davis had spoken of during many of our therapy sessions finally, registered. I seized days, weeks, months, and four years, starting during the worldwide imposed pause button to write, *Walking a Tightrope Backward in High Heels*. While initially a painfully cathartic exercise, this effort gave me the space needed to forgive myself and let go of an unsuccessful marriage. I remain eternally grateful to my pastor for the permission to do so.

I leaned into affirmations by leaders from across the spectrum, erudite and renowned writers, gifted poets, academicians, gifted artists, and, of course, activists, and well-known celebrities I had selected with great care. Positive thoughts and affirmations were required to refuel my soul and comfort me during the tough times, the inconvenient times, the uncomfortable times, and those lonely painful times when I was steamrolled by that career boulder waiting for it to roll away. Every day, I repeat, every day, I needed internal and external cues and signals to motivate me during the fog of adversity. My faith and hope propelled me forward.

Finally, I found solace and acceptance in my new reality that hearts never break even. I left regrets behind, chartered a new course of action for resurfacing my bumpy road with the gumption, (i.e., moxie) my mother taught me.

Carpe Diem

CHAPTER SIXTEEN

PASSING THE BATON A.K.A. LEGACY

"The greatest gift of leadership is a boss who wants you to be successful."
—Jon Taffer

Here is my sermon! Women elected officials must walk on water to be equal to the men occupying the seats of power. Black and Latinx women elected officials must sprout wings to walk on water to fly higher and may still not be equal. We fully recognize the cliffs, glass ceilings, and inequality when we decide to accept the mantle of public service. As lions, many predecessors have managed the double standards that come from the good, the bad, and the ugly of politics for the change we work to see.

We are counting on the next generation of women to carry on what we have started, including breaking the glass ceiling. Young women like my daughter, Brielle, Hon. Katherine Gilmore Richardson, and former staffers, Candice and Haniyyah, and Taylor and Samantha and Gabriela, and thousands of others like them will have to carry on what we have started. My former colleagues and I may craft all the public policies we please but how they will be executed will depend on the work ethic of the young women we coach. We expect these ambitious young women to sit where we are sitting and when we move on or are called home, attend to those matters we thought were important. They will move in, move up, and manage our corporations, our businesses, our churches, our universities, our healthcare institutions, and our government. Our success will give them broad shoulders to stand on, and their career outcomes and level of success will be the judge of our effectiveness.

All our works, our books, our achievements of any scale will be questioned, judged, praised, celebrated, affirmed or not by them. They will give rise to the caterpillars who will become the butterflies people of color in our country have been waiting for. So, it behooves us to be confident and at ease when our work shines a bright light on inequalities that persist. As we pay attention to the next generation hand off the torch and pay it forward, we can be assured that these dynamic young women's achievements will indeed shatter ceilings and scale cliffs. By acknowledging their good work today and rewarding their enormous potential through mentorship, we plant seeds for their nonnegotiable demands and the kind of confidence that inspires them to be more and do more always with excellence. Doing so does not diminish us. Those of us in the ring ready to pass the baton should examine our hearts. Do a real gut check and assessment of what we must pass on.

No one can cultivate or build a legacy if we are not intentional in our actions to invite and bring young people to the table. As the only woman at-large member, my staff and I made it a big deal to intentionally celebrate Women's History Month. With a bullhorn, we used the month of March to speak to our constituency, women voters, the stuck Neanderthals, the devoted listeners of WURD Radio, and anyone else who did not understand that women and the role we play among all the stars in the universe matter. With redundancy, we spoke loudly about the visible, and invisible barriers, and never-ending challenges women face in their professional endeavors and workspace.

My staff and I understood that the best leaders do not focus on just half of the world but lead for everyone. Our stomping gave us an opportunity to identify the young, fierce tribe marching up the hill.

As a veteran, my job to recruit other women began once I ascended to a place of influence. My work was never done. I didn't rest on my laurels because I understood it is never just about having a seat at the table; it was more about what I did once I gained a seat at the table. This was reflected in our women's history month and year-round programming. Once I sat in the coveted chair, I made sure to pull up chairs for other women. My self-imposed next assignment was not to settle into the bench but to reach back or across the bench and pull the next young woman along. Sometimes young stars have not yet recognized the fierce in themselves, so even if she is kicking and screaming, pull her along. Sit them right next to you.

Rearing the next generation of leadership is the best advice I can give a woman in politics because you will need other women at the table. If you don't make room for another woman, you, my dear, may end up on the menu or your issues may end up on the scrap pile. Lifting and advocating for younger, emerging women leaders whose voices may be choked or smothered by the power structure and the old boys' network is imperative. Supporting these women authentically is yet another responsibility to take on. Wear the cape as their fierce champion. Be a steadfast confidant, a resource, a listener, an ear, and a guidepost. When you encounter a woman, you care about in any circle, your family, your village, your workspace, and most importantly, a woman of color whose career is being attacked or publicly demoralized or financially taken advantage of, speak up. Rally additional allies. HELP HER. Resist being silent. Silence implies complicity.

There are dozens of gifted, promising young women like my former chief of staff, now Councilwoman Katherine Gilmore Richardson, and the former city treasurer, Rashia Johnson, whose seats at the table had to be protected. Like them, there are many more who, when encouraged, like diamonds in the rough, will shine brightly if given the chance. At their crowning moments, these young women will rise to the occasion, surprise you, and never disappoint.

Guidelines for Building a Legacy

"At last, the time comes to decide, whether to turn the page or close the book." —Tanzeel Lane.

Moxie women like the women of Delta Sigma Theta Sorority, Inc., *flex*. This quality was first observed and articulated by my former boss, State Senator Vincent Hughes. They choose or elect to pass the torch and embrace the value of building a bench. With decades of experience in their chosen fields, they have tackled, endured, and survived the impediments, the hurdles, the crises, and the glass ceilings. Moxie women have the responsibility to reckon with the question: what time is it? The answer and beauty of the question lies in having a bench. Women who lead today will experience great satisfaction when they make it a practice to mentor, coach, and prepare promising young women to come off the bench and accept the torch. Herein lies a win-win proposition. Mentors sharpen their leadership skills in the mentoring process, and the reciprocity of joy is indeed priceless. Australian women's cricket team's highest run-scorer, Beth Mooney reminds us that, *"women behind you are looking for the next step. Light the way."*

Fear may be one of the major reasons leaders do not intentionally plan for the inevitable leadership handoff. Seek to be selfless and opt to be intentional about leadership succession which can be an organic process or not. You decide what is comfortable for you. "It's *important to make way for those new voices and ideas so that the country and the world continues to evolve."* —Michele Obama.

I had reached the point of flexing. What does one do with forty years of knowledge about how our government works? Hopefully, this book might answer and shine light on that question. After privately deciding and before formally announcing my decision not to seek reelection to a sixth term, consistent with protocols, I called and met with my chief of staff, Katherine Gilmore Richardson, to inform her of my decision.

Katherine Gilmore Richardson, like me, is a Girls' High graduate, a proud member of Zeta Phi Beta Sorority, Inc., and now the Honorable Councilwoman. She was my perfect successor. I met 15-year-old Katherine when she personally stopped me and handed off a handwritten note while gardening in my yard. Thanking me and inspired by speech remarks I had delivered at GHS; this seedling of a new acquaintance led me to follow Katherine throughout her undergraduate and graduate school studies. Katherine has an amazingly inspirational story. Born to a teenage South Philly mother, she was adopted at birth by loving parents who raised her and her sister. She attended the Philadelphia High School for Girls and West Chester University. With ten years of affiliation with my office from college intern to ultimately returning to my office as a young professional, she held every staff position (except public relations) with excellence. She was exceedingly equipped with the knowledge and the "how to" of the legislative process. As the mother of young children, she saw the city through their eyes. Issues of education, public safety, job creation, and criminal justice reform felt urgent and important to her. After quiet thoughtful consideration with her family, she decided to enter the ring to champion those causes with the hope of a better outcome for her children. She decided to run for City Council at-large because of her love for the city, the love of her children, and her desire to move our city forward. I was one of her co-chairs.

Katherine Gilmore Richardson reminded me of myself. She embodied the qualities of a younger me, and always, as I did, acted on and practiced the Girls' High motto, *Carpe Diem*. I knew I wanted to pour into her, and I trusted my instinct. Investing in her meant encouraging her spirit that was already modeled on the belief that collective work and responsibility, a.k.a. Ujima, has a role in community building. Giving this firecracker opportunities and challenges that stretched her capabilities for almost two decades, built her self-confidence, and enforced her rubber band principle (stretching as far as one can go) which reinforced her professional development and readied her for campaigning. Katherine did 99 percent of what her three co-chairs (Ryan Boyer, Jonathan Saidel, and I) requested and advised. More importantly, she showed up for all campaign-related events, ward meetings, transit stops, playground ceremonies, senior citizen centers, Divine Nine meetings, AND she raised the mother's milk to handsomely finance her 2019 campaign, ready to tell her story, ask for votes, and appeal to Philadelphia voters. With a heart full of gratitude, passion, and no entitlement her tireless efforts carried the day excellently!

This emerging young leader proved and showed to the 45,070 Philadelphia voters what I always knew, she was young, smart, hungry, fired up, and ready to go! Kathy exhibited the qualities required to be a successful candidate. For the 109 days leading to the May 2019 Democratic Primary, this millennial mother of a blended family of three, ages fifteen, six, and four, raised the money for her campaign war chest. Kathy traveled to every corner of the city, meeting with all sixty-nine wards of the Democratic Party, some of them twice, covering all 142.6 square miles that included dozens of women's organizations and churches. She presented before the Divine Nine, the RCOs, a.k.a. Resident Community Organizations, and impressed enough of the majority of her new constituency base to place fifth. She was amazingly Amazing!

While stomping for her election, I brought Katherine forefront and center. Ernest Owens of *Philadelphia Magazine* appreciated this. He clearly understood my intentions, and to his credit, was the first to snag Katherine Gilmore Richardson's remarkable story after I officially announced my retirement from City Council. Less than thirty days following my announcement in February 2019, he interviewed "the vice president of Young Philly Democrats about her platform, challenging the perception that she's an 'establishment' candidate and about why Black women are needed in politics now more than ever." Here is what preparation, grit, and fierce looks like.

You're one of the youngest candidates running in the primary. How is your platform different from those of the many others who are also vying for City Council?

My platform is different because I bring and have the experience to get things done. I will shift funding priorities to middle neighborhoods to help families keep, preserve, and stay in their homes.

You've just left your post as chief of staff for Councilwoman Blondell Reynolds-Brown. How do you plan to challenge the perception that you're an 'establishment' candidate?"

I am an experienced candidate…I worked on the ground in government, and I know how to get things done in city hall. Lots of candidates will talk about what they will do, but not how they plan to get it done. City Council is a team effort. I am the only candidate with ten-plus years working behind the scenes in the City Council in every position. While I have worked full-time for more than a decade, I am also a millennial on the City Council. We are the largest age group in the city, and in the latest midterm elections, we were the largest voting bloc.

Reynolds-Brown recently announced that she's not running for reelection, there's a possibility that another Black woman won't replace her in representation on the

City Council. Why do you think it's important for Philadelphia to elect a Black woman specifically for City Council at-large?

When Black women vote, whoever we vote for wins. Black women have been and continue to be the lifeline for the Democratic Party both locally and nationally. For the last twenty years, there has always been at least one Democratic African American woman serving City Council at-large: the late great Augusta Clark from 1980 to 2000, and Councilwoman Blondell Reynolds-Brown from 2000 to 2020. In a majority-minority city, it would be a disservice to African American women if we lacked citywide representation. When I am elected, (speaking the affirmative into the universe) I will be the youngest African American woman ever to serve on the City Council at-large.

Another piece of advice I often share with aspiring hopefuls is that as a public representative, before you open your mouth, you will be assessed and scrutinized by the way you dress. So, care about your presentation and fashion decorum. Take a page from former First Lady Michelle Obama and House Speaker Nancy Pelosi's stylebook. These women always show up looking well-appointed and fabulous! Conservative chic worked for me for twenty years but have fun showing your sense of style with your fashion choices and jewelry and always have a set of pearls! *"Style is knowing who you are, what you want to say, and not giving a damn."* —Gore Vidal.

As women and particularly as Black and brown women, we don't have the luxury not to give a damn about what we say. When in the political leadership ring, we must always be conscientious about the words we utter. We do not and will never get the pass of dereliction of duty like number 45 and many leaders like him are given every day.

Endeavor to tell the truth. Be honest and direct but avoid being cruel. In your communications, you can do both. Never believe for a second that you are not an influencer. WE ALL ARE.

Limit worry about criticism. If you have a weak spirit and are void of a spiritual foundation to guard and restore your soul regularly, electoral politics is NOT FOR YOU. Remember, politics is a contact sport. Jesus had critics. Trust that your warts will be revealed or exposed, and when that happens, you will be exploited by your critics. Two of the best books I read early in my career were Dale Carnegie's *How to Win Friends and Influence People* and *How to Stop Worrying and Start Living*. These timeless books provided me with the psychological armor and essential interpersonal tools required for living among naysayers, most of whom are sitting in the stands and pointing fingers from the bleachers. Remember Jill Scott's edit. *"Everything ain't for everybody."*

I am eternally grateful to Rev. W. Arthur Lewis, one of my early former bosses, the Executive Director of the Philadelphia Opportunities Industrialization Center. I am convinced that he saw my ambition and encouraged me to take strategic steps that would nurture my career. His most memorable instruction to me that I have shared with the young women I coach is this: *"Your career is a marathon. It is not a sprint."* Never have truer words been spoken. It was Rev. Lewis who urged me to take the Dale Carnegie year-long public speaking course. I took his advice and made a self-investment in my professional development. The course paid dividends for my career.

Dale Carnegie presented a menagerie of strategies to manage worry and criticism. *"Unjust criticism is often a disguised compliment."* Everyone will have an opinion, including those who would never have the spine to walk in your shoes. They are usually the Monday morning quarterbacks typically sitting on the sidelines saying what they would have done. Of those offering unsolicited advice while sitting in the bleachers hiding behind the social media handles, ask yourself a few questions that will help you screen the noisy noise.

Are they a part of your intimate circles of family and friends? Are they someone you would have a discussion with over a glass of wine after hours to iron out or talk through your difference of opinion? Do they see through an alternative lens completely removed from the reality of those whose life chances you are committed to improving? Does their wealth get in the way of their ability to show compassion for those vulnerable citizens you are devoted to helping? Do the sideliners understand that government exists to solve societal problems, many of which the private sector will not touch? If you cannot answer these questions about the critics who don't matter, learn to dismiss them, and keep your distance, including those you love. Accept that there will be times when you must exercise discipline and stop trying to convince people. Stop arguing and simply let them be wrong. This may be difficult initially and will feel like a new muscle you have to build. As my mom always said, "It takes all types of people to make the world go round". Despite your good deeds and best efforts and intentions, you will not be exempt from the pitfalls or criticism. Accept this.

So, build your precious memories within the one limited commodity, your time. Become quietly indignant about avoiding those people who dwell in the negative column or don't respect or appreciate your chosen career space. Believe this. Protecting your emotional health and deciding who and what you want in your personal emotional space and inner circle is not a weakness. It's wisdom. Instead, analyze your own mistakes, critique yourself, and be kind to yourself. When and after you do, practice the mental muscle and Move on!

The June 2019 edition of *Oprah Magazine* featured a column penned by the co-chair of the Women's March on Washington, Linda Sarsour, titled, "Beyond Belief." She discusses qualities such as appealing to people's humanity that I believe are seedlings for cultivate the next generation of leaders. For those who can do little for you, genuinely meet them where they are. It may be the college intern who asks for thirty minutes during their internship, or the senior who hits a bureaucratic stone wall trying to get their broken furnace repaired through a city housing agency. Model. Patience. Sarsour challenges us, "*We activists want people to hear our arguments. . . . Step up for those who can't.*" Pick any issue. You don't have to look far, and you will find someone who has been thrown away. Start in the corner of the world you occupy. Use your intellectual spine and be brave enough to emulate Maya Angelou's instruction, *"Be the rainbow in someone's clouds."*

When you select the one young woman you desire to pass the baton, instruct her to adopt the Navy SEALs mantra. *"Get comfortable with being uncomfortable."* Are you prepared, are you ready to be challenged at community meetings? How about your family at Thanksgiving dinner? What about in your car when you are taking your teenager to school? How about at the dance studio when you are waiting for your child during class? Brace yourself to restate your opinion and your position to the darndest. Prepare yourself to allow grace to the audacity of those you have never met and will never meet again after you defend your position. Sarsour says, "*You need to have the courage to have tough conversations.*" Refrain from being a wimp. Brace your heart and your head. Say and alert the other parties, acknowledge, and confess that this is a hard conversation. Do the work. Meet neighbors. Invite them to your home. Attend community meetings. There will be too many more than you can count. Roll up your sleeves. Show up at the mosque, the supermarket, the YMCA, and the public music venue. Wherever two people are gathered. Just show up and DO THE WORK!

This is my recommendation and my opinion. The next generation of elected leadership must be concerned about saving our planet, a.k.a. climate warming. Join hands with the Greta Thunbergs or the

Katherine Gilmore Richardsons of your region and challenge local leaders to deal with the issue of the climate, the environment, and sustainability. Demand that your local peer leaders reckon with this one truth stated over sixty years ago. *"The supreme reality of our time is the vulnerability of our planet..."* —John F. Kennedy. The intractable issue of gun violence and its culture that has saturated and seized too many of our urban communities is one of the biggest public health epidemics that is killing our children. This complicated, layered, messy Second Amendment dilemma yearns for and will require collaborative, transformational leadership across levels of government that thinks outside the lines. The next generation of women leaders will be charged with this intractable public policy unresolved assignment.

Remind the next generation of leadership that the only place where success comes before work is in the dictionary. As stated more plainly, *"opportunity follows struggle. It follows effort. It follows hard work. It doesn't come before."* —Shelby Steele.

Women tend to raise eyebrows when we build our careers in spaces traditionally reserved for men. The world of electoral politics is certainly one of those spaces, although we should be encouraged by the record number of women who were inspired, stepped up, and ran in 2018. Let's not mimic or adopt any of the obtuse behaviors formerly practiced by men in positions of leadership and responsibility. Effective leaders are decisive, lead with core values, and set a clear vision. Their emotional intelligence creates an environment that fosters a sense of community for everyone and not a select few.

Be honest with that rising star in your sphere of influence about the hurdles, the hiccups, and the disappointments sure to accompany her milestones of achievement. Like a straight shot of whiskey with no chaser, avoid sugarcoating the bruises that are ensured with building a career. In the words of the extraordinarily talented and gifted Oscar and Grammy award winner, Jon Batiste, "*There are highs and there are lows, that's life. Strap in!*"

Don't be afraid! Do it afraid! Amy Morin's book provides for us women and, I am sure, applicable for men, tools that encourage us to push through our fears to seize own our success. Gift yourself her book, *13 Things Mentally Strong Women Don't Do.*

To create a new chapter, we must change our old thinking and create new habits. Every stage of our lives requires a new way of thinking and doing. Education has its levels, and so does life. To do better, we must be willing to learn, relearn, and dive into unfamiliar territory and experiences that will scare us but stretch us to do more and be better in new unfamiliar spaces. Adopt the attitude of a champion. Elementary thinking will never get us to the mastered life we dream of living. *"In character, in manner, in style, in all things, the supreme excellence is simplicity."* —Henry Wadsworth Longfellow.

Know that image matters. While my daughter and I have a generational difference of opinion about political correctness, I firmly believe that as women, image matters, and image matters more for African American and Latinx women. Never forget the double standard. While not always obvious and seemingly silent, the double standard is quietly lurking. This enemy of racism and sexism still exists. Fellow Girls' High alum and brilliant writer, Bebe Moore Campbell, stated in a 1984 *Essence* magazine article, *"Assessing your professional image means grading yourself in all the categories that matter most: communication, grooming and dressing, team playing and networking. Whether you are aiming for a higher position or hoping to start your own business, your image can make the difference between the chump change of mediocrity and the big bucks of success."* Any bold woman contemplating running for elected office must reckon with the fact that this harsh reality is as true today as it was in 1984, be you a millennial, like my daughter, or old school, like her mother.

As you examine and sometimes reexamine your spirit, check your people skills, most specifically your Emotional Intelligence, a concept first introduced by Daniel Goleman. Literature devotes much research to this controversial topic in the workplace. Kristin Cardinale, Ph.D. discusses in her book, *The 9–5 Cure*, that EI, "refers to a person's ability to manage her own emotions and the emotions of others. There are five fundamental elements to EI; knowing your emotions, managing your emotions, motivating yourself, recognizing and understanding the emotions of others, and managing relationships and the emotions of others." If you decide to enter the unforgiving world of electoral politics or any public space that calls for leadership responsibilities recognize that all the elements of EI require personal, intentional, continuous work. *"Suddenly you just know, it's time to start something new and trust the magic of new beginnings."* —Meister Eckhart. I agree. Your instincts will never lie. You just know.

> *"Walk to the edge. Listen hard. Laugh. Play with abandon. Practice wellness. Continue to learn. Choose with no regret. Appreciate your friends. Lead or follow a leader. Do what you love."*
>
> —Mary Anne Radmacher.

Commit to cultivating a legacy. Give your time, your talent, your seasoned experience, and your tested voice. Look forward without guilt and with a clear heart to pursue those new horizons and unknown territory. Understand that your time is your time. Noooo. Your time is not up, and you are not too old. As Hollywood actress Taraji P. Henson stated in an interview for the premiere of *The Color Purple*, *"Time is up when your heart stops. As long as you have a beat in your heart you have what it takes to make your dreams come true."*

By the way, in addition to all she stood for, the other compelling fact, unknown to my critics, which led to my decision to unequivocally endorse candidate Katherine Gilmore Richardson was her accurate assessment of voter patterns. Demographics matter. Now you can see why I was so proud to share her story while traveling the campaign trail once she decided to run for City Council at-large. Councilwoman Katherine Gilmore Richardson, along with Brielle's shero, AOC, Congresswoman Alexandria Ocasio-Cortez, made it crystal clear that these Generation X women hold the promise of tomorrow. I am confident these women will go the distance, and go on to do great things, locally and nationally for all the right reasons.

Leading, I hope, by example, I want to see these promising young women, who have gotten off the sidelines using their eagerness, intelligence, and bright-eyed dreams, to step into their life's calling. As Oprah Winfrey would say, *"Your real job in life is to figure out as soon as possible what your purpose is, who you are meant to be, and begin to honor your calling in the best way possible."*

If there were women to hand the baton to, Katherine and Alexandria exemplify the best. When they arrive at the table, they understand their assignment: to bring other eager women to the table and pull out the chair for them. They fully understood that each one brings one is about building beyond self. Being an active member of a tribe of women who model the value that behind every successful woman is a woman who has her back, is something we honestly believe in. I learned at age twenty-two that it is never about you. As the oldest of seven children, my Mom made it clear to me in no uncertain terms and with no use of foul language that I had the duty and responsibility to be an example always. This included showing through my actions and my choices that dreaming is not enough. We must set goals, and then nurture and nourish our dreams and the dreams of others we care about. Demonstrate by example that one must be willing to pay the price to do the work, the repetitive work, the boring monotonous work, always with excellence as your handprint while in pursuit of those dreams. Supporting Katherine Gilmore Richardson modeled the example I had been taught by my Mom.

Councilwoman Katherine Gilmore Richardson's letter aptly expressed why my decision to leave not only was my personal decision but affirmed that passing the baton and my legacy in the world of electoral politics was well intact and in good hands. My heart remains full and appreciative. I want to share this letter with you. She wrote:

To My Forever Councilwoman,

Writing this letter has been one of the most difficult tasks I have undertaken since our first meeting in the fall of 1999. To quantify the magnitude of your impact is a very difficult task. Bob Proctor stated, "A mentor is someone who sees more talent and ability within you, than you see within yourself, and helps bring it out of you."

To say you are a mentor is an understatement. After meeting you when you were just elected to Council and not yet sworn in was the beginning of our journey together. Your words, work ethic, and presence were distinctive. I started in your office as an intern and volunteer, serving in every role except communications, and ended my career as your chief of staff. You successfully passed the baton, gracefully and flawlessly. I could never have been elected to the City Council without your passion, gumption, and unwavering support. You were wise enough to know that you wanted to experience the width of your career and not just the length of your career.

You pioneered what it means to walk on a tightrope backward with high heels on, blindfolded, being a wife and working mother while meeting the relentless demands of being an elected public servant. I had the privilege to have a front-row seat to your day-to-day life in City Council. While most days I know were not easy, you met the challenge each day head-on. You unknowingly showed me how to lead while always being present for your daughter.

I watched you up close and personal, often making tough decisions on important legislation to improve the quality of life for all Philadelphians. I have seen you fight tirelessly for women, children, and families, and as a mother of young children, there is nothing more important.

When you were elected in 1999, you were the only African American woman elected at-large in Philadelphia's City Council. Today, I am honored to now hold your seat as the youngest African American woman ever elected in City Council's history. Thank you for paving the way for me and so many women. Your example allowed us to dream big and if that did not work, dream bigger.

Steven Spielberg once stated, "The delicate balance of mentoring someone is not creating them in your own image but allowing them to create themselves." Thank you for allowing me to create myself and leave a LEGACY for the next generation of women leaders.

We Journey On, Councilwoman Katherine Gilmore Richardson

Ultimately, thanks to my daughter, who during COVID nudged me annoyingly to tell my story, I am sharing with any political hopeful or layperson tools and strategies that can be useful as they embark on any non-traditional career such as a career in electoral politics.

Carpe Diem

CHAPTER SEVENTEEN

DEAR PAST, THANK YOU FOR THE LESSONS LEARNED

Life isn't life unless it tests you. My daughter's generation says, "Life be lifin'." It certainly did me. Full of highs, lows, experiences that ached beyond tolerance and heartbreaks. Were I not spiritually grounded, the pain I experienced from my career fumbling could have broken me. But here is the good news. Life also offers new beginnings, and as my youngest sister would say, "Every day is a new, fresh start." Despite my harsh reality at the time, I held on through the good, the bad, and the ugly times, knowing and believing that after every storm comes a clear blue sky, sometimes accompanied by a rainbow. I remained hopeful that what didn't kill me would make me stronger. My mom's adage stuck in my soul. "Nothing good or bad lasts forever."

My career misstep was just one chapter and not my whole story. Scripture reminds us, "*Weeping endures for a night.*" My weeping was quite a bit longer. Through the nightmare, I kept fragments of my Pollyanna belief and showed respect even to some not worthy. My patience was helped along because I had a mom who raised me to never compromise my character even when there was reason to do so. What had occurred in my case was not criminal, my actions were unethical. If my treasurer had disclosed and recorded, "my" story would have ended differently. In fact, mine would be a different story. Knowing in my heart that no ill will was intended, I continued to look for the good in people hoping they too would see the good in me. This period of my life proved that good people with no hidden agendas still exist in the world of politics. The support I received buoyed me even as the dissenters aimed to destroy twenty years of my commitment to my constituents and public service.

Pray you never find yourself in a public debacle or chaotic career quagmire. When the non-blissful experience knocks at your door and you catch yourself reflecting and dwelling on the past, you will follow Zimbabwean politician, Roy Leslie Bennett's advice, view the past as *"a place of reference, not a place of residence."* This will be insanely difficult to do as bullets fly and the sting along with the remnants of the sting will hurt repeatedly for weeks and months going forward. Each morning, when you put your feet on the floor, talk to yourself. Journal. Memorize "I Rise" by Maya Angelou. Read a daily passage from *Grace for the Moment* by Max Lucado. Avoid becoming an M&M—memories and mistakes! Move On! Recognize that even the strongest among us are not exempt from the unforeseen gut punches life will throw our way. What we do with those surprise and painful events will be a better measure and a test for who becomes the victor.

If you enter the world of electoral politics, profession or industry, as you build your career, know that as you distinguish yourself among the many, there will be lots of applause and pleasantries. Enjoy those moments, but realize, those pleasant experiences may not count. Most of those easy moments could have been an empty use of time in the face of disaster. It is during the tough times, the ugly times, the painful times, and the times of doubt that the only thing that endures is character. The unforgiving world of electoral politics will show you who you are and what you are made of.

There may exist successful individuals who can easily forget or dismiss their mistakes. I am not included in that group. I felt compelled to share my lessons so interested women especially Black and Brown women can be mindful of the potential pitfalls. The lessons learned from this firestorm were many. As a God-fearing woman raised by a faith-filled mother, I learned that nothing is impossible with God. During my tenure as a city councilwoman, stuff happened that did not turn out as planned. At all times, it was important to face whatever goes wrong. Despite the fear, face your lions, confront your fear, and with God's grace accept the consequences. It is principled to persevere despite the fears. I repeat. Be fearless!

Former First Lady Jill Biden, a woman who has endured heartaches and loss publicly, reminds us to have comfort in knowing that "*at some point in our lives, we will all be broken or bruised. The morning always comes, and the seasons always change.*" She, a woman of faith, embraces that reaffirming scripture verse, "*weeping endures for a night, but joy comes in the morning.*" —Psalms 30:5. The toughest part about enduring catastrophe is that you cannot push the fast-forward button. The second First Lady of the United States, Abigail Adams, remarked in one of her 1,100 letters to her husband, second US President John Adams, "*Great difficulties may be surmounted by patience and perseverance. You simply cannot rush your way through or out of the painful experience.*" So, get ready, fasten your seatbelt. Strap in. Face the music and, if you can, dance to the music as if no one is watching.

Here are my top 22 life lessons learned:

1. "*Life holds no promises as to what will come your way. Life makes no guarantees as to what you'll have.*" —Dena D. Iaconi

Not only is it human to err, but it is also inevitable. There are no perfect people, but broken people who learn from their mistakes can enjoy a harmonious life. For the most part, we grow because of our mistakes, not despite them. Seeking to be a perfect public servant, free of scandal and controversy, is a mountain to climb. While the feelings of embarrassment are unforgettable and will never be comfortable, an immediate public statement of an error is a victory of the highest order. It was and it is the adult, reasonable, and responsible action your staff, campaign supporters, and contributors expect you to take. Own your SSS—stupid stuff stumble. Immediately. This chapter is not the only chapter or the last chapter of your life. Remember you are the author and the artist who holds the pen and paintbrush.

Dr. William Augustus Jones of Bethany Baptist, the Church in New York, once stated, *"A setback is only a setup for a comeback."* Failure can be used as a stepping stone of faith and a lesson that breathes wisdom into the spirit. The Bible is a portfolio of people who, by the power of God, told despair and defeat to take a hike. Joseph's life is a profile of falling and rising. Moses failed miserably early in life; that is why he had to leave Egypt. Hannah's perseverance and trust that God was watching even in her weariness, reminds us that God is faithful even in suffering.

2. Persistence. *"Nothing in the world can take the place of persistence. Talent will not; nothing is more common than unsuccessful men with talent. Genius will not; unrewarded genius is almost a proverb. Education will not; the world is full of educated derelicts. Persistence and determination alone are omnipotent."*—Calvin Coolidge.

3. It takes a difficult experience to get a temperature reading on yourself and others. Never become discouraged or disappointed by friends you expected to show up but didn't. You will be pleasantly surprised by the angels who do show up, many of whom

are observers of your work. They will likely attribute your mistake in judgment to your head and not your heart. If you belong to a supportive group, as I did your Sorors will rise. For me, this was exemplified by the intangible bond and sisterhood of Delta through one of our guiding principles, compassion. My firestorm revealed countless supporters and contributors, all of whom were paying attention to the hard news. However, despite the daily news spin, believers and many others reached out with encouragement, and help, some anonymously, some financially. Others will quietly pray for a successful rebound. The art of living when under fire requires us to meet challenges each morning when we drop our feet to the floor, head on. Those uncomfortable, painful, bruising experiences associated with my campaign mistake ironically provided the unexpected fuel I needed to rebuild my confidence and renew my faith when I was most vulnerable. I learned during this period when we long for a life without difficulties, we must remind ourselves that, *"Oaks grow strong in contrary winds and diamonds are made under pressure."* —Peter Marshall. I have grown to accept that after divorce, you do learn to live in a new norm. Life moves on with or without your renewed and better self.

4. Despite the fear, persevere and face the music. Indeed, during those moments of despair, it was not a matter of trying to eliminate all the inequities and double standards, but rather doing my best to facilitate and effect change to rise above them. Believe firmly that there will always be more people with good hearts even in what appears an imperfect world.

5. One key to rebounding is not to seek perfection. It is a burden. Avoid it. A former staffer, now an advertising and public relations executive, challenged me once about why seeking perfection is not realistic. I learned from Jason and finally reckoned with the fact that the key to success is not perfection but rather making peace with doing and giving my very best when pushing

forward. I learned that where you stand and the direction you are going are keys to pushing through the rough patch as you fulfill your commitment to a job well done. When on the bicycle, keep your back straight. Seek to keep your balance while trudging through the storm in the valley.

6. Identify people who can provide the needed expertise to advise you on how best to operate and take corrective action on multiple fronts, simultaneously. Deputize. Determine what YOU must do and what someone else can do to help you. Set priorities. Recognize the interdependence of decisions. Determine who will be affected and the consequences. Set timelines, deadlines, and time limits, some of which may be influenced by external forces. Set up new controls and auditing techniques. Follow up. Verify. Follow up. Verify. Follow up. Critique your new systems in the campaign organization. Set your new course. Then leap with eyes wide open!

7. Be the robin who sings in the rain. The robin possesses the singular trait of singing when the storm has silenced all other songbirds. When the rain comes and the sun does not shine, we still have reason to rejoice. *"No storm can shake my inmost calm while that refuge is clinging. Since Christ is Lord of heaven and earth, How can I keep from singing?"* —Robert Wadsworth Lowery.

8. *"You never know how strong you are until being strong is the only choice you have."* —Bob Marley. This lesson was glaringly clear to me, as a woman separated and going through a divorce. Daily my daughter observed how I navigated those 7:30 a.m. morning calls while driving her to school. Often, she heard me say, "Allow me to spend thirty minutes of quality time with my daughter this morning while I take her to school. Know that I will return your call after 8 a.m." I had to be strong about not shortchanging my daughter's quality time with me.

9. Your signature is sacred. Guard it with your life. While I signed my campaign expense reports, I did not make it a standard practice

to stop and READ the reports before signing them. Not reading my campaign reports was inexcusable and did not exonerate me from the penalties or the unprecedented fines imposed by the city's Ethics Board. In the newspaper dated Tuesday, February 26, 2013, the headline read "Ex-aide reaches ethics settlement. Former treasurer pleaded guilty to stealing from Blondell Reynolds-Brown's campaign and another political action committee." His omissions and statements of key information about spending put me in scalding hot water and I became the torch bearer of the consequences for campaign filing misconduct. Who the violator was became insignificant. No one cared. This was a case of *respondeat superior*, the superior is responsible. When you sign your signature to anything, any document, any report, any letter, any email you are fully, totally, completely, solely, and explicitly responsible. Period!

10. It is important to admit your failure, immediately. Denial and dishonesty will be assumed if you delay. So, don't deny. Don't delay. Act swiftly. Square with your supporters during the tough times. The value of honesty with those who love you and who want you to overcome the rough patches that are sure to come, is discussed more comprehensively in the book by Yale University Professor Nicholas A. Christakis, *Apollo's Arrow*. Read it.

11. You must re-embrace the phrase made popular by President Obama in his first run for the presidency with a "Yes I Can" attitude. With a finite amount of time to accomplish my goals for the 2015 primary election, the time had come for me to put my sadness in the rearview mirror and get busy. I no longer had the luxury of being unproductive. My career needed retooling, and time was my new enemy. I implemented the three magic words, A "Yes I Can" attitude. In the September 1985 issue of *Essence* magazine, Susan L. Taylor's "In the Spirit" editorial was entitled, "You Can.": *"Our lives are the sum total of our thinking and our actions. You can decide to win. Decide to set goals and work*

towards accomplishing them . . . Decide to trust that God is on your side and that life has good things in store for you if you agree to take the necessary steps to achieve them. You can be the winner."

12. *"An arrow can only be shot by pulling it backward. So, when life is dragging you back with difficulties, it means that it's going to launch you into something great. So just focus and keep aiming."* —Paulo Coelho. *"Failure is the great informant. It tells us where success is not. Hence it points us indirectly to the land of possibility."* —Unknown.

13. *"Nothing good or bad lasts forever."* My mother, left to raise seven children all under sixteen years of age alone with no life insurance, had to figure out how to feed us, clothe us, raise us, and inspire us to achieve her number one expectation and demand—secure a college education. I witnessed my mom, my hero, move us from a two-bedroom house to a six-bedroom home following the untimely death of our father. She shouldered the burden while grieving her loss, and never allowed the circumstances of this tragic, life-altering event to derail her. My mom never complained.

14. Believe that eventually, all the pieces will fall into place. Until then, with strict discipline, hold firm to your recovery action plan. While not visible at first glance, know that everything happens for a reason. Probably my favorite passage in the Bible, Ecclesiastes 3:1–8, tells the story of King Solomon and his philosophy, *"There is a time for everything and a season for every activity under the heavens."* The January 2013 edition of *In Touch Ministries'* article, better articulates the meaning of this passage. *"In Every Season, GOD discusses how each of us experiences life in seasons. Spring is for beginnings. Summer is a time for labor and growth. Fall is for harvest. Winter is for withdrawal from activity, rest, and even death of what has come to the end of its time. To be fully healthy, our lives require each one of these seasons at its due time. The key is to recognize what season we're in and then embrace life to its fullness. Rather than seeing these variations as random, we are to recognize*

human experiences as a tapestry woven of times." Bible scholar Iain Provan eloquently states, *"We all experience points in life at which our situation seems so far from what we initially expected that we end up feeling hopeless or even completely lost. During the winter season when we lose relationships, our health, or our reputations, we cannot become discouraged."* None of the aforementioned are an option. It is required that we believe and have faith in knowing that God has a purpose and plan for our lives, beyond the current stupid stumble.

15. Do not allow the fumble of the individual you trusted to be the cross around your neck that buries you. It is not your yoke to carry.

16. Do what arms you to rejoice in the mornings at the start of a new day. Kneel and express gratitude, meditate, journal, listen to inspirational music, and have a morning call with that one individual who is guaranteed to lift your spirits. When you rejoice amid your difficulties, you are giving the enemy a black eye who doesn't know what to do with people who keep giving God praise despite their circumstances.

17. The only time you should look back in the rearview mirror is to see how far you have come. You cannot dwell in the past. It hurts too bad. Let it go. I repeat. LET IT GO. The stare in the rearview mirror will make you sad and slow your pace of recovery. Your backward glances should serve only as a reminder and a red light not to cross that street or dark alley again. Pastor Terry Davis advised me during one of my sessions eight years post my debacle and far more eloquently than paraphrased here, that lingering in that rearview is unhealthy and counterproductive. More importantly, you'll miss the new opportunities displayed on the front window before you.

18. When you run into the individual who is responsible for or who contributed to the stumble, you will remember that avoiding certain people to protect your emotional health and who dampen

your spirit is not a weakness, it's wisdom. When you run into that rare breed (and you will) who wants to rehash the past to justify their conduct and their flawed decisions at your expense, make peace with the saying *"Karma is a patient gangster."* —Unknown.

19. It's the detours in life that make us better. It's the bumps in the road that test what we are made of and who we are. Embrace and believe the fact that opinions, especially by onlookers who have never been in the ring, do not define your reality. Never allow a stumble, a misstep, a bad choice, unbridled criticism, uninformed gossip, or informed gossip to define who you are. The incomparable wise poet Maya Angelou said it best. *"I can be changed by what happens to me. But I refuse to be reduced by it. Just like hopes springing high, still, I'll rise."*

20. One thing for certain and two for sure: *"A lie can travel halfway around the world while the truth is just getting its shoes on."* Such is the nature of intentional propaganda.
—MSNBC, *Morning Joe*, Joe Scarborough.

21. Transitions are hard. Make them. Many of us struggle with moving forward in unchartered territory and choppy waters, especially after a career fumble. This is normal. We become gun-shy because we can barely swim in the quagmire much less envision a new dream. Dream anyway. Don't allow self-imposed mind games to determine what we can or cannot do next. The quickest way to lose focus on the future is to dwell on the past. I repeat when the past calls, compartmentalize it. Dump it in the voicemail or the spam file of your memories. Sometimes the exposure, the breakup, is the blessing. So, show yourself approved, exercise that mental muscle, and move on.

22. Resilience is the big word in recovery and bouncing back from setbacks. Much has been written on this topic. Andrea Evans credits a few writers in her Harvard Business Review article, "What Resilience Means, and Why It Matters." She discusses several qualities and strategies for bouncing back from

unexpected setbacks. In *Firing Back: How Great Leaders Rebound After Career Disasters*, Jeffrey Sonnenfeld and Andrew Ward cite five steps one should employ to recover from a career catastrophe to match or exceed former accomplishments: *"decide how to fight back; recruit others to help you emotionally; don't be afraid to criticize the people who let you down; buck yourself up to try again; find a new mission that renews your passions to create meaning in your life."*

Al Siebert, PhD, author of several books on resiliency, defines resilience as the *"process of successfully adapting to difficult or challenging life experiences."* His five levels of resiliency are:

a. Maintain your emotional stability, health, and well-being. This is essential.
b. Focus outward on the challenge or problem that must be handled. Research findings show that problem-focused coping leads to resilience better than emotion-focused coping.
c. Focus inwardly on the roots of resiliency, strong self-esteem, self-confidence, and a positive self-concept.
d. Well-developed resiliency skills include the attributes and skills that demand the courage to continue taking responsibility for your actions.
e. Learn the talent of serendipity, the highest level of resiliency. This is the ability to convert misfortune into good fortune. Resilience teaches us to finish strong.

During my crises, every morning I had to find grace to embrace the scripture, Psalm 118:24. *"This is the day the Lord has made; we will rejoice and be glad in it."* Resilience, therefore, is not optional. Finishing strong was my only option. This was required of me. Why? My daughter, while silent during the turmoil, was always watching. I learned five years later after she graduated from Syracuse University during COVID-19 that she was also always listening. She shared with me how she often heard me speak firmly but nicely to folks reminding those calling early in the mornings before 8:00 a.m., that my daughter was my top priority. She quoted my refrain. "Allow me to get my daughter to school on time this morning." My faith was tested. Like Helen Keller instructed, *"Look the world straight in the eyes."* Daily, I looked the lion in the mouth and vowed with some indignation, I shall not be eaten! Do not allow the malice of a few to be the cross that chokes you around your neck. Burn the midnight oil. After the storm, do what you always have. Re-anchor your work ethic. Do the work. Consistently. Mark your work with excellence. Get busy. Be unapologetic with your grind. Do not ask for permission. Reclaim your career. Recognize that you have the right stuff and that you are enough to reboot your GSD (get stuff done) attitude. Now execute your encore! Do the obvious. Show up. Work hard. Wait, watch, and work smart again, again, and again. Remind yourself that the view of your new beginnings will be glorious. Be like a gymaholic. *"Results happen over time, not overnight."* —M. Darhower. So, reboot your spirit. Each morning nurture and coax your new goal. Beat the temptation not to be consistent. Be patient. Remember progress is always slow and incremental. Reboot your work habits. Win with the discipline required of habits. Your new habits will frame the destiny of your next chapter. Your new habits will matter.

23. Let Go. Forgive yourself and believe in a fresh start. The biggest challenge that has tugged at my heart for almost ten years has been to move past the failing of my marriage. At this writing, I still get emotional. Tears still stream. With lots of counseling, therapy, and prayer, I was advised that I finally had to learn to forgive myself for the career blunder and forgive my daughter's father. That doesn't mean I now accept his position, behavior, or decision he made around Brielle's education. It does mean, however, being at peace

with the most important parental decision I made for our daughter during my marriage: Brielle is the beneficiary.

24. *"Some people come into our life as a blessing—while others come into our life as a lesson; so, love them for who they are instead of judging them for who they are not."* —Yolanda Hadid.

    Stated more poetically, I have reckoned with that winter season of my personal life and now better understand this. *"Life is not about waiting for the storm to pass . . . it's learning how to dance in the rain."* —Vivian Greene.

25. Accept the Zen proverb, *"Obstacles do not block the path, they are the path."* Members of the press and, specifically, *The Inquirer*, were aiming to bury me and discredit my work. Despite the transparency I displayed during the group candidate interviews with the editorial board in May 2015, it was never enough. Made up of mostly white suburban men sitting on high, casting invisible wands on who should be elected in the city where they did not reside, was typical. After that circus and round-robin of questions, I did not secure *The Inquirer's* endorsement for the 2015 May Primary election. Their non-endorsement showed many that one monkey does not stop the show. In the end, I excelled and won the 2015 Primary election. My campaign leadership and I mastered how to navigate the road blocks. One of my favorite famous Hollywood actresses, the talented and beautiful Diahann Carroll, described it best. *"Climb the hurdles and weather the storm."* We did!

26. Sorry looks back. I can testify. Worry looks around you. Faith propels you forward. It is important to take stock of our lives often and be aware of the voids. Seek to fill those empty spaces with people who will pray for you and experiences that feed, nourish, and enrich your soul. Spend your quality, limited time with women who love you unconditionally, with no competition. Women who believe, "you got this" kick butt kind of energy.

27. You will arrive on the other side of the storm with a new third eye and a deepened intuition. Embrace your new reality. Psychotherapist Lori Gottlieb reminds us that, *"most big transformations come about from the hundreds of tiny, almost imperceptible, steps we take along the way."*

28. In the dark times, there shall also be singing. In the end, we all win! My faith taught me that walking through the fire refines and redefines us and deepens our trust in God's faithfulness. So, hold on, don't let go. While wounded, encourage yourself daily. Pick yourself up. Don't complain. Please. Do not fret. Do not whine. It's annoying. No one cares. Moving through your day, one hour at a time, one day at a time, one week at a time is all that's required to reclaim your life. Know that the trial has made you stronger, and more circumspect. I suspect you now have a story and a testimony. *"When we long for a life without difficulties, remind us that oaks grow strong in contrary winds and diamonds are made under pressure."* — Peter Marshall.

29. During my grief therapy sessions after the loss of my mom, I learned about the work of Swiss American psychiatrist, Elizabeth Kubler Ross, best known for identifying the five stages of grief experienced by the dying—denial, anger, bargaining, depression, and acceptance. *"The most beautiful are those who have known defeat, known suffering, known struggle, known loss, and have found their way out of the depths. These people have an appreciation, a sensitivity, and an understanding of life that fills them with compassion, gentleness, and a deep loving concern."* You will go through all the stages.

30. One of the most beautiful revelations about recovery from a career firestorm or tripping off the tightrope is one's openness to be vulnerable. It is liberating.

So how do you survive?

- With intention, keep your spirits high.
- Figure out what medicine you need to take each morning that will fuel your day with hope and swallow it.
- Accept that *"you can't go back and change the beginning BUT you can start where you are and change the ending."* —C.S. Lewis.
- Read scripture, or an inspirational passage, listen to your favorite song, or adopt a new practice, meditate.
- Purify your spirit. Look the lion in the mouth and say daily, I will not be eaten.
- Know you are in charge of how your story is going to end.
- Self-talk is magical. Journaling is cathartic. Write it down!
- Manage your anger because the breakthrough is coming. Don't miss the victory coming through on the other side because you're too angry to notice.
- Be encouraged. When you win and show up for the next Inauguration Ceremony at one of the country's National Historic Landmarks, The Academy of Music stage, close your eyes, embrace and savor the metaphorical expression often best expressed by adventurist and mountaineer, Bhawna Dehariya, *"The best view comes from the hardest climb."* Relish in the science and metamorphosis instruction of the butterfly. At the end of the tiny egg process, we see and marvel at their beauty never remembering the imperceptible changes they endure to achieve their beauty to rise as a spirited beautiful, purple butterfly.

CHAPTER EIGHTEEN

RECOVERY

Recovery is about progression, not perfection. —Bill W.

Make a choice. Quickly! Decide whether to either fight back to restore your reputation or not. If the answer is fight and not flight, the next question is to decide how. The January 2007 *Harvard Business Review* examined the tests of a leader: *"Real leaders don't cave in. Defeat energizes them to rejoin the fray with greater determination and vigor. They must take steps to recover their heroic status, in the process proving to themselves and others that they have the mettle necessary to rediscover their heroic mission."* I fully understood that I had too much to lose. So, as minister and inspirational author Rigel J. Dawson advised, I was, *"Willing to eat the crow of embarrassment just as readily as I'd devoured the cake of congratulations."* I dusted off my hurt pride and got about the business of doing.

The Strategies For Recovery Are Numerous. Adopt And Practice New Activities That Foster New Habits. Here Are The Steps I Took.

1. **Let Go**: The actions and steps I took to regain and recover from my personal embarrassing, emotionally exhausting, and expensive setback were many. I had fallen off the tightrope and lost my

balance when I lost my marriage. It took me close to ten years to fully recover financially, emotionally, and psychologically. Only after Brielle's father remarried did I come to grips with the fact that it was time for me to start anew. I applaud everyone who lives Samuel Johnson's belief, *"to marry a second time represents the triumph of hope over experience."*

2. **Release** The Pain: Karen Salmansohn advises in her book, *Open When . . . Letters to Lift My Spirits*, that our ultimate mission after being hurt and deeply disappointed is to *"release the pain of the past and allow karma to kick your offender's booty."* My youngest sister, Alesia, would remind us that forgiveness is a choice. The healing and restoration of self is harder. Forgive, but never forget their names. Memorize and practice one of Barbara Ellen Johnson's devotions. *"The past cannot be changed. Opinions don't define your reality. Everyone's journey is different. Judgments are a confession of character. Overthinking will lead to sadness. Things always get better with time. What goes around comes around. It's okay to let go and move on. You only fail if you quit.""*

3. **Accept:** I accepted that the voters and my constituency knew my reelection had been compromised. I took responsibility and reminded everyone *ad nauseam* that my goal was to reconstruct my career.

4. **Take Action:** To re-establish your hard-earned reputation, you must see your future, plan, and act strategically, intentionally, swiftly, and with a clear purpose. The severity of your situation will be glaringly obvious. So, move quickly. Recruit a select group of professionals to help you emotionally, intellectually, politically, and spiritually. Engage them directly, candidly, and openly. This highly selective tightly woven new group of comrades that surround you are selfless people who care about you, your future, your survival, and your comeback. They are called angels. Provide all the harsh details. Minimize any additional surprises the press may reveal. Admit your mistakes. Treat your trusted advisors who have decided

to give you their talent, time, and treasure with honesty, integrity, and respect. *"An error gratefully acknowledged is a victory won."* — Caroline Gascoigne.

5. **Be Resilient**: Fight for your reputation. Recognize that obstacles are put in our way to see if what you want is worth fighting for. Resiliency becomes a requirement in the face of adversity and sadness. Those mornings when you open your eyes after long and lonely nights after having difficulty falling asleep, rewrite your goals on that notepad beside your bed and focus on who will be the beneficiaries of you staying the course. Exhaust your God-given potential and go further. Act boldly. Be audacious. Proceed always with grace and gratefulness. Repetition of what arms you to rejoice in the mornings at the new start of a new day must be intentional.

6. **Build a Professional Team**: Selectively organize your task force. It will be separate from your social network of family and friends, although anyone from your social network with unique and applicable skill sets can be invited to be on your task force. This special strike force of professionals must each bring expertise that helps you navigate the shark-infested waters ahead. A *Harvard Review* article stipulates, *"research has shown that slight acquaintances are more helpful than closer friends in steering you"* toward recovery.

7. **Confidentiality:** It has enormous currency and must become the North Star. Seek to proceed, with caution, where and when you disclose confidential information as *"Bush ha ayz."* —Hyacinth I. Swaby-Holder. Translated, *"There are ears in the bushes. When you talk, be careful of your surroundings; beware of eavesdroppers."*

8. **Prepare and Research:** Do the homework. Identify a public relations guru with solid experience in crisis management to help you craft language that reassures the corrective action will be immediate. Release a statement that speaks of your intentions to deal with the oversight, omissions, and mistakes which, when corrected, will reveal a clean slate, and reveal the pathway back to restoring your reputation.

I was and am forever grateful to the angel, Sue Jacobson, of Jacobson Strategic Communications, who appeared unsolicited after she read the initial headline. During my dark season, she volunteered to convene a young group of millennial PR firecrackers in her beautiful home during the first week of my crisis. Skillfully, they helped me prepare and navigate for the avalanche of media torpedoes they knew were pending. That team of young women schooled me about a new niche in communications called, Crisis PR. Another angel, Richard R. Harris, Esq., a Village Dad, a.k.a. The Fixer offered guidance in a related episode with another Black female so-called, "consultant" who misrepresented herself during the protracted nightmare. A proud member of the Divine Nine, the Omegas, Chi Delta Chapter, made at the University of Maryland, Richard is "The Man" when you need to get out of a quagmire you did not create. There is a code of honor among the parents and the children of the Village Home Team. Richard honored The Village's unparalleled devotion to each other, unceremoniously, during this dark time and whenever he was called upon, he delivered. For the writing of my memoir, I questioned Susan about her willingness to come to my aid, unsolicited. Her response was, "Blondell, I felt the press was being unfair to you." So, get busy. Collaborate, create, and map out an agenda and action plan with your new trusted advisors who will coach you and guide you, expecting nothing in return. Establish realistic goals and develop problem-solving strategies with benchmarks and timelines. Develop a series of events to boost your name and neutralize the firestorm from those humiliating press reports and the trolls on social media who know neither victory nor defeat. There will be many. Do not allow the press to define you. Exercise strict discipline in the execution of the agreed upon Action Recovery Plan that you and your crisis intervention team construct.

9. **Cleave and Leave:** Make a mental note of those who will take steps backward when you get knocked down. Waste no energy getting angry, just be mindful of who they are, and post-recovery, deal them with caution and, "a long-handled spoon."

10. **Stay Motivated:** Read about others who had career stumbles, even disasters, and took back their lives. This exercise will be restorative. Memorize the motivational message, "*Storms make trees take deeper roots.*" —Dolly Parton.

11. **Speak Up:** Since I had given them a reason to target me, the "got you" reporters who never sought or desired the full story used my circumstances to address issues unrelated to my situation. The Philadelphia press corps, namely Fox 29 for example, with their own agendas made my very public dilemma worse than it had to be. A white male reporter from the *Philadelphia Inquirer* looking for a bigger headline about derailing the career of Congressman Chaka Fattah made me his pawn for the bigger fish he was after. When this happens, you may have no choice, but you do. Choose not to accept the reporter's skewed, often uninformed, or ill-informed, spin of your story. Rebut by asserting yourself when telling your story and pointing out misinformation in theirs. Seek out a seasoned experienced Crises PR professional who will mitigate the negative episode. Be gracefully politely indignant.

12. **Be Intentional:** With the objective of getting our voice out there to rebut erroneous information, my team and I made the intentional decision to call *The Philadelphia Tribune*. I was counting on their objectivity. I remain eternally grateful to Robert W. Bogle, President and CEO, for the opportunity to go before his editorial board to be questioned vigorously without prejudice. His team of journalists allowed me to tell "my

story." Their next day headline read *"Councilwoman Pleads Mea Culpa."* I was grateful to the *Tribune* for allowing me the space to explain my unvarnished full story while acknowledging my role and poor judgment in the career debacle. I faced the editorial board with deep remorse that was heartfelt, avoiding at all costs the "woe is me" disposition.

Show up with your mettle. Then prove your mettle again, again, and again, and again. There is no time for self-pity or helplessness. It is vitally important to remember that no one cares, so show yourself approved and worthy of rebuilding your life. No one has respect for wimps.

13. **Mind Your Health**: Kathleen Barton discusses the obvious in her article, "Resilience: A Must-Have Characteristic in Today's Workplace." "A good diet and regular physical activity help alleviate stress. Resilient people take care of their bodies and minds. They exercise regularly, take time for relaxing activities, and maintain balance in their lives." We all know, of course, that self-care practices promote well-being but may look different for each of us. Pray and ask for the capacity to forgive the jerk that torpedoed your career. Because you forgive them doesn't mean you accept their duplicitous deceitful conduct. Hardly. Never again. As stated earlier, forgive them for you so you can let go and move on with your life. Accept that this new pivot will not be a cake walk.

14. **Maintain Your Sense of Purpose**: In Japan, there is a practice called *ikigai*, a concept of life purpose. Research has shown having a sense of purpose reduces mortality and yields lower levels of the stress hormone cortisol. In a study of nearly 7,000 older Americans, those who revealed that they had no sense of life purpose were twice more likely to die within four years, compared with those who had a sense of purpose. Amy Morin, LCSW, in her essay titled, "The 7 Tips for Finding Your Purpose in Life," links feelings of "a sense of purpose" to positive health. Make sure, even in your darkest times that your purpose is clear. You have a reason

to wake up every morning even if it is to return your life to its intended path before the chaos.

15. **Moxie Up**: Elected and public officials who make mistakes are not allowed to appear vulnerable even when harsh blows render them prostrate. This is the time to stand taller than your fear so that you can mindfully drive toward your renewed, satisfying future, despite the curve balls, speed bumps, and broken stop lights on the road ahead. There are many websites, helplines, and online counseling services available to help us get through the dark tunnel. Corrie Ten Boom authored several books about healing through difficult experiences. Her words reveal truths we need to remember in our daily lives: *"When a train goes through a dark tunnel, you don't throw away your ticket and jump. You sit still and trust the engineer."* All I can do when I hear this metaphor is shake my head. Prolific American novelist, Mercedes Richie Lackey declares, *"If only. These must be the two saddest words in the world."* So, get busy and move on.

16. **Trust God**: No matter how dark your situation gets. Faith matters. Susan L. Taylor stated in her September 1987 *In the Spirit* editorial titled, "The Art of Living," *"Learning to put God first, moment to moment and in all things, gives us divine assurance so we never feel alone. We know we can overcome any obstacle."* Therefore, stay encouraged. Keep going. The lion must never win. No matter what, the lion must not win. And remember, it is God who says you are coming out.

17. **Never Quit:** Quitting is never to be an option. Just **Don't Stop**: Daily, even after my snafu, I prepared for my reelection. During the two years leading into the 2015 Primary election, I doubled down on my efforts. Social media which had evolved significantly from 2011 to 2015 emerged as a major platform for promoting and marketing campaigns. My campaign team mastered social media and used it to advance and elevate my visibility and our campaign message. In addition to the traditional means of

learning about and promoting events of all types, we successfully and effectively incorporated the use and the power of social media. Additionally, I traveled to every corner of Philadelphia to tell my story to anyone who would listen and to boldly ask for their votes and their volunteerism. It did not matter if I had been invited to the event, program, or gathering. I did not care. I went everywhere! *"Because true winners never accept any temporary failure as a final defeat. Great men and women fail, no doubt about that. Almost every biography of a great leader includes stories of defeat, failure, and setbacks. Great generals lose battles. Famous singers lose record deals. Great athletes lose games, championships, and sometimes their jobs. But the common quality they all share is a refusal to quit when failure comes; the unwillingness to accept defeat; the determination to fight back from misfortune."* —Charles Paul Conn.

18. **Focus**: Welcome this fact. *"Life is like a camera, you focus on what's important, capture the good times, develop from the negative, and if things don't work out, take another shot."* —Ziad K. Abdelnour.

19. **Make Sure Your Goals Have Deadlines:** When on a mission to achieve a goal, while not exactly behaving like a bull in a China shop, you should come close. Much to the surprise of many, I was determined to take another shot at the next election. Yielding to those who thought I should not run again and those who felt my career was over was immaterial. Period. Many were never authentic or enthusiastic fans anyway, so why give weight to their opinion? In the end, I won the 2015 Primary election, despite a millionaire candidate who had self-financed spending as much money as I had, close to $250,000. I'm eternally grateful that my reputation was restored, and my work over many decades of service was restored, validated, and convincingly so.

20. **Know That A Comeback is Assured**: At an annual luncheon event hosted by the Philadelphia Visitors and Convention Bureau, I was approached by an African American female executive for one of our city's banks. It was our first time meeting.

We were in line rushing to get our coats to return to our offices. Bumping into each other, she whispered to me, "Your setback is a setup for the comeback," and never skipping a beat, she moved on. She was one of those citizens, a woman, paying attention and rooting for me. This corporate citizen and now minister, Rev. Michele Lawrence, later became one of my spiritual advisors. She was right. The comeback is always stronger than the setback.

21. **Attitude of Gratitude:** Express appreciation to anyone and everyone kind enough to drop you a note, an email, or a text encouraging you. Personally thank friends who care enough to include you in their busy lives and pause long enough to send you a word or two reminding you to look forward as you move yourself out of the valley. Return their goodwill. We live in a digital age. However, I am still old-school and firmly believe handwritten personal notes speak volumes when expressing gratitude and appreciation. The act itself is a short, to-the-point four-sentence note that takes less than five minutes. Anyone who has given their precious time to make your life better is worthy of a tangible gift in a personally handwritten thank-you note. By the way, I should have invested in Hallmark cards. I should have stock in Hallmark. Maybe I will create my line of Blondell's Thank-You cards for Moxie Women next. Start a gratitude practice. Incorporate the consistent practice of stopping at some point during your day to acknowledge the gifts and blessings in your life.

22. **Journaling:** I love to write, so I decided to follow my daughter's example and start a gratitude journal. Tamara Levitt, voice of the Calm app, reminds us that, *"gratitude asks that we make a conscious choice to focus not on what we lack, but on what we have; not on what's wrong, but what is right."* The amazing faith-filled therapist, Dr. Denise Ray Shields, another dynamic miracle of a woman who supported me during the crisis leading to my 2015 reelection,

showed me how to better embrace my losses. During COVID, she sent me a text saying, "*God favors you. Think about it. Take stock of the good. You will see that the good always outweighs the bad.*" This touching reminder brought tears to my eyes. Maya Angelou's instruction is, "*If you must look back, do so forgivingly. If you must look forward, do so prayerfully. However, the wisest thing you can do is be present in the present, Gratefully.*" My! My! My!

23. **Embrace The Lessons Learned**: Time will teach you to gradually learn how to reframe your view of that story. With a fresh lens and renewed perspective, acceptance of your new NOW enriches you with compassion, empathy, and best of all, wisdom revealed due largely because of the painful experience. The unhealthy alternative is becoming emotionally charged at the mention of that episode, which means you are stuck in the valley of regret. Do yourself a favor, don't live there. *"Never cut a tree down in the wintertime."* — Steve Jobs.

24. **Be Patient:** During that dark rocky season, Judge Genece Brinkley, another angel of a friend, gifted me the book, *Prayers That Avail Much*; the chapter on patience teaches: be careful not to make permanent, consequential decisions when you are emotional during the storm. WAIT. Be encouraged. Be patient. Wait. The storm will pass. The spring does come. The sun will rise again.

25. **Reset:** Be fearless in your pursuit to RESET and reboot what sets your soul on fire. Get more comfortable to "*be who you are and say what you feel, because those who mind don't matter and those who matter don't mind.*" —Dr. Seuss.

26. **Reclaim**: Not rebounding from the setback is never optional. I needed to secure once again my most important intangible resource, my reputation. Tarnishing and destroying the reputation of elected officials when they stumble is fodder for the press. Beware.

"In your life's journey, there will be excitement and fulfillment, boredom, and routine, and even the occasional train wreck. But when you have picked a dream that is bigger than you, that truly reflects the ideals that you cherish, and that you can positively affect others, then you will always have another reason to carry on." —Pamela Melroy.

Carpe Diem

CHAPTER NINETEEN

SELF-CARE MATTERS

"Be still for a moment. The world will wait." —Unknown.

Overscheduled as always, every morning I would rush out, harried, and breathless to take Brielle to childcare, Powell Elementary School, and later the Agnes Irwin School for Girls. Mom would remind me to slow down. I was always content seeing my mom leaving the house at the same time every morning, with her gym roller bag filled with essentials and a snack. Mom was so conscientious about her physical fitness and wellness. This continued until my mom's health became compromised and started to fail after her fourth fall eighteen years later after moving into her mother-in-law's suite.

"Blondell, please slow down." These were the commanding words my mom in her soft-spoken voice would regularly utter whenever I whizzed through her attached mother-in-law suite on the first floor of our home. As a mother and a wife, I was accustomed to my role as nurturer and caregiver taking care of family and leaving my needs for last. Being intentional about stealing time took a back seat to all my other responsibilities and was not a priority for too many years.

Still, as a former dancer, one always needs to be in tip-top shape. During my years on the City Council, my attention to optimum conditioning slipped. However, I did manage to eke out a little time for moderate self-care making weekly trips to the sixth floor of City Hall for my walks with weights in hand. Twenty-four months after my departure, in a funk, I was far from practicing self-care. From our upbringing, the basics of clean, healthy eating were a rote habit for my sisters, brother, and me. The staff never had to ask what I wanted to order for lunch. They knew: a Caesar salad, no croutons, salad dressing on the side. I kept extra virgin olive oil, a healthy staple, and water in my office fridge.

After my first full term in office and before she retired, Councilwoman Marian B. Tasco, a senior and highly respected Democratic Party leader and veteran member of the Council, would stop by my office and admonish me for not taking breaks. So much more can be said about the fearless Marian B. Tasco. What a trailblazer! What a woman! Even when she disagreed with your policy stance, she pushed women to do more and be more than their potential revealed. I am a grateful beneficiary of her Southern swagger! Like a mother would to her child, she would chastise me for not taking a break to do anything but council business during the Council summer recess. Deliberately, she invited me to join her and her close circle of friends, Joann Bell, and Soror Linda Miller to the Jersey shore to ensure I took an R & R break. No work bags were allowed.

Once I was elected to the leadership circle, stepping away from Council meetings became increasingly more difficult and, at best, unacceptable. Council leadership brings another thick layer of responsibilities, duties, and a need to be present for formal Council hearings and last-minute legislative developments. Attendance at informal sessions following hearings was mandatory. An escape to the council president's office to recap with the other member of our three-legged stool, Councilman Bill Greenlee, was always uplifting. In my spirit I recognized it was becoming less and less satisfying as a respite and was no longer adequate to serve as my antidote to the sometimes stupidness of long workdays.

When squeezing time and getting to the gym became impossible, I terminated my 12th Street Gym membership. It was the one place I could escape and zone out with my music and ear pods and no one knew my name. That worked for a couple of years until someone recognized I was one of the seventeen. Interruptions to ask questions about City Council legislation became constant. My limited time at the gym to punch in forty-five to sixty minutes became a wish, and with my precious anonymity lost, the time had come for me to abandon Plan A and find an alternative means to stay physically fit. The stress was constant and palpable. I needed to find a way to stay sane. Figuring out an alternative means to manage my mental health in between the endless nine days a week, endless days, Council formal and informal meetings, briefings, hearings, emails, and phone calls became imperative. Whenever an empty hour appeared on my schedule, I began a new, if irregular, practice after leaving a hearing in Council chambers. I would head to my office, grab my ten-pound weights and ear pods, proceed to the stairwell, and tackle the seven flights of stairs walking every other step.

Conditioned to know our body is our most precious possession, as choreographer Harold Pearson from Philadanco used to preach, "*Girl, it would behoove you to take care of it.*" I knew I needed to do better.

In 2017, I was experiencing stress like never before. My mom's health was deteriorating fast. Thanks to my sister Pandora, for years my Mom had a steady, daily routine of self-care at the West Philadelphia YMCA. Mom was exceedingly conscientious about her weight and appearance and even ailing would kindly admonish me when she would notice that due to my spreading bottom, my pants were a little too snug. In my mom's eyes, this was not cool. I counted myself pretty lucky to have my in-house weight accountability captain nudging me to stay within my 155–160 lb., a fat size ten for my entire twenty years in City Council. The death of my mom in 2017 ushered in a blue period for me. Added to the stress of my career blunder, I was simply on autopilot. Self-care was the last thing on my list.

I cannot identify the precise moment or period in 2018 when I began to feel empty and depleted. The feeling was stark. I can say and now admit with the benefit of hindsight that I was also still depressed and still grieving the passing of my mom.

I vividly remember attending a city hall gathering hosted by Islander Councilwoman Maria Quiñones Sánchez and feeling irritable, bothered, and unhappy. This feeling was rare and unusual, as Maria's office was one of the rare places in city hall, where I would run to recover from a long, exhausting, mentally fatigued day. It was almost two years after my life-changing experiences, compounded by the loss of my mother and I had not started grief counseling.

Wobbling through the emotional waves of memory and loss, it was amazing that I recognized at some point, I had hit an invisible wall. Emotionally, I was depleted, drained, and burnt out. Being a helicopter Mom was exacting and being an empty nester was even more sobering. My invisible wall finally revealed itself after I lost my mom. It was clear the time had come to recalibrate and reassess my career, my friendships, my goals and my future as a single mom of a new college graduate. This new state of living spurred my need for greater attention to self-care. I also realized that my mental health was a very important part of my self-care, and I took it very seriously. *Breathe* magazine in its April 2021 edition, discussed that, at some juncture, one must get in touch with their "*V.I.T.A.L.S. Values—what's most important to you in life? Interests—what are your passions? Temperament—your innate preferences? Activities—what does the rhythm of your life look and feel like? Life mission—what gets you up in the morning? What inspires you? Strengths—what are the talents and the emotional parts of your character?*"

By January 2019, I had not examined my V.I.T.A.L.S. The discovery was I had been long been running on empty. Twelve months after I departed from Council, in addition to being in a funk, the almighty COVID-19 hit. When the 2020 pandemic hit, for the many like me who longed to push the pause button life did not allow, it was a blessing in disguise. God knows I am one of the thousands thankful for the opportunity the pandemic provided me to again spend quality time with Brielle, and to my delight, become a better cook, a very therapeutic activity indeed. During the pandemic, a group of my sorority sisters stayed connected through our new daily group chat to help each other through that unprecedented global trying disruption period we all faced. One of the Sorors sent an in-your-face challenge to our group. This challenge was for the dreamers who dream and were willing to dig in and do the work required to make that dream come true. I, like most of America, was glued to the television, so her message resonated with me. I had left city hall a year previous and was contemplating my next career move. I had new and unfilled dreams, but I remained uncertain of my next steps. Watching death all around and realizing that life is fleeting, I took that message as a sign to *carpe diem* to act on the dictate my daughter had already suggested. Because of this jump-start message, I began to dig deeper and lean into a long-held dream of mine—becoming a book author. While it all felt so daunting, I fully understand there is no substitute for doing the work. Soon afterwards every morning for weeks I woke up to my cup of Joe, painstakingly organized the boxes of dozens of files and photos, heeding Julie Thorn's inspirational words, "*If you don't sacrifice for what you want, what you want becomes the sacrifice.*" I got busy.

Quarantine not only forced me to prepare mentally and physically to make a major new change in my life. It also allowed me the time to be more intentionally devoted to self-care. Parenthetically my lack of self-care was noticeable to a couple of dear girlfriends of the Travel Crew. Having girlfriends in your inner circle, who care about you and your well-being is another miracle. They whisked me away for a glorious weekend at the Poconos Spa and Retreat to celebrate my sixtieth birthday in grand style. Their instruction to me was to just, "show." It was a memorable experience that exemplified the beauty of true friendships. I am forever grateful to these fabulous, successful career women who were also walking the tightrope. Their generosity of spirit and their subtle way of sending me a message that self-care should not be the letter Z in the alphabet was priceless.

Self-care is more than just eating healthy. Mental, emotional, spiritual, and physical fitness is about getting and staying centered on who you are at your core. Spending time in solitude is when you are most likely to hear and process thoughts and actions calling and burning in your soul. My best example was the time I spent during those four cold days in January 2019 alone in contemplation that led to my firm decision to step away from center stage and the public arena of the City Council. It was during that alone time at my Happy Place, ABC Summer Wind, that I came to grips with the revelation to choose a new direction for Act IV of my career and my life.

One of my many aha moments during the pandemic was awakening to the fact that endings were very hard for me. My evidence of this insight was I had kept boxes of memorabilia from my marriage for ten years, my Mom's library of books, on a variety of topics, on everything about health, the brain, herbs, and encyclopedias on home maintenance, and more. They came in handy. Turning the page on a chapter that had required courage and faith was tough, harder than I imagined. Sobering and indescribable, COVID-19, which had literary stopped the world with a microscopic virus, put in perspective with a level of gravitas, an impulse I had not fully appreciated. Life can be fleeting and not promised. Like millions around the world, I was forced to Be! Still! Facing my losses was now inescapable. My self-maintenance was upgraded to self-care. COVID-19 helped me to rediscover what true self-care looks like.

Self-care can be achieved in small ways with small, focused tweaks in one's daily routine. While I was familiar with the 21/90 rule, the pandemic allowed me to practice this habit more consistently. "It takes twenty-one days of inspired, committed action to change a habit, and ninety days of inspired committed action without deviation to create a lifestyle. The secret weapon is inspired committed action—a simple premise that when applied without deviation can be transformative." —*The American Way* magazine 2019 article, written by Sanyika, titled, "Inspire Yourself by Following This Simple Principal."

Being older now, and since losing my mom, I have a new approach to self-care that is more wholesome and selfish. Those who know me well also know that my favorite place on earth is walking or sitting in a chair with my music. Give me my *O, The Oprah Magazine*, and my favorite spirit, yes, that kind of spirit, and some water to gaze at, and I can find Zen for hours. The one place I can immediately shift my thoughts from overdrive to calm is the beach. An interesting tidbit I learned also during COVID is that mental health experts affirm that the two ancient antidotes to stress are nature and water to the physical body. Research and scientific evidence corroborate that a relaxing time at the beach watching the waves can be a mood booster. Jenny Roe, PhD, director of the Center for Design and Health at the University of Virginia, who studies the mental and physical benefits of these so-called blue spaces states that "Water has the quality of magic." The beach, a.k.a. my happy place, has been and will always be my retreat from the chaos and the hard balls life throws.

The Power of Friendship

Before the pandemic, I had the good fortune to be a part of a group chat that greeted us with a spiritual blessing and scripture daily. During the pandemic and since my newly adopted self-care practice and habit forever going forward requires me to spend a few minutes every morning reading from one of my library of inspirational books that offer daily positive affirmations on my night table including my bible. Sharing my inspiration for the day with my siblings, my Sorors, the Travel Crew (TTC), The Village Moms, Jamilla and

Vernease, and an assortment of Penn Staters is a newly adopted daily morning practice that mimics learning ballet dance technique all over again. I love it! This new "habit" nourishes my day.

While it was difficult to build new friendships in the often-unkind world of electoral politics, cultivating lasting relationships with some amazing women brought me so much joy. In retrospect, I will confess two things. One, I am firmly convinced that The Village Moms, the Travel Crew, and a short list of longtime friendships from Danco, Penn State, and CORE saved me from burnout and despondency. Two, I can now submit that one reason among many that led to my pivotal surprise change for others was my emotional burnout. My sister Pandora's expression would best describe that feeling I tried to dismiss in this way. "I'm over it!"

Through a couple of painful lessons about friendship, I came to appreciate that self-care includes surrounding yourself with uplifting friends far removed from the world of politics. Family, the anchor of my life, provided a safe space and joy. On occasions, my colleagues and I, the Islanders, would escape to that mountaintop home in Puerto Rico.

I have had the good fortune to call upon the cherished relationships I treasured long before my arrival on the fourth floor of City Hall Council Chambers. My age-old friendships minted it at Girls' High with Terry, Janice, Jennifer, Valerie, Diane, and Carolyn, and longtime friendships seeded and cultivated further at Penn State will forever hold a special place in my heart. Linda, Marcia, Yolanda, and my Best Buddy of the Philadanco Dolls, Jamilla. These cherished friendships I continue to enjoy and appreciate today. Collectively these women never took invisible steps backwards and were the rocks that allowed me to solidly stand on when my footing was wobbly.

A gazillion books have been written about friendship, what it is, and what it looks like. What counts most to me are good friends who just "show up," no questions asked. While on the campaign trail,

Sandi LeBlanc, who cooked Brielle's favorite mac and cheese during my 2015 campaign, Terry, who wrote that first $2,500 check to help me kick start the payment of the $40,000 in fines, Devon Allen who saw me downtown and scolded me for not giving myself grace, Brian and Alesia who sent the initial check for me to reimburse my campaign account. Friends who never keep an accounting of what "I did for you." Friends who just did and DO and in doing help you keep your sanity! Friendship is the toughest thing to explain but one of the most precious encounters you can make in life. While I made a few friends after I entered politics, it was my friendships, pre-politics that became the stars in my life. Scheduling time with The Village Moms was relatively easy because of our unwavering commitment to our Village children and their well-being. However, Council demands and duties forced me to often sacrifice quality time with my sisters, my Sorors, and the Travel Crew. But here is the beauty of everlasting friendships, *"You don't always see them, but you know they're always there."* —Unknown.

Choosing to be in the presence of those who nurture your spirit with intention and no agenda except to share joyful times is a key to self-care. Humans need connection and joyful connections can carry you a long way spiritually, psychologically, and emotionally. My Travel Crew morphed and coalesced into a delightful place of refuge during the last ten years of my Council career. Through an abundance of great times, these women gave me a safe space with no judgment, happiness, and laughter in unmeasurable ways, that I could never imagine. Masters in self-care and fun times The Travel Crew's keen awareness and sensitivity to my inability to devote time to self-care further revealed that our collective professional relationships had evolved into endearing lasting friendships. I adore these women because our careers were 360 degrees different from my own. I was always a student in their presence. Their savviness in the hospitality and tourism industry is and remains unmatched and admirable. What are the lessons?

1) Seek out, show appreciation for, and celebrate other women in opposite unrelated careers from your own. You will learn from and be inspired by the mutually beneficial authentic love for each other.
2) Develop a principle or spiritual system that strikes the delicate balance between work and rest. The world will wait. Prioritize rest.

Carpe Diem

CHAPTER TWENTY

WAKE UP RUNNIN'

"Our goals can only be reached through a vehicle of a plan, in which we must fervently believe, and upon which we must vigorously act. There is no other route to success." —Pablo Picasso.

There is no shortcut to success. If you want to catch a star you must wake up runnin' daily. Wake up runnin' means a preparedness to take risks, albeit calculated, but risks, nonetheless. Have a plan B, know what you are willing to sacrifice, and the discipline required to attain your goal. This mindset is the only way you win. No shortcuts! No substitutes! Though there may be detours, you want positive results at the journey's end. Seldom will this happen if you lack insight, foresight, and action that comes from consistent, hard, and smart work.

I have been there and done that as a candidate running for an elected office six times. On the campaign trail, I often told bright-eyed lawyers running for a judgeship who often whined and complained about the road ahead what I had been told by my former boss, Congressman Chaka Fattah, "Please, don't complain about it, Be about it." When you make the difficult decision to run for a judgeship or a dog catcher, be prepared to do the work, all the work, all day, every day sun up to sun down for the entire run of the campaign. Think of it as a marathon. If everything about the process surprises you, then it is clear you didn't prepare even for the dress rehearsals. Preparation, repetition, dry runs, and moxie are not just for a while on the campaign trail, but they are constants in life. Preparation acquaints you with the possible obstacles, repetition allows you to work out the kinks in the plan, dry runs allow you to simulate the most likely scenarios you meet along the way, and moxie is the attitude you bring to the table. If you find yourself whining, check it. Because anything less than a moxie attitude, suggests you are not ready, built for and prepared for showtime and clearly not ready to wake up runnin'.

As a dancer in my twenties going to auditions, 99 percent of them in New York City, I had to venture into unknown and uncharted territory. I was no triple threat. Dance was my only creative discipline. I couldn't carry a tune, and I never studied acting. But I was young, bright-eyed, and excited about the possibilities of making my dream come true. I felt I could beat the odds. My mom thought I had lost my mind, and as my golden geese gave advice, she thought she would save me from the steep mountain climb ahead. Knowing my dream was on the top of the mountain, my attitude was please, Mom, allow me to figure it out. For over a year, I made my weekly Amtrak trips to the Big Apple to audition. I scoured for dance auditions in *Backstage*, a publication for performing artists interested in the world of entertainment. Yes, I had the fire in my belly, and I woke up every single day…runnin'.

That was all good but let me give you a few more facts. I was five feet, three inches tall, which was quite short for a dancer at that time, twenty-eight years old, and lived in Philadelphia. As you know from my story, I drove back and forth to Atlantic City, performing two shows six days a week, and slept under our make-up tables happy as a bedbug. When Fattah offered me a position a decade later with a two-hour commute each way, I seized the day, *carpe diem*. My Girls' High indoctrination had revealed itself again.

While you may wake up runnin', put the regrets on a shelf. Do you until you know from the inside out that the door will not open? Whatever your circumstance, your motivations, your aspirations, your challenges, your endeavors, and your setbacks, in your professional or personal lives, get up in the morning and run like hell. There is an old oral African story that goes like this. *"Every morning in Africa a gazelle gets up. It knows it must run faster than the lion or it will be eaten. Every morning in Africa a lion gets up. It knows it must run faster than the Gazelle or it will starve to death. So, at the end of the day, it does not matter if you are a lion or a gazelle. When the sun comes up, you had better be running."*

Earl Graves Sr., founder of the premier entrepreneurial magazine *Black Enterprise* promoted his teachings in a quarterly newsletter, *The Black Enterprise Professional Exchange*. Through the newsletter, Mr. Graves covered a range of topics and strategies for Black professionals. His inaugural newsletter provided a menu of suggestions to help Black folks battle and navigate tough and tricky career decisions.

Tweaking from my professional experiences, and a few of his suggestions, I began my reboot. I drafted a defined future career plan. Being intentional and strategic when defining my goals helped me better integrate the skills I brought to the table. With these skills I possessed, 1. I needed to develop my new career as an author. Understanding the road map of the publishing industry would help me pivot when and if unexpected curve balls or opportunities appeared in the road ahead, so I have much to learn. 2. I must *master my interpersonal skills and the lingo* of my new career so I will be able to relate to everyone, from the senior VP, or managing editor all the way up to the CEO and publisher. 3. *Be productive. Meeting deadlines* implies well-honed time management skills. Be about it. 4. *Develop sharp analytical skills.* Most superstars in the workplace have made their reputation on their ability to integrate facts and figures and make the right decisions based on their findings. Therefore, success trackers are found in positions responsible for the bottom line. 5. *Write well.* If you do not write well, learn to write well. Invest in yourself and take an online writing course. Nothing is worse than submitting a sloppy report with typographical and grammatical errors and inaccurate information. It's not only important to understand how to write a good report, but you must also learn your supervisor's style, and honor it. 6. *Be well-read and develop diversified interests.* Part of any business, irrespective of sector, is conversing with clients and contacts. You can't talk about business all the time. Never go out with a business associate without having glanced at the latest front page of the local newspaper (or your social media news alerts). 7. *Engage in social networking.* Social networking has value and involves establishing business contacts at dinners, tennis games, professional conferences, conventions, and the golf course.

8. *Show interest in all aspects of your company or the organization.* Reading memos and promotions, year-end reports, and government regulations not affecting your department but your company, may seem boring, but constant updating is necessary, especially considering the increased and never-ending downsizing, mergers, and acquisition activities.

While these nuggets of career advice were presented and discussed by Mr. Graves in the late 1980s, they still have great value, purpose, and relevance today. *"At the banquet table of nature, there are no reserved seats. You get what you can take, and you keep what you can hold."* —A. Philip Randolph.

I have finally learned to embrace change and the new self-imposed station in my life, i.e., the writing of my career experience in electoral politics with a memoir lens. Brielle has finished law school and has started her journey into womanhood as a young junior lawyer chasing her dreams. She is not a dream hunter. Brielle is clear that dreaming is a wonderful thing, but dreams without a plan and work is a wish. My prayer is that I have been a good example and prepared my daughter sufficiently for the joy laced with the strategies required to confront and face the curve balls of life that are sure to come. I appreciate who I have become. I can and do, without exception, ask for no permission to just be still most often at my slice of heaven, the beach. This new space is like a new muscle I had to build. My mom would be proud.

YES. You can act with intention on behalf of others AND be intentional about the directive Stanford University Law School Professor Gregory Ablavsky advised his law students. *"Engage in radical self-kindness."* The two are not exclusive. This approach to self-care is another example that selects choices in our careers as in legislative matters do not have to be an "or". Your choices can be an "and." Choices can be an *and*. This practice and approach to legislation remains my favorite lesson learned from my Council BFF, Councilwoman Maria Quiñones Sánchez dictates.

> I hope that you become enriched and enlightened by the antidotes, the stumbles, and the valuable lessons learned and recognize that the kindness and goodness received from others reveals this revelation best expressed by fitness trainer, Lynne Schroeder, *"Lifting others up is great strength training."*

> Indeed. These selfish angels, save us during those seasons of weariness and despair. Their generosity of spirit lifts us, and magnifies the notion that, *"If a blade of grass can grow in a mountain cliff, a human being empowered with an invincible faith can survive all odds the world can throw against her tortured soul."* —Robert H. Schuller.

My battery soul survived. I praise God. Still! As you read through these pages, remember, *"Everyone has a copyright of their own life."* —Hilton Als. Walking on a tightrope backward in high heels, blindfolded is mine. In the darkness, I learned a lot during my interrogation of Blondell. *"Vulnerability is the birthplace of love, belonging, joy, courage, empathy, and creativity"* —Brene Brown.

While contemplating or waiting to get in the ring, self-motivation, honing techniques, and mastering the dance of your career, will get you ready for your premier performance. Become possessed with perfecting writing skills, research skills, cultivating relationships across sectors, reading campaign reports, studying voter patterns, and building your database of everyone you have met since birth. The latter becomes the seedlings for the network essential for the launch of your campaign. Once you successfully execute your campaign plan and win the prize of victory, the real work begins.

Framing your legislative agenda stems from the awareness of the myriad issues and problems facing the community you wish to serve locally, regionally, and nationally. Having a fundamental knowledge of those issues is paramount. Learn the breadth and depth of these issues. Read everything related and become a sponge. Tackle and track the demographics and trends, and seek out creative, orthodox, and unorthodox solutions to issues. And just when you think you've got it, that's when the work begins. Knowing and having a grasp of the issues is not enough. The real work begins when you must decide which of those myriad issues you'll wrap your arms around to champion. The list of issues in underserved communities is unlimited. It includes everything from affordable and accessible childcare and housing, business and economic development, employment and job trends to education and skills training, arts and culture, hospitality and tourism, the environment and sustainability, technology, and more. Solving every issue presented will be impossible so it's best to decide which issue you feel most capable of influencing to a positive outcome. Decide based on your experience, interests, training, and skill sets. *"Take the time to deliberate, but when the time for action has arrived, stop thinking and go in." —Napoleon Bonaparte.*

This is what politicians are elected to do, and it is their responsibility to deliver to the best of their ability positive results.

It is also imperative to examine one's spirit before and after a successful election. Did the win inspire you further or drain you? Is this truly your life's calling? Can you go the distance? If the answer is yes then teach others how to navigate this political terrain successfully, including other colleagues. To be effective you will need and require support for the passage of legislation from your colleagues.

If your fight is for social progress, you walk the tightrope between realism and hopefulness. Craft language for the ideas and ideals of those issues you firmly believe are possible and present them in a way that can scale barriers. Last, and most importantly, adopt the mantra of a former US senator, the forty-sixth president, Joe Biden. When negotiating for the constituencies that look to you for hope and finding solutions, be strategic. Allow no one to tell you what their priorities are. Remember to trust and verify. Tell them, *"Show me your budget and I will tell you what your priorities are."* Richard Kreigbaum states in one of my favorite books on leadership, titled *Leadership Prayers*. *"The budget declares the operative values and priorities of the organization. It also declares our investment in future directions. The budget is a leadership plan, and budgeting is a leadership process."*

Budgets are kings, queens, jacks, and jokers. The money behind a project will determine its success or failure. Mayor John F. Street, former Finance Chair, and former president of the City Council was a masterful guru with the city budget and well respected by then Mayor Ed Rendell for his remarkable knowledge and skill in the negotiation of the budgeting process. During my tenure, two more standouts came to my attention, President Darrell Clarke, former protégée of Mayor Street, and Councilwoman Maria Quiñones

Sánchez, who seized the role of Council's Appropriations Chair. They were exceptional stewards of the city's budgeting process, and the Greater Philadelphia Chamber of Commerce agreed with my humble opinion. These two colleagues were budget gurus whom I admired greatly.

Mastering the delicate balance between juggling dense, difficult, and competing legislative demands and the myriad unlimited needs of a city with a grossly limited city budget becomes the norm for a legislator. Stack this stress on top of making hard choices about what issue or issues, all of which are important, will have to be sacrificed. Welcome to the intoxicating tug and pull that exists for all legislative victories and losses. Striking the delicate balance as you walk the tightrope to meet the competing interests and demands of interest groups is exhausting. If you are in the world of electoral politics for the right reasons, then seeking mutually acceptable agreements without giving in becomes an attraction. I loved this aspect of my work. The application of the tenets of Roger Fisher and William Ury's book, *Getting to Yes, Negotiating Without Giving In*, my go-to manual before many of those hard-nosed negotiation sessions, helped me to underscore Ann Landers's opinion of this book. *Getting to Yes, "Teaches you how to win without compromising friendships."*

In the end, what mattered most about the nurturing relationship and finding common ground was exemplified by Street. He fostered and cared about my success and the success of several on the City Council. Mayor Street had many infamous sayings. One of my John Street favorites was *"Everyone can have their say, but only nine will get their way."* He and his Council ombudsman and advisor, George R. Burrell, Esq., had a clear vision for the city and goals aligned with that vision for selected Council members. Further, they were strategic in their offerings of legislative ideas that might advance or strengthen that Council member's profile and legislative record. I was grateful to be in the small group. They knew that I, as a freshman member of the Council, cared deeply about one core constituency, our city's children and youth. Thus, when the subject of tax breaks for corporate Philadelphia reared its big head, they knew my prevailing question was bound to be, what is in this deal for our city's children?

By my third term in the City Council with twelve years of legislative experience, I had risen to a leadership position in the Council, and I had achieved a modicum level of success with a reputation as a champion for improving our city's educational outcomes, making issues impacting children and families, women's rights, health care, and the arts as my signature public policy issues. My style was never to seek the spotlight and show off which I found disingenuous, but unfortunately, as an elected official, one must get comfortable tooting their own horn. I found this uncomfortable as my training was to just do the work consistently, confident the results and outcomes would ultimately speak for themselves. I learned what had to be done throughout my tenure including limiting self-praise during election cycles. My focus on getting things done and conducting myself in a manner that would make others, most especially African American Latinx women proud of my work as their City Council at-large representative mattered most. I achieved that balance.

One of my early lessons learned when crafting legislation was honing the skill of carefully selecting legislative language. Relentlessly choosing words that flawlessly capture the intended goal and yet with a nuanced fragility that in the end does not offend those who must make the concessions is difficult at best. This too is another example of walking the tightrope backward! Here is what I believed and knew for sure as I steadfastly held my position to what I wanted for our city's children: a society is often measured by how it treats and values its women and children.

Philly Pre-K Citywide Childcare initiative made possible through the city's unprecedented, sweetened beverage tax deserves praise. As a former educator, I was one of the nine reliable votes for this legislative measure. By far, this initiative was the one signature impactful legislative achievement during his disappointing tenure as a shadow mayor. Regretfully, however, mayoral successes can and do get overshadowed quickly. We all have short memories of the good that elected officials do. Hard to explain how too many of us have long memories of the negative. What too often sticks in the memories of voters is how elected leaders conduct themselves, and manage and handle a crisis during chaos, turmoil, and controversy.

When you decide to get in the leadership ring, you accept that unbridled often uninformed criticism is one price of leadership that comes with the territory. While every mayor's accomplishments matter, ultimately one's legacy is measured by how one navigates and manages the tough, nerve-shattering times accompanied by the sleepless nights. Ajeenah Amir, a former Kenney administration staffer, summarized it best. *"You meet the times, or the times meet you."* ("Inside Jim Kenney's Terrible, Horrible, No Good, Very Bad Year," Phillymag.com, Josh Kruger, 12/5/2021) Google it. Read his assessment. I agree and need not say anymore.

What not to do? Yeah, I know. Worrying. OMG. There is not enough to be said about worrying, except that you suffer twice. Worrying is an exhaustive misuse and abuse of your imagination. Manage it. Choose to hone a new skill. Sharpen an existing skill. Learn to kick worry in the teeth. STOP IT!

What I know for sure is strength in spirit is what we gain from the madness, the prolonged anger, and the heartache that we survive.

In 1985, after a breakup with a former boyfriend who asked to marry me three times while all I wanted to do was dance, I purchased a framed poem from a Hallmark store. Today it still sits on my bookshelf. Even in my twenties, I searched for poetic inspirational messages and passages to hold my heart together during difficult life episodes. I had to relearn and re-memorize, " A Few Words of Caring" following my very painful and difficult divorce.

"After a while, you learn that love doesn't mean leaning, that kisses aren't contracts, and presents aren't promises. And you begin to accept defeats with your head up and your eyes open, With the grace of a woman, not the grief of a child. So, you plant your own garden and decorate your own soul, instead of waiting for someone to bring you flowers, And you learn that you can endure . . . that you really are strong, and you really do have worth, and that with every new tomorrow comes the dawn." —Unknown.

What I can say to you as an aspiring elected official is this: if you feel the tug of your heartstrings for public service, expect very few thank-yous for a job well done. Make sure the rent you pay for living is indeed the rent you want to pay and be certain you understand that your service to others will require sacrifices of unmeasurable proportions. My word of caution is to be clear-eyed about how willing you are to do this important work consistently, tirelessly, and without complaining. Examine your heart and trust your answer to these questions. If you are a working mom devoted to being a present mom, meditate on this question—can my service to others give my life daily purpose, nine days a week, thirty-two hours a day, while I honor my role as wife and an engaged helicopter parent? Electoral politics is a place where you must arm your heart to embrace the surprises, dissonance, and discoveries.

As you read on, you will discover that politics is a contact sport that requires a thick skin. No wimps are allowed. You will also discover that life's challenges when confronted with absurdities and adversity are not meant to paralyze but rather designed to reveal what you are made of. I hope that my story pulls at heartstrings and touches the nerves of women who dare to walk the tightrope of marriage, motherhood, demanding careers, and fulfilling friendships, all while squeezing in time for self-care. Accept that perfection is not in the cards. NOT EVER!

Last, I must tell you that service to others is hard. Everyone will have an opinion about you, your work, and what they believe you should be doing. When you step into the boxing ring sometimes in the face of criticism, remain steadfast. Electoral politics needs noble, selfless women like you, who are driven to act: women who dare to change things for the better and make a small difference while serving others. Every community needs conscientious citizens with big hearts who will link arms with like-minded women and men to face the wrongs of society. Underserved families and under-resourced communities yearn for worker bees who will give their best to right their grievances. The world longs for doers who will resist the silence and dare those who hang in the wings of the stage with their fingers crossed lying dormant when injustice rears its ugly face. James Baldwin said it best in his essay written to the *New York Times* in 1962: *"Not everything that is faced can be changed, but nothing can be changed until it is faced."* Therein lies our hope, no longer a wish. It becomes a belief. Hope gives us the ability to look at things as they are and still with confidence and hard work believe that better days are coming. I join you and remain confident that women from all walks of life will continue to do the necessary work to tackle and shift the paradigms, albeit incrementally toward fairness and justice for all. *"The wise with hope support the pains of life."* —Euripides, 484–407 BC, Greek dramatist. I agree.

My story is for all women. This reality applies to women in other nontraditional fields as well as those seeking to make a difference in their community or the C-Suite. I specifically want to note the moxie women who are committed to making a small difference in the corner of the world they occupy. These women who are ordinary women, single, separated, divorced, married, or widowed, part-time workers, minimum wage earners, or full-time execs, these women all have one thing in common, they are all driven, confident, and clear about making their dreams real and devoted to missions bigger than themselves. These women fully understand that no one can pursue their dream but the woman in the driver's seat of her car. They elect to make a positive difference in their chosen professional field, cause, or special interest, never complaining.

My role now as a veteran is to offer guideposts that inspire young women to meet their moments of opportunity while bracing themselves to tackle unexpected and harsh moments. To offer a hand when they get knocked down because no one is exempt from experiences that tarnish their best efforts. With failure, they must rise again. I ask that as a moxie woman, you trust that you can meet and exceed your potential, the things dreams are made of. There are no shortcuts or substitutes for the hard work required. No substitute for the self-examination that must proceed with your decision to step into the ring. In her 2011 commencement address to Harvard University, Africa's first elected woman, head of state, President of Liberia, Ellen Johnson Sirleaf proclaimed, *"The size of your dreams must always exceed your current capacity to achieve them. If your dreams do not scare you, they are not big enough."*

When you arrive at the decision-making table, your power includes showing up prepared. Of all the commentary from a 2006 interview with Wendy Ginsberg of the *Philadelphia Business Journal*, she encapsulated and titled the article, "From Philadanco Dancer to Councilwoman, Blondell Reynolds-Brown, You should always come prepared." I was completely satisfied with her summary of our session. Get busy and take the time to plan. One of my staff mantras was: "Prior, proper planning will always prevent the replay of a painful performance." Recruit and identify your new team. Build your inner circle of professionals who show by their actions that they love you, appreciate you, and want to see your success in the good times and your recovery following the ugly times. You will discover in your process that there will be folks, and not necessarily your family and friends, who can provide the needed expertise to operate in multiple fields and disciplines simultaneously during your recovery process. In crises, determine what YOU must do and what someone else can do for you. Set the priorities. Recognize the interdependence of decisions. Set deadlines and time limits. Then stick to the schedule.

I cannot say enough about planning. For the skeptics and those who practice the ad hoc approach to building your career, consider another one of my top ten books in my library on leadership, Gabriel Hevesi's book, *Checklist for Leaders*. He devotes an entire chapter to planning.

> *Leaders Plan. Staying successful requires the courage to change directions. To dump, when necessary, is a major strength of the past. To adapt quickly to new situations. Those who don't plan to fall behind. Organizations can't live on past successes, sticking to their old ways, their old procedures, and their old products. Past success offers no guarantee of continuity without planning, thinking ahead, and anticipating change. If you miss the train, the distance between those on board and you—still on the platform—increases fast.*

Citizens who choose to leap into electoral politics know at the door the service you provide and the work you do on behalf of others will be no crystal stair. Showing appreciation is always a welcomed gesture. Taking the time to practice the age-old courtesy that is dying slowly, a handwritten personal note provides an uplift to one's spirit that is incalculable. Show appreciation to those who walk the tightrope of service to others. Seek to be creative in your approach. You will discover paying it forward and lifting others is rewarding and great fuel for your soul. Your sense of satisfaction is priceless.

Whether a job seeker pursuing employment, as a dancer in an audition, or as a political candidate on the campaign trail, here is one fact. *"You must knock on doors until your knuckles bleed. Doors will slam in your face. You must pick yourself up, dust yourself off, and knock again. It's the only way to achieve your goals in life."* —Michael Uslan.

To all the dreamers, I say, look for courage, especially when in danger. It is okay to be scared. Do it afraid. In the tasks you seek to achieve, listen for the wisdom that will speak softly later. Rise daily with fortitude to tackle your dreams. Most of all, *"Do not be anxious about anything, but in everything by prayer with thanksgiving let your requests be made known to God."* —Philippians 4:6. Be steadfast. Don't complain. Do the work. Seize the day! Make your dreams of today be seedlings for the triumphs of your tomorrows. LL Cool J assures us that, *"There are no deadlines on your dreams."*

While pursuing your dreams with eagerness and zeal, every step along the way, be mindful of how you treat people. Blogger and author Mandy Hale, affectionately known as, "The Single Woman," echoes one of my mom's repeated refrains. *"Be good to people. You will be remembered more for your kindness than any level of success you could attain."* Your kindness will be repaid in dividends when you no longer hold the position or stature. So with grace be that girl! Unapologetically, BE THAT MOXIE WOMAN. Soar!!

THE PLAYLIST COMPENDIUM

- Music is my Sixth Sense
- *Be Sure* by Teddy Pendergrass
- *Better* by Hezekiah Walker
- *Black Butterfly* by Deniece Williams
- *Blessed* by Charlie Wilson
- *Blessed* by Jill Scott
- *Break My Soul* by Beyoncé
- *Breakeven* by The Script
- *Careless Whisper* by George Michael
- *Celebrate Good Times* by Kool and the Gang
- *Cold, Cold World* by Kenny Gamble and Leon Huff
- *Dear Momma* by Tupac
- *Don't Worry, Be Happy* by Bobby McFerrin
- *Don't You Worry* by Jonathan Butler
- *Fast Car* by Tracy Chapman
- *Flight Time* by Donald Byrd
- *Flowers* by Miley Cyrus
- *For The Love of Money* by Kenny Gamble and Leon Huff
- *Girl On Fire* by Alicia Keys

- *Gratitude* by Earth, Wind and Fire
- *I Gotta Feeling* by The Black-Eyed Peas
- *I Just Can't Stop Dancing* by Kenny Gamble and Leon Huff
- *I Rise Up* by Andrea Day
- *I'm Every Woman* by Chaka Khan
- *I'm Every Woman* by Whitney Houston
- *If I Could Change The World* by Eric Clapton
- *If You Believe* by Lena Horne
- *Imagine* by John Lennon
- *In The Midst By It All* by Yolanda Adams
- *Just Dance* by Lady Gaga
- *Let Them In* by Billy Paul
- *Let's Dance* by David Bowie
- *Life Goes On* by Lena Horne
- *Life Is A Song Worth Singing* by Teddy Pendergrass
- *Livin' Your Life Like It's Golden* by Jill Scott
- *Long and Winding Road* by The Beatles
- *Love and Hate* by Wale
- *Love Will Find a Way* by Lionel Richie
- *My Life* by Billy Joel
- *Never Break* by John Legend
- *Places and Spaces I've Been* by Donald Byrd
- *Please Don't Stop The Music* by Rihanna
- *Reach Out and Touch* by Diana Ross
- *Respect* by Aretha Franklin
- *Revelation 19:1* by Stephen Hurd
- *ROAR* by Katy Perry

- *Rock With You* by Michael Jackson
- *Sadie* by The Spinners
- *Shut Up and Dance* by Frontman Nicholas
- *Sign of The Times* by Prince
- *Smile Happy* by WAR
- *Somebody Prayed For Me* by Dorothy Norwood
- *Somebody That I Used To Know* by Goyte featuring Kimbra
- *Something I'm Going Through* by DJ Rae and David Morales
- *Sorry, Not Sorry* by Demi Lovato
- *Stomp* by The Brothers Johnson
- *Superwoman* by Alicia Keys
- *Thank—You For Being God* by Travis Greene
- *Thank You For It All* by Marvin Sapp
- *That's What Friends Are For* by Elton John
- *The Potter's House* by Tramaine Hawkins
- *The Power of Love* by Luther Vandross
- *The Road Less Traveled* by Joe Sample
- *The Sound of Silence* by Paul Simon
- *Waiting On The World to Change* by John Mayer
- *Where Are We Going* by Marvin Gaye
- *Why We Sing* by Kirk Franklin
- "Wind Beneath My Wings" by Bette Midler
- "Work" by Rihanna
- "You Can't Hide From Yourself" by Teddy Pendergrass
- "You're a Winner" by Curtis Mayfield & The Impressions
- "You've Got a Friend" by Carole King and James Taylor

GRATITUDE AND ACKNOWLEDGMENT

"No act of kindness, no matter how small, is ever wasted."
—Aesop

Gratitude is a very difficult emotion to express, so until we find a more appropriate word, thank you will have to do. No experience occurs in a vacuum. All experiences happen with the intervention or uplift from family, parents, siblings, children, spouses, close friends, colleagues, admirers, protagonists, and distractors or haters associated with you and that life experience.

Our dreams, aspirations, careers, hobbies, achievements, and failures begin or end with a thank you. Somebody in every aspect of our lives impacts who we are. What we become is partly attributed to those who touched our lives along the way. Justice Thurgood Marshall once quipped, *"None of us got where we are solely by pulling ourselves up by our bootstraps. We got here because somebody—a parent, an Ivy League crony, or a few nuns—bent down and helped us pick up our boots."*

To my sisters, Yvonne, Cynthia (posthumous), Angelina, Jill, and only brother, Angelo. Sisters Pandora, Alesia, and Brian (brother-in-law) were needed angels at my darkest hour. Love youu. Thank Youuu.

CORE, Founder, Congressman Chaka Fattah, 2nd C.D. and The Fattah Organization. I am grateful for those individuals that I surrounded myself with who pushed me and nudged me to stretch and maximize my potential and others who lifted me higher because of my potential. My Kitchen Cabinet George R. Burrell, Esq., David Forde, Esq., David L. Hyman, Esq., Sandra Dungee Glenn, Terry Grayboyes, Hadji Maulomian, Esq., Melonease Shaw, Wayne L. Walker, Esq., and Pandora Woods. I bow to YOU.

My Campaign Strategist and guru, Gregory Naylor, Campaign managers: Willie Jordan, Sandra Dungee Glenn, Hon. Cindy Bass, and Tracy Hardy. To my campaign, contributors, led by President Darrell Clark, my Finance Committee members, and the thousands of contributors of the Friends of Blondell Reynolds-Brown. The Olde School Dance Party Steering Committee, led by the dynamic duo, Pandora Woods and Matthew McDonald, were unmatched.

To my former City Council colleagues whom I completely enjoyed working with and learning from over the twenty years. Listed by Councilmatic District:

Frank DiCicco, Mark Squilla, Kenyatta Johnson, Jannie Blackwell, Michael A. Nutter, Carol Campbell*, Curtis Jones Jr., Joan L. Krajewski*, Bobby Henon, Richard T. Mariano, Daniel J. Savage, Maria Quiñones Sánchez, Donna Reed Miller*, Cindy Bass, Marian B. Tasco, Cherelle Parker, Brian J. O'Neill, W. Wilson Goode, Allan Domb, Angel L. Ortiz, Juan Ramos*, Bill Green, Ed Neilson, Derek S. Green, Esq., David Cohen*, William K. Greenlee, James F. Kenney, Thatcher Longstreth*, Jack Kelly, Dennis O'Brien, Al Taubenberger, Frank Rizzo, Jr., and David Oh. *Deceased

Mentee: Hon. Katherine Gilmore Richardson, Philadelphia City Councilwoman at-large.

The Women of Delta Sigma Theta Sorority, Inc. Philadelphia Alumni Chapter: The Village Moms, we selflessly leaned on each other as I walked the tightrope. Marcia, Loretta, Bridget, Jeannette, Ingrid, Sheila, Robbie, Lisa, and Natasha. I love you.

My beloved Travel Crew, Wanda, Delilah, Sandi, Cassandra, and Deadra. My former bosses, Willie F. Johnson, Joan Myers Brown, Robert W. Sorrell*, Rev. W. Arthur Lewis*, Hon. Senator Vincent Hughes, Congressman Chaka Fattah. Edwina A. Baker*, Onah Weldon*, Sorors Barbara Daniel Cox*, Hon. Councilwoman Marion B. Tasco, and Dr. Constance Clayton; C. Delores Tucker*, Ernesta Ballard,* Mary Hurtig, Hon. Councilwoman Augusta A. Clark*, President Anna C. Verna* and Joann Bell. These trailblazers and coaches cared for and offered solicited and unsolicited career advice throughout my growth as a developing professional and elected official.

Mayor John F. Street for my appointment as a Robert Wood Johnson Fellow. To my early technical assistants, Jamilla Toombs and Pandora Woods. Robert Mendelsohn, now an angel, selflessly served as the photojournalist for my entire twenty years in City Council. My spiritual advisors: Pastor Keith Miller, Pastor Michele Lawrence, Pastor Terry Davis, Pastor Kevin Johnson, and brother-in-law Pastor Brian Jacks. Thank you, Sorors Judge Renee Cardwell-Hughes, and the Philadelphia Urban Affairs Coalition President, Sharmaine Matlock-Turner, for your selflessness, guidance, coaching in early morning private meetings, and just plain kindness. Vanesse Lloyd Sgambati and Nancy Moses, a publicist and award-winning author, respectively, these women filled my basket of dreams with inspiration and Brielle A. Brown Esq., became my book accountability coach and captain.

Special Thanks to Former Staff and Colleagues 2000–2020, Honorable Katherine Gilmore Richardson, Francine Brown, Marlene Goss, Debra Brown, Jamal Haywood, Jason Lewis, Hadji Maloumian, Esq., Craig McLaurin, Leslie K. Carter, Joseph Meade, Steven Chintamen, Esq., Sylvia Purnell Muldrow, Mark Clark, Samantha Pearson, Vance Coles, Gabriella Raczka, Luz Colon, Zeyna Rodriguez, Dawn Crump, Rodney Settles, Taylor Daukaus, Jerome Dorsey, Julian Thompson, Esq., Chip Fattah, Alisesha

Vaughn, David Forde, Esq., Kellan White, Eileen Frierson, Michael German, Barbara Glenn, Candice Woods, Anna Marie Strawberry*, Adrienne Williams*, Holsey Gillis*.

*Deceased

And finally, *Muchas gracias, merci beaucoup, danke schon, arigato, spasibo, mahalo, shukriya, asante sana,* and a thousand times in any language would not be sufficient to adequately express my gratitude to those who touched my life during my twenty years in City Council, filled with joy and, at times, difficult but uplifting experiences. They all laid the foundation and blueprint for me to complete this memoir. Until we find a word that is more appropriate, thank you will have to do. If I missed anyone, please attribute it to my head, the less than perfectly organized files spanning twenty years, and not to my heart.

Special Thanks to: Chris Brennan/ @ByChrisBrennan/ Brennan@phillynews.com

African American WISDOM, Quinn Eli, 2003 *Politics,* even with double standards still firmly in place, Karen Heller, *Philadelphia Inquirer,* 2007.

A salute to Robert Mendelsohn, the unselfish and kindest photographer and photojournalist of my City Council career.

Visit my website, www.Moxie.BRB.com, to view the gazillion moments and experiences Robert captured.

ABOUT THE AUTHOR

Blondell Reynolds-Brown forged her legacy as a Philadelphia City Councilwoman at-large, where she emerged as an accomplished legislator and fierce champion for women's advancement. During her tenure, she authored dozens of transformative bills that became law, focusing on expanding opportunities for women, children, and families. Her legislation created lasting changes across multiple sectors, from increasing women's representation on boards to strengthening leadership roles in nonprofit and government spaces. Reynolds-Brown's impact extended to the arts, minority and women-owned businesses, LGBTQIA rights, and environmental initiatives.

Her commitment to public service began long before her political career, shaped by her experience as an educator, community activist, and parent. For two decades, she served on the Philadelphia City Council, winning five consecutive citywide elections before surprising many with her decision not to seek a sixth term.

Currently, Reynolds-Brown serves as a Senior Advisor at Frank DiCicco Associates, where she continues to influence public policy. Her passion for mentoring the next generation of leaders shines through her signature initiative, The Celebration of Moxie Women, where she coaches young women and girls to reach their full potential.

A proud Penn State alumna, Reynolds-Brown holds both a bachelor's and master's degrees in elementary education. She maintains deep roots in Philadelphia and remains an active member of Delta Sigma Theta Sorority, Inc. Philadelphia Chapter. A recipient of dozens of awards, she was recognized as one of Pennsylvania's 50 Most Influential Women in the book, *VOICES*.

www.ingramcontent.com/pod-product-compliance
Lightning Source LLC
Chambersburg PA
CBHW050257010526
44107CB00033B/1413/J